Praise for *Innovative Team Selling*

"I have worked with Eric Baron for more than 25 years—as a colleague, as a client of his, and as a co-consultant. The insights in this book are extremely valuable—in particular in the current world, where team selling of complex customer propositions becomes both more central and more challenging at the same time. Bringing together an understanding of consultative selling, team dynamics, and leadership is a powerful combination that will help many teams to dramatically enhance their effectiveness. This book is a powerful tool for anyone who seeks to enhance the effectiveness of selling in today's environment."

—**David A. Nadler, PhD**
Vice Chairman
Marsh & McLennan Companies
(Author of *Champions of Change* and *Building Better Boards*)

"Fully leveraging sales resources is critical for businesses to succeed in today's dynamic, global economy. Eric Baron explains, in *Innovative Team Selling*, how sales teams can collaborate to derive innovative solutions to help their clients solve their business problems."

—**R. Glenn Hubbard**
Dean and Russell L. Carson Professor of Finance
and Economics
Columbia Business School

"Individuals can obviously do great work, but high-performing teams consistently produce better results. *Innovative Team Selling* explores how sales teams can collaborate to develop innovative solutions for their clients. We've successfully worked with Eric Baron and his team to deliver these concepts to our client-facing professionals. I'd encourage any organization that believes in team selling to consider what Eric has to say."

—**Karen Peetz**
President
BNY Mellon

INNOVATIVE
TEAM
SELLING

INNOVATIVE
TEAM
SELLING

HOW TO **LEVERAGE YOUR RESOURCES** AND **MAKE** TEAM SELLING **WORK**

ERIC BARON

WILEY

Published by John Wiley & Sons, Inc., Hoboken, New Jersey
Published simultaneously in Canada

For general information about our other products and services, please contact our Customer Care Department within the United States at (800) 762–2974, outside the United States at (317) 572–3993 or fax (317) 572–4002.

Wiley publishes in a variety of print and electronic formats and by print-on-demand. Some material included with standard print versions of this book may not be included in e-books or in print-on-demand. If this book refers to media such as a CD or DVD that is not included in the version you purchased, you may download this material at http://booksupport.wiley.com. For more information about Wiley products, visit www.wiley.com.

Library of Congress Cataloging-in-Publication Data:

Baron, Eric.
  Innovative team selling: how to leverage your resources and make team selling work/Eric Baron.
     pages. cm
  Includes index.
  ISBN 978-1-118–50225-9 (cloth); ISBN 978-1-118–64640-3 (ebk);
  ISBN 978-1-118–64636-6 (ebk); ISBN 978-1-118–64550-5 (ebk)
  1. Selling.   2. Sales management.   3. Teams in the workplace.   I. Title.
  HF5438.B265   2013
  658.85—dc23   2012049845

Printed in the United States of America

10 9 8 7 6 5 4 3 2 1

In Memory of

Sandi Rotkoff

Without whom this never would have happened

Contents

Introduction

M y first book, *Selling Is a Team Sport*, was published more than 10 years ago. The world has undergone monumental changes since its publication as technology, globalization, and unparalleled competition have made succeeding in business so much more difficult. Innovation is no longer a luxury; it's a necessity for every organization if they want to stay in the game and ahead of their competition. Effective sales teams who understand how to leverage their resources can contribute significantly to any organization as they address the challenges they encounter in this competitive environment.

Organizations are comprised of intelligent, talented, committed, and effective people. We all know that individuals can do great work. But teams outperform individuals. We know that intuitively, and there is tons of research to back that statement up. Of course, there are situations where an individual might outperform a team when given a specific task. But nobody is smart enough to always assign a task to the one right individual who will outperform the team. It just doesn't work that way. Teams do better than individuals, and when they work together well they can accomplish great things.

This is a book about how effective team selling works. Our emphasis is on innovation, collaboration, teamwork, differentiation, and leveraging resources. Sales teams have the potential to do remarkable things. They just need to learn how to reach their potential. The intent of this book is to provide the reader with skills, techniques, methodologies, and approaches that will enable their teams to work together more effectively and derive innovative solutions for their customers.

The process of successful team selling is essentially comprised of three distinct components. First is the dynamic of how the sales team works together internally to develop strategies, recommendations, and solutions that address their clients' needs. They must learn how to conduct outstanding meetings. To do this they need to understand concepts like meeting dynamics, facilitation, roles and responsibilities, generating and developing ideas, leveraging each other's expertise, managing conflict, and gaining commitment. The first half of the book focuses on this *internal component* of team selling.

Second is how a sales team works together to make outstanding team calls. This is the *external component*. Whether it's two people meeting a prospective client early in the process, several colleagues making a formal presentation, or many members of the sales team participating in a Finalist Presentation, they need to do this in a customer-focused way that is both memorable and unique. How sales teams present themselves, how they connect with their customers, how they work together, how they demonstrate understanding of the client's situation, how they tell their story, and how they build upon each other's comments all contribute to the impression they make. These factors significantly impact the likelihood of their success. The skills required to make outstanding team calls are what the second half of the book explores.

There is an important third overarching component that impacts the entire team selling process: the *planning and coordination* required in day-to-day interactions. Sales teams can't just come together when it's time to strategize or when it's time to visit the client. They need to consistently collaborate. They need to communicate on a daily basis. They need to be thinking about the customer all the time. When they get together, they need to review each member's understanding of the customer's needs and look for unique ways to address those needs. The teams have to consistently leverage the collective expertise of the organization. They need to listen to different points of view. They need to plan and rehearse prior to their client visits. And they must always be held accountable—to the customer, to the organization, and to each other. This, too, will be discussed throughout the book.

This book is about improving the process behind selling as a team. You will see, as we investigate innovative team selling, that process refers primarily to *how* individuals work together. Whether it's with your colleagues, your teammates, your customers, your friends, or your children, how you interact greatly impacts whatever you hope to accomplish. What you have to say, or what you suggest, or even what you think is often dwarfed by the way you interact. Most of the information about team selling that is currently in the marketplace discusses what teams need to do, how they are comprised, and what their goals and objectives should address. That is important information. But there isn't much out there about *how* they do it. That's what we will explore together.

For sales teams to reach their potential, it is critical to understand the power of process awareness. Whether they are planning for a presentation, working together in developing a strategy, problem solving to derive innovative solutions, or meeting with their clients, how they interact drives everything. Unfortunately, process rarely gets the attention it deserves.

Ralph Waldo Emerson said, "What you are speaks so loud I cannot hear what you say." This exemplifies the power of process. Sales teams can work effectively and efficiently, both internally and externally to derive creative, innovative solutions for their clients. Adding process sensitivity to the sales team's toolbox enables them to work like a well-oiled machine when they attack problems, uncover needs, and pursue opportunities. Understanding the importance of process enables teams to tell their story in a well orchestrated, beautifully coordinated, extremely polished and impressively professional manner that will differentiate them from their competitors every time.

In the 30-plus years that The Baron Group has been training sales professionals and sales managers, we have had the opportunity to observe tens of thousands of sales calls; some were in person, but most were in simulations on video. Participants in our programs practice the skills they learn by using cases we develop on video. As a result, we have acquired a body of knowledge that is based on what salespeople do, whether they are working internally or externally; whether it's face to face or on the phone; whether they are selling products or services; and whether they represent major corporations or smaller firms. We have learned much from them and as a result the concepts we teach are consistently tweaked, modified, or enhanced.

Early in our firm's evolution we won a job that we really had no right to win. We were too small, too young, and too inexperienced. But we won it. That happens sometimes, just as when you don't win jobs that you should have. The client told us that they selected us, not just because they liked our product, but because they liked how we worked together, how we gave the impression that we enjoyed each other, and how we demonstrated our ability to complement each other. There was more to it, of course, and our ability to demonstrate our understanding of their situation was huge, but the way we worked as a team played a big role in our winning that piece of business. I never forgot that, and much of what team selling is about can be summarized by that experience.

The Baron Group's roots trace back to Synectics® Inc., now called Synecticsworld. After earning a degree in chemical engineering, I worked for Union Carbide for eight years, holding positions in technical sales, sales management, and marketing. By accident I had the opportunity to work in the Personnel Development Laboratory (PDL), which was a group dedicated to training Carbide's sales professionals. The PDL was way ahead of its time back there in the 1970s, and we had the opportunity to work with people like Mac Hanan, Chet Karrass, Rosabeth Kanter, Earl Rose, and Barry Stein.

It was at PDL that I met Synectics and fell in love with the pioneering work they were doing in creative problem solving, innovative teamwork, and meeting management. I left Union Carbide to join Synectics, where I spent five wonderful years. It was at Synectics that I became intrigued with the notion of applying problem solving skills to the sales process. My colleague, Kate Reilly, and I left Synectics to found Consultative Resources Corporation (CRC) with Jonathan Whitcup in 1981. I left CRC to start The Baron Group in 1992, because my interest had evolved more toward team selling and relating innovation to the sales process.

When I wrote *Selling Is a Team Sport*, I introduced our sales process and demonstrated how sales teams could apply it to their day-to-day activities. I took the consultative selling model, built upon it by infusing it with problem solving skills and techniques, and demonstrated how by using it, sales teams could become more effective. But the book started with the selling model and related it to teams.

This book takes a very different approach in an effort to enhance the concepts and increase the uniqueness of the approach. *Innovative Team Selling* begins with the sales team, not the selling model. The early focus is on what the team needs to do to get its act together and do brilliant work. That is the starting point. So in essence this book turns everything upside down. Investigating sales teams and exploring how they can use sophisticated selling skills to do marvelous work is quite different from starting with the sales process and explaining how teams can effectively apply it. This reframing of team selling will be an exhilarating exercise and you will make many connections throughout the process.

With that in mind the book will once again take a hard look at some proven problem solving skills and explain how sales teams can use them to generate innovative solutions internally, and then leverage these concepts to impress their clients externally. It will explore meeting dynamics and introduce ways to use that knowledge with both colleagues and clients.

And we will look at state-of-the-art selling skills that every member of the sales team can use whenever they interact with their customers.

To help accomplish this, a story is woven throughout the book. This fictitious story is about a sales team, led by their team leader, Sam Jamison. The team is comprised of 10 individuals from different functions. You will see how the team works together from the time they receive a Request for Proposal (RFP) that provides them with a marvelous opportunity, right through the day that they give their major presentation. You will see how Sam manages the team. You will observe the team as they strategize. You will watch them try to clarify the customer's needs. You will walk through their customer visits with them. You will see them rehearse before the big day. You will be there when they develop the big idea that helped them win the business. And you will even get a sense as to how they think and how they manage their own insecurities.

As you observe Sam and his team, you will benefit from watching them put into action what we have learned over the past three decades from the many outstanding salespeople with whom we have had the pleasure to work. Their story is based upon a real story. Everything they experience is based on actual situations, either our own or those of our clients. Their situations can apply to any organization regardless of their business, their size or their history. We made this example complicated, and it relates to a manufacturing company, but the dynamics can apply to any organization's sales opportunities.

Sales teams who understand how to use process as a tool to build relationships, understand their clients' needs, make great recommendations, and orchestrate both their internal and external meetings, will outperform their competitors every time.

You will notice as you read this book that we use the terms *customer*, *client, buyer*, and *prospect* interchangeably. We don't do that to confuse you. We do it to ensure that whoever reads this will be able to relate to the concepts we offer.

Every example we give, every anecdote we introduce, and every situation we include in the story about Sam Jamison's team is based on real events with only the names changed for obvious reasons. Everyone in our firm, including yours truly, has serious sales experience. We know what it is like to lose a job we should have won. We know what it's like to travel for hours only to learn that the customer can't see you. We know what it's like to be told you won a job only to have it go elsewhere for political reasons. We even know how it feels to be thrown out of someone's office—if not literally, at least figura-tively. And, of course, we know how sweet it is to win new business, close deals, and emerge victorious.

So when you read this book, please keep in mind that it comes from people who have been there. Our research is based on experience, and the concepts we introduce have been tested in the best laboratory of them all—the real world.

I conclude by referencing my business partner for 12 years, David Hauer. He was with me during a critical period of our evolution and made significant contributions. David often referred to what we taught as "applied common sense." The first few times I heard him use the term I didn't appreciate it and I shared that with him. But he continued to use it, and as time passed I realized he was right. Much of what we teach is common sense. I hope that, as you read this, you'll realize that much of what we say are things you either do, or know you can do, or realize you should do, but don't do as often as you'd like. Much of what we include are the things successful salespeople incorporate into their approach. This book will help make the principles associated with team selling practical, usable, manageable, and, yes, ways to apply what is really common sense.

Enjoy the experience.

1 The Celebration, or Why We Need Sales Teams

I t was not your typical business dinner. The group was a bit more jubilant, bordering on being rowdy. They had just arrived and you could immediately sense that unlike similar events, the evening was getting off to a fast start. Usually the excitement builds at these kinds of dinners, but not tonight. The high-fives and fist pumps were flying around the room before people took off their coats.

Sam Jamison, the sales professional and team leader who had arranged for the team to celebrate their recent success, was glad he had requested a private room. He had a feeling that things could get noisy as the evening moved on. And why not? This was their evening. They earned it.

The group looked pretty much like any group of business people that you'd see in a restaurant on a weekday night. Whether it's an off-site, a national meeting, or just a group traveling together, dinner is usually part of the agenda. And like any team, there were those who were thrilled to be there, those who attended a bit reluctantly, and the majority who accepted these kinds of events for what they were and did what they could to make it a fun evening. But again, this particular group seemed different.

Like any of these dinners, it was another night away from home for those who attended. Sam knew that. So when he sent out the invitations, he was very careful to position this as a celebration. Because that is precisely what it was.

Dinner had just been ordered when Sam tapped his wine glass a few times with his spoon in an effort to quiet the group down so he could make a few opening remarks. He had been thinking about this moment from the day he received that memorable phone call informing him that they had won the contract. He usually liked to speak extemporaneously at times like these, but from the minute he heard the good news, he knew that this deserved a bit more thought. After all, how often do you hear a client say "Congratulations, Sam! You won the business. And it wasn't even close!"?

As he tapped on his glass for the third time, he was amused at the difficulty he was encountering in trying to get this group to give him attention. They were downright giddy. And it was still quite early in the evening. "Okay, here we go," chortled Frank Prince, the always-upbeat R&D manager. "I learned a long time ago that there is no such thing as a free lunch, so I guess we'll have to listen to Sam." The group gave Frank a polite chuckle, and a few people raised their eyebrows, but it did quiet them down. And finally Sam was able to share his prepared remarks.

Surprisingly, in light of the time he put into preparing what he would say, he started with one of those terribly overused clichés: "I could not have possibly accomplished this without you." Nobody said anything, but you could see that in spite of those somewhat patronizing words, he had finally gotten the group to listen. But then he immediately corrected himself. "Let me say that a bit differently. *We* never could have done this without each other." That got everyone's attention.

He continued, "Everyone in this room, and I mean *everybody*, as well as the few members of our team who couldn't make it tonight, played a significant role in our winning this business. That's what makes this so special. It's not just the size of the contract we won, it's what we did together to win it." That's when even the more skeptical members of the team finally tuned in.

But Sam was far from being through. "You know as well as I do that the odds were stacked against us. But we worked together and developed not only what proved to be an incredible proposal, but a presentation that blew the clients out of the water. We won the business hands down. And that's why we are here tonight celebrating this mind-boggling accomplishment." The group spontaneously gave him an enthusiastic round of applause.

He then did something quite unusual. He asked each person to look around the room and acknowledge the other members of the team. "Just take a minute and look at your colleagues," he said a bit sheepishly. "Don't say anything. Just look around and see who we are." So they did. It felt a bit awkward, even contrived, and a few people found themselves looking at their shoes as opposed to their colleagues, but most of them appreciated what Sam was trying to do.

He wanted everyone to realize what an incredible team effort this was, and he wanted each of them to enjoy every minute of this very special evening. "I'm sure as you looked at each other you realized once again how talented a group we are," he said. He wasn't worried about overdoing it as he praised the team. He just wanted them to know how much he appreciated each and every one of them.

He then said a few words about each member of the team. He kept his comments brief, but was careful to include each person, even those who could not attend. He talked about how Francine from Marketing provided the team with incredible data about the competitive landscape. He credited Tony from Distribution for his thoughtful comments at the presentation about "just-in-time inventory." He recognized how articulately Helen from IT explained how the transition would be seamless if we were to win the business.

When he sensed the group was getting a bit antsy, he kidded Joe from Contracts about his tolerance and self-restraint when he had to deal with the prospective client's Procurement Group. He told a funny anecdote about how Jerry from Manufacturing reworked his slides six times before he felt comfortable talking about his quality standards. He enthusiastically recalled how Lesley from Customer Service triggered the big idea that he truly believed made the difference in their winning the business. The team applauded enthusiastically at that particular remark, and Joe said, "Let's drink to that." Which they did, and after lots of clinking of glasses, Frank, who would be the first to admit that he was incorrigible, said, "What is this, a wedding or a business dinner?" He just couldn't help himself and the group appreciated it.

Sam realized it was time to wind down, but he quickly referenced the brilliant benchmarking work that Valerie from Market Research had done to help them price their recommendation. And he poked fun at Charlie from Operations about how he had never seen him in a suit and tie prior to the Finalist Presentation. That got the best laugh of the night.

He mentioned every member of the team, including his Sales Manager and his Sales Assistant, and concluded his remarks with the same message that he used to begin: "We could never have done this alone. Without everyone's contribution this never would have happened." And then it was time to stop, particularly since Frank said, "Enough already, let's eat."

It was a great moment. Some of our best days in business are when we win big jobs. This was the third biggest contract that Sam's company was ever awarded. To win it required many players and many points of view. Many functions were involved. The entire team contributed to the research, the planning, the strategy sessions, the development of the proposal, and of course the Finalist Presentation. They did a fabulous job and tonight they were celebrating what they had accomplished. It was the final chapter of a wonderful story.

They met as an entire team regularly, but sometimes they worked in subgroups. They communicated day in and day out. Each team member submitted status reports on a regular basis. They diligently reviewed and revised their proposal over and over. They rehearsed their presentation several times. As a result, they won the business. And as the client said when he told Sam that they had been selected, "It wasn't even close."

That is what team selling is all about. When teams understand and leverage their expertise, they can do extraordinary things. When they allow themselves to tap into their creative potential across functions, and develop innovative solutions for their customers, they can differentiate themselves in ways that are hard to match. *Innovative Team Selling* presents an approach that every organization, regardless of its size, structure, and offerings, can adapt to and apply every day. And it is something every company must take seriously.

Teams have the ability to get things done efficiently, quickly, and collaboratively. And they can do this extremely well. They just need to learn how to apply these basic, but critically important and surprisingly sophisticated, concepts:

- How to conduct productive internal meetings.
- How to make outstanding team presentations.
- How to plan and coordinate the process on a day-to-day basis.

This is the three-legged stool upon which team selling sits. If sales teams effectively perform these critical activities, they will outperform their competition every time.

Why Sales Teams?

There are many questions you may be asking, the first of which is why? Why do we need sales teams? Can't salespeople just get the help they need and use their resources without having to involve so many people in the process?

Isn't this in some ways counterproductive? Do we really want to risk complicating the process with so many personalities and so many conflicting points of view? In today's fast moving high tech world, can't we do all this stuff electronically? Don't other functions have enough to do? Since most meetings are a waste of time anyway, will this really help?

These are certainly reasonable questions to ask, even if they are somewhat challenging. We look forward to answering them. And our answers might come across as somewhat steadfast. That's because we are convinced that teams outperform individuals. Many studies, including what the *Boston Globe* described in 2010 as "a striking study by the MIT Sloan School of Management professor shows that teams of people display a collective intelligence that has surprisingly little to do with the intelligence of the team's individual members."[1] The article further states, "Intuitively we still attribute too much to individuals and not enough to groups." This is interesting stuff. In today's complex world, nobody has the ability to do it all by him or herself. The *generalist*, that talented individual who could do it all, is history.

Leveraging Sales Teams

The sales organization has a very specific role in any business. They are charged with bringing in new business, while maintaining and building existing relationships. If that oversimplifies the role of this critical function, we apologize. But that's what they do. They know that it's all about the customer. Sales has the responsibility of constantly determining and demonstrating their understanding of the customer's situation, and explaining what they can do to satisfy their requirements and add value. But to compete today, Sales must know how to take advantage of the depth of their organizations. They simply have no choice.

Virtually any sales organization will be more successful if they learn how to leverage their resources and tap into their collective expertise. To do this, they must conduct effective meetings that address business opportunities. When team members have the opportunity to get together to collaborate, speculate, and innovate, they can accomplish great things.

---

[1] Carolyn Y. Johnson, "Group IQ: What Makes One Team of People Smarter than Another? A New Field of Research Finds Surprising Answers," *Boston Globe*, December 19, 2010.

If they can figure out how to corral those resources, they'll inevitably derive innovative solutions that will help differentiate themselves from virtually everyone else.

At the same time, they need to explain articulately to clients and prospects how well they understand their needs and objectives. This is perhaps the single most important thing that any sales professional or any sales team must do. Few actually know how to do this. And finally, they must clearly demonstrate how their products, services, and ideas can help their customers accomplish their objectives, satisfy their needs, and take advantage of their opportunities.

These are the keys to success in sales, more so today than ever before. You need to understand the clients' needs, use your resources to derive innovative solutions, and demonstrate to those clients how you are different from your competitors. It all comes down to these three challenges. Addressing them is mandatory in today's extremely competitive global environment. Anything less will fall short. And sales teams can play a major role in making this happen.

Now, much of what appears above is pretty basic stuff that you probably heard the first time you attended a basic sales training program. Most salespeople know that they need to figure out their customer's needs, come up with good solutions, and explain the solutions in ways that the customer can understand. No big deal. What you might not know, however, is how much better you can do this if you leverage your resources, particularly when you tap into different functions throughout the organization. And though it may seem obvious, this rarely happens.

Most organizations simply do not take advantage of their collective expertise. Whether it's because of the silo mentality conundrum, the structure of the organization, the way salespeople go about their business, the lack of leadership, or even compensation structures, team selling still hasn't become totally embraced by most sales organizations. They talk about it often; they just don't do it. The reality is that innovative team selling is the exception, not the rule. That is nothing short of a missed opportunity—a huge missed opportunity.

Let's go back to that celebration for a minute. Sam wasn't just blowing smoke. He didn't plan this celebration so that he could shine in front of his colleagues and managers. He was recognizing the team for what they had done. He knew better than anyone else how critical each of them was in winning the business.

From the time the RFP was received he knew he could not do this alone. In fact, his immediate instinct was to decline the opportunity because it appeared to be too big for his company. He came very close to not responding. A few of the people he discussed it with, including his manager, were quite skeptical about their ability to compete. When he first read that 32-page document, he was surprised at the anxiety he experienced. He usually embraced these kinds of opportunities with heartfelt enthusiasm. But not this time. His initial reaction was that he couldn't see how they could pull this off.

But Sam was not one to walk away from a big deal. So, consistent with his company's policy, he put together an internal proposal requesting approval to move forward and invest the time and money required. Once he received the go-ahead, he formed what Steve Waterhouse would call a "vertical team" in his thoughtful book, *The Team Selling Solution.*[2] The team would work together for this one particular project. It was Sam's responsibility to sign them up, get their commitment, and utilize them throughout the process.

The ball was in his court and he knew he would do everything he could to make it to the finals. He kept telling everybody, "It's just like the playoffs in any sport. Once you get there you have a chance." He knew that if they could put together a proposal that demonstrated to the prospective customer their creativity, their innovative approach, and the things they could do that were unique, they would have a shot at winning the business.

And that's precisely what he did. As soon as he received approval, he sat down with selected resources and scoped out their response to the RFP. They spent significant time doing this and found themselves doing some thoughtful problem solving. He assigned different people to contribute to specific sections. He clarified everyone's role and got the buy-in he needed. He verbalized his expectations and gave others the opportunity to do the same.

As the proposal was developed, he managed the process diligently, and when necessary he pushed back or asked for more. Prior to submitting the proposal, a subgroup convened and reviewed it very carefully, line by line. And when he was informed that they were selected as one of four finalists, he convened a series of meetings to develop the formal presentation. Once that was locked in, the team conducted several rehearsals to ensure that they were ready.

---

[2] Steve Waterhouse, *The Team Selling Solution* (New York: McGraw-Hill, 2004).

There is no way that Sam could have done this alone. As Sam said many times throughout the process, "I hope the other guys are doing this alone. They don't have a chance if they aren't tapping into their resources the way we are."

We don't want to make this thought bigger than it is. Sales teams, or at least the concept, have been around forever. This isn't something you haven't heard about or experienced before. We know that. In the early days a sales team might have consisted of a sales manager and his or her direct reports. They would convene every so often to talk about the state of the business, share success stories, and occasionally work on customer related problems. Sometimes a Marketing Manager or Technical Resource or Distribution Coordinator would be invited to attend a meeting to help when needed. This played out on a bigger stage at annual sales meetings and business related off-sites.

But the concept of cross-functional sales teams didn't really become prevalent until the 1980s, and even then they weren't used very often. If a major opportunity presented itself, a team would be assembled for that initiative, but in general sales did its thing and asked for help when necessary. Rarely were specific teams assigned to specific clients or specific business opportunities. You would hear about sales teams from time to time, but in the day-to-day business environment you did not see them used very often.

But as globalization became a fact of life, and technology soared, more and more organizations realized they simply could not compete unless they tapped into their collective expertise. The result was that the notion of developing sales teams became more and more common, and many organizations will tell you they use a team selling approach today. The definitions and approaches vary, as does the level of successful implementation, but most companies, regardless of the industry or their size, will claim to use a team selling approach.

There simply is no other option. To compete today demands tapping into the resources of your organization, whether you are 10 people, 100 people, or 100,000 people. If you choose to avoid getting on that train, you will find yourself waiting at the station for a very long time.

The Human Factor

Like anything else, saying it and doing it, particularly doing it well, are two very different things. Team selling is not something that just happens because someone in the C Suite thought it would be nice to do. It takes time, effort, commitment, and energy. Lots of it. Because the minute teams come into play, human dynamics play a role. And that complicates things dramatically.

There are many interactive components associated with team selling. After all, human beings are involved. They are all worthy of our attention. How colleagues feel about being a member of the team, how much their colleagues value them, and to what degree they are included day-to-day, can have significant impact on the team's success or failure. How team members' ideas are treated, how their opinions are respected, and how their points of view are accepted all play a tremendous role in the long-term success of any team.

The way meetings are conducted, whether it's the whole team or sub-groups focusing on specific issues, and the corresponding behaviors of the players, play an important role. How the team interacts in front of the customer will often determine whether they are selected or not. And those brief conversations every day can in the long run greatly influence the overall performance of the team.

All this and more impacts a team's ability to accomplish its objectives. It isn't as simple as putting the team together and letting them do their thing. They need to learn how to maximize their potential. They must learn how to address these issues. They need to get their acts together. The good news is that they can.

Let's return to the celebration one more time. There was a lot going on that Sam wasn't aware of. As sensitive and aware as he was, and as hard as he tried to understand his team, there was much that he missed. These kinds of things happen to everyone. They aren't good or bad; they are the dynamics that occur between and among people that usually happen beyond our awareness. We aren't clairvoyant. We miss stuff. It happens a lot.

For example, Sam didn't know that when Frank from R&D made his somewhat sarcastic comments about Sam's opening remarks, his intent was to let Sam know how much he appreciated all that he had done. It was his way of showing affection. His primary motive was to quiet the group down as opposed to having fun at Sam's expense. Not everybody interpreted it that way, but that was his intent.

When Sam kidded Jerry from Manufacturing about his slides, he did not know how frightened Jerry was prior to the presentation, and how much Sam had helped build his confidence. Jerry was a bit embarrassed when Sam complimented him at the dinner, but the first thing he said to his wife when he got home that evening was that he had been recognized by the team leader in a positive way. And he felt great about it.

When Sam made his encouraging remarks about his sales assistant, little did he know that she hoped this would help lead to her promotion. She was thrilled that he had gone out of his way to recognize her contribution. And when he talked about the self-restraint that Joe the Contract Manager demonstrated, he was not aware that his remarks made Joe a little uncomfortable. Joe could come on strong when he negotiated, but he was really a sensitive guy, and a comment like Sam's could make him uneasy.

When the group applauded Lesley for her big idea, nobody knew that she had to fight back a few tears. It was a very proud moment for her. She was truly exhilarated. And finally, Sam could not possibly know that as Helen listened to him rave about her IT presentation, all she could think about was how this was the first time she had been invited to an event like this and how gratified she felt about being there.

There was no way for Sam to know all these things. And if he worried about how people would react to what he said all the time, he would say very little. That applies to all of us. We never know what people are thinking. But that doesn't mean that we have to approach our interactions as if we were political candidates, knowing that every word we utter will be scrutinized. Nor do we suggest that we all become armchair psychologists. We just need to realize that it's important to understand that groups and group dynamics are complicated subjects. We need to be sensitive to this if we want to get the most out of our resources.

Sales teams can be even more complicated. They are hard to manage and harder to lead. But they are absolutely necessary. They can do great work if managed and led properly. They can help any organization differentiate itself. They can be the key variable in the winning business equation. But they must learn how to work together effectively and reach or exceed their potential. Sure, it's hard work. But it's very manageable, particularly if you have the necessary skills.

Synectics®, Inc., the granddaddy of them all when it comes to corporate creativity, said this very well: "Involvement is the prerequisite to commitment." If your team members are involved in the process, they will be committed to the results. Sales teams who understand this and team leaders who make it happen will enjoy unparalleled success.

The key is to understand the skills, processes, techniques, and concepts that are required to make innovative team selling work. It should never become just another catchy phrase. It can become a basic tenet of corporate life. How to make it work is what we will explore together.

Some Things to Consider

What

Anyone who leads a sales team must realize the importance of recognizing the members of that team. Whether you win a job or lose an opportunity, it is important to let each team member know how much you value their contribution. It can be done formally or informally; just be sure to recognize the members of your team.

How

At one extreme it can happen at a celebration dinner like Sam's. At the other it can be in a team meeting or even on an individual basis. The key is to include everyone. Even when you lose, your team members need to know that you value their contributions. And public recognition is something most people appreciate very much.

When

Do it sooner, not later. Any successful coach will tell you how important it is to give feedback as soon as possible. If not, it seems less important and won't be as relevant. So whether you win that big job or learn that your client went in another direction, meet with the team or individuals and express your appreciation.

2 Meetings, Bloody Meetings

John Cleese coined the term in this chapter's title. It is the title of a very funny training film that he produced years ago. The movie demonstrated the horrors that we all experience in meetings, and offered some thoughtful ideas about how to address them. And as only John Cleese could do, he made the points in a most humorous fashion.

But this chapter is not a review of a 25-year-old training film. It will instead explore some of the reasons that cause so many meetings to fail, and suggest some of the things you can do to make your meetings more productive. If sales teams are going to work together effectively, they need to conduct effective meetings. Otherwise they will have a hard time developing innovative solutions for their customers.

Meeting regularly with your team is not a prerequisite for collaboration, but it sure helps. As we said earlier, conducting effective internal meetings is one of the three critical components of Innovative Team Selling.

One way to begin thinking about meetings is to do what someone suggested I do at my older daughter's wedding. I was told to take a few minutes, stand alone with my wife in a quiet corner, and just observe what was happening. "Everyone from your world is there," she explained. "Just take a few minutes and watch what's happening. When you are involved in the event you won't see it; you need to look at it from a distance. If you don't do this, you'll miss something special."

What great advice that was. I have offered the same suggestion dozens of times to friends, relatives, and even acquaintances. Any time I hear that someone is celebrating a big event, whether it's a wedding, milestone anniversary, important birthday, graduation, or even a retirement party, I suggest this. Try it yourself; you'll be amazed at the extraordinary perspective you'll gain when you remove yourself from a situation and watch from a distance.

So why am I telling you this? You aren't reading this to learn how Uncle Harry and Aunt Melissa can get a better view of their 50th wedding anniversary gala at the Rotary Club. I'm sharing this with you because the same concept applies to meetings. If you were to quietly stand in a corner and observe one of your meetings from a distance, you would find that to be most enlightening. Many things happen simultaneously in meetings, and looking at them from afar yields new and different insights.

We have had the luxury of doing exactly this. Our company has video-taped thousands of groups conducting meetings as a key component of our training programs. Our professional staff has facilitated thousands of meetings for our clients. We have seen all kinds of meetings in all kinds of settings in locations all over the world.

As mentioned in The Introduction, our firm, The Baron Group, can trace its history back to Synectics,® Inc., now called Synecticsworld. They have been researching problem solving meetings, the creative process and group dynamics since the early 1960s. They have applied what they learned to offer a variety of services that have their roots in creative problem solving and innovative teamwork. They apply their body of knowledge when they both teach their courses or work with their clients to solve business problems or explore new opportunities.

What we will introduce here is based not only on research, but also on practical experience. Being there, and observing firsthand what contributes to or detracts from the success of any meeting is something we have been privileged to do for decades, originally at Synectics®, and on our own. What we have learned can help any team work together more effectively and more creatively. This, of course, includes cross-functional sales teams.

So What's the Problem?

Let's start by thinking about what you might observe if you were to stand in that corner to learn about your meetings. For starters, you'd probably see a group of conscientious people who want to accomplish their objectives. Nobody goes to meetings with the intent of sabotaging them. Sure, that might happen once in a while because some bozo is out to prove something, but in business that's usually the exception and not the rule.

As you watch the meeting evolve, you'll see some good, solid thinking happening. You'll witness the generation of many ideas. You might see the person who called the meeting clarify the objectives and refer to an agenda. You might even see participants build on each other's ideas. You'll see lots of good things taking place as they do in most meetings.

But at the same time you'll observe things that prevent meetings from reaching their potential. It probably will not start or end on time. Some people will show up late; others will leave early. The agenda will not be crystal clear and some people will not even be sure as to what it is. Others may wonder why they were invited.

Some participants may not listen to each other as well as they could, and they will ask questions that could easily be misinterpreted. Ideas will not always be treated warmly, and too often participants will try to push their ideas rather than explain them. The intentions behind certain actions will be confusing and the anticipated outcomes for the meeting might be fuzzy. And if an action plan is developed, it probably will not outline specific next steps assigned to selected individuals.

Now this is not an ideal situation. And this doesn't even take into consideration the very present distraction of mobile phones or computers or other electronics that can be major detractors to productive meetings. We can't avoid mentioning the wise guy who makes people uncomfortable, or the whiner who keeps complaining, or the confused participant who keeps digressing, or the bully who takes control. Yes, lots of things get in our way when we come together as groups.

This may sound a bit exaggerated, but as you know from your own experiences, any variety of these elements can likely affect your meetings regularly and can make meetings very frustrating experiences. My former business partner, David Hauer, spent many years in the advertising business before joining us. He often told groups how when he returned home at the end of the day and his lovely wife, Barbara, asked him how his day went, too often his response was "awful . . . I was in meetings all day." Sound familiar?

So why does this happen? Meetings are comprised of intelligent people who want to accomplish their objectives. They are committed to their work and want to be successful. They rarely suffer from a lack of knowledge or expertise. Whatever information they don't have available, they can access.

So again, why do meetings often leave the participants feeling frustrated, disappointed, and annoyed?

The answers are surprisingly obvious. In fact, before we go any farther, and ask yourself what you think is the single biggest reason that most meetings fail? It may be something listed above, and that's fine. Take a minute and do this.

This exercise is one of several we'll ask you to do. They'll be short and sweet. Doing them will make this a better learning experience for you.

Here are some other reasons our meetings don't accomplish our goals: People don't spend enough time planning their meetings. They are so busy, and their days are so full, that they just don't have the time to do it. That often results in agendas that are overly aggressive or dreadfully incomplete. They typically don't have a structure or some kind of model to use and reference once they get started.

It doesn't stop there. They don't know how to navigate their way through meetings. When it comes to listening to each other; generating, building upon and responding to ideas; clarifying intentions; or managing resistance, most participants in meetings just aren't as skilled as they would like. These are skills they never learned. There are rarely courses like Meeting Management 101 in college.

You may have thought about how most teams do not adequately define their roles and responsibilities. As a result they aren't sure who should be doing what throughout the meeting. And finally, you usually don't know precisely what to expect of one another, and therefore tend to either be overly cautious or too demanding. There are other issues for sure. These are just the ones we hear most often and plan to discuss moving forward.

If you find all this to be somewhat disconcerting, not to worry. Most of these items are what we call *process related issues*. We need to differentiate between *content* and process. In simple terms, content is the *what*, and process is the *how*. When groups don't reach their potential, process is usually the culprit. Virtually every issue listed above is process related. The good news is that every one of those issues is manageable. Every one. Teams can learn to be more sensitive to process and if they do they will perform better every time they interact. Stay tuned.

The Interactive Meeting Model

So how do you improve your meetings? We will begin by presenting a generic model, a framework if you will, which we simply call the "interactive meeting model" (see Figure 2.1). It is deliberately generic, since different versions of

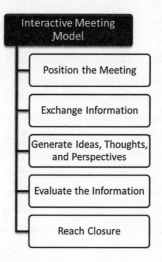

FIGURE 2.1 The Interactive Meeting Model

this can be applied to problem solving meetings, sales calls, coaching sessions, strategy sessions, negotiations, and even consulting assignments.

The model has five specific phases and we will discuss each briefly. When we relate this to the innovative team selling approach we will carefully review and dissect the different phases in detail. Like any sequence, it is simply a roadmap. It tells you where you are, where you were, and where you hope to get. You don't always follow every step in the process, but when you do, it helps you accomplish your objectives.

Position the Meeting

In phase one of this model, we start with the concept of *positioning*. It's a funny word and not one you use every day in business discussions. But every interactive situation needs to begin with positioning. Simply put, this refers to what you need to do to get your meetings off to a good start. It includes actions like making sure the participants are comfortable, explaining the approach that will be used, establishing ground rules when necessary, and answering relevant questions.

Positioning includes clarifying agendas and ensuring that everyone buys in. It means establishing how much time is available and assuring the group when the meeting will end. And it means setting the stage for whatever is about to happen so surprises are avoided.

How you position your meetings sets the tone for everything. Creating a healthy atmosphere for every meeting is extremely important, particularly when you are attempting to solve problems.

This isn't rocket science. Participants simply need to know what the person who called the meeting hopes to accomplish. They need to be comfortable. They need to understand what will happen. And they need to know what is expected of them. If everyone is on the same page, they will feel more comfortable, will be more focused, and will contribute more effectively. If you get buy-in early through effective positioning, you are less likely to have to deal with push back later.

Whether it's something as personal as a coaching session, as important as a sales call, as complicated as a negotiation, as exciting as a finalist presentation, or as convoluted as a creative session, effective positioning always results in a more effective and productive experience. It is critical to establish a healthy climate for every meeting before you start. If you do, your meetings will be much more productive almost every time.

Exchanging Information

Phase two of the model involves exchanging information. We believe that this is the most important phase of any interactive process. It varies depending on the situation.

If you are problem solving, this is when you define the problem and clarify expectations. If it's a sales call, this is when you learn as much about the customer as possible by asking questions to determine their needs, problems, and opportunities. In a negotiation this is when you get your respective points of view on the table and clarify both areas of agreement and differences. And in a coaching session this is when the manager provides his or her subordinate with feedback in order to begin the discussion.

In any interactive situation, there is a need to exchange information, though it's always situational. When problem solving, sharing less information can actually lead to more creative solutions. Conversely, when you review needs determination as a key step in the consultative selling process, you should passionately express the importance of asking as many questions as possible in order to truly analyze the customer's situation.

Exchanging information isn't as easy as it seems. As you watch a group interact, it is easy to recognize when people aren't listening. That isn't because they don't want to; it's because of other things getting in the way.

You can also see how easy it is to misinterpret why certain questions are asked. And you'll see that often people have a difficult time articulating their positions.

When we explore the sales process, many of us take the position that questioning may be the single most important skill of all. There is a direct correlation between your ability to effectively ask questions, and how many deals you close. One of the best ways to utilize the sales team is to get them very involved in the needs determination part of the sales process; before, during, and after client visits. Often your colleagues will ask questions that you didn't consider, and they will acquire information and hear needs that you may have missed.

Having said that, one of the interesting things about questioning is how asking lots of questions can antagonize people. We hear so many examples of sales professionals asking questions with the best of intentions only to turn off their clients. People often use questions for reasons other than obtaining information, and that can impact the level of authentic communication. We need to be aware of that.

The way people react to questions is their parents' fault, not theirs. "Sure, blame it on the parents," you may be thinking. "That makes it easy." You're right, of course, but when it comes to how people react to questioning, it relates to how we were raised. Let me explain.

When you were young, chances are pretty good that your parents spoke to you in question form. So when someone asked, "Would you like to take a bath?," regardless of your answer, you quickly found yourself sitting in the tub. Or if someone asked, "Are you ready for bed?," before you could tell them you weren't, you were wearing your pajamas.

Now they weren't setting you up; it's just a simple way to communicate with youngsters. But as you matured, you realized that this questioning stuff wasn't all it seemed to be. And you soon realized that these questions weren't seeking answers as much as they were making statements. That's one of the reasons that as adults you tend to be skeptical and even suspicious of questions.

If you don't believe this, just think about your immediate response the last time you came home on a Friday night and your significant other asked "Would you like to see Hal and Betty tonight?" Chances are pretty good that the reservations have already been made at the local Italian restaurant. Get the point?

So this information exchanging stuff can be difficult and even a bit convoluted. If questioning, listening, and explaining are the building blocks, you need to be aware of how difficult these tasks may be. But sales teams can learn to do this effectively in both their internal and external meetings. When they do, good things happen.

Generate Ideas, Thoughts, and Perspectives

Phase three is the part of the process that most people like best, because this is when you get to speak. In a problem solving meeting it's when you offer your ideas and share your expertise. In a selling situation it's when you tell your story, explain how you can help, and demonstrate what you know. In a negotiation, it's when you start to look at the available options in order to reach a mutually acceptable conclusion. And in a coaching session, it's when you suggest how your people can improve. It's the fun part of any interactive situation.

The problem is the tendency to do this too quickly. Participants offer ideas before they completely understand the problem. Sales professionals offer recommendations before they truly understand their client's needs. Negotiators put options on the table before they have agreed upon the issues to resolve. Coaches offer subordinates ways to improve before getting buy-in. In each of these examples they clearly want to help. But the tendency to present too soon actually works against them.

One way to look at phase three is to think of this as a *privilege that has to be earned*. You simply do not have the right to explain how you can help in any meeting—internal or external—without doing the discovery work required in phases one and two.

You have heard many horror stories about salespeople presenting before they completely understand the customer's situation. It happens all the time. They often miss opportunities because of this. Without earning that privilege, it's hard to make customer focused recommendations.

When you are problem solving, phase three encourages you to offer your ideas, perspectives, suggestions, thoughts, and insights. When you are in this mode, it is important to suspend evaluation. There will be plenty of time to do that in phase four. Think of phase three as generating the raw material. In phase four, you develop those ideas and transform them into solutions.

This phase of the model is extremely important for sales teams, both in their internal and external meetings. This is the phase they enjoy most. But they must always keep in mind that as gratifying as it is to offer ideas, perspectives, and insights, their biggest challenge is to avoid doing this too soon.

Evaluate the Information

If phase three is the fun part, phase four is where the real work of any interactive situation happens. One last time, let's relate this to different kinds of interactions.

If it's a problem-solving meeting, you'll develop the selected ides. One of the keys to creative problem solving is to suspend evaluation early. You'll have plenty of time to evaluate the selected ideas diligently later in the process. Generating ideas is the easy part. Turning them into solutions requires some effort.

In coaching sessions, this is when the manager has to deal with the resistance he or she encounters. If the person being coached pushes back, then the manager has to resolve the differences. That can be challenging. In negotiations, putting options on the table gives you the chance to be creative and demonstrate your flexibility. But when you have to take the other parties' position into account and work together to develop win/win solutions, it can become a bit daunting.

But it's when you are in selling situations that this is by far the most uncomfortable part of the process. Whether they are one-on-one visits, joint calls, or even team calls, sales professionals tell us that resolving objections is what keeps them up at night.

Determining needs and making recommendations isn't easy, but you know how to do this and usually do it very professionally. It's when the customer objects that things can get testy. That same elegant salesperson, who did everything so efficiently, so articulately, and so comfortably, can immediately transform into a pit bull when customers resist. There is this basic tendency to get aggressive or defensive when you encounter resistance. When you are in this phase of any process, it's important to maintain your professionalism and work with the customer, which is not easy. So we will devote significant time to exploring objection resolution and what sales teams can do to help when you encounter resistance.

Phase four is the most difficult part. This is when what is on the table is being judged, whether it is a group reviewing ideas or the client assessing a recommendation. That's when the rubber hits the road. Working in teams has so many advantages. One of those is working together to successfully manage this part of the process.

Reach Closure

The ultimate objective of any interactive situation is to reach conclusions that are acceptable to all. It doesn't always happen, of course, but this is how you want to end.

The challenge is how you do it, and more importantly, how you communicate it. Too many meetings conclude without action plans, without next steps, and without accountabilities. As a result, weeks can go by without anything happening. You put the time in to reach some kind of conclusion, but then you never see the results of your efforts. What's more frustrating than that?

Every meeting needs to end with a specific action plan. A model that has worked for us is what we call the "Four W's". Without the assigning of next steps and associated accountabilities, you'll waste a ton of time and create a lot of unnecessary anxiety every time you interact with others. Who wants to do that?

To quickly end the mystery, the Four W's refer to *who* will do *what* by *when* and with help from *whom?*

The *what* is nothing more than a clear description of the next step. It is specific and includes the key points that were agreed to in the meeting. It needs to be thorough enough so that anyone can look at it in a month and know precisely what was expected to happen. Usually three to four action items are sufficient. You agree to this first because until you know what has to be done you can't in fairness assign someone to do it.

The *who* (not to be confused with the rock group) is the champion. This is the person who will make it happen. This is the individual who is accountable. It's his or her baby. If it doesn't happen, this is the person who has to explain why. If it does, he or she gets the credit. This is where the buck stops. Accountability is critical when teams reach decisions.

You can't railroad someone into being a champion, though some managers may feel the need to assign specific tasks and that is their prerogative. Usually people volunteer to take responsibility and the manager must approve this. You don't want a junior person to take on a task that is meant for a managing director. Teams can figure this out. But in any meeting, you need to know who is going to take the results of the meeting and implement them.

The *when* is pretty obvious, but let's not make any assumptions here. The most successful meetings we have observed end with specific next steps and associated target dates. Often the manager will assign or approve those steps. But implementation is increased dramatically when action steps are tied to specific dates.

Try to avoid cloudy time frames like "third quarter," but instead assign specific dates to each action item. And of course, the champion has to agree. It's important to be realistic here. You want to maintain the enthusiasm and excitement when you accomplish your objectives, but don't set up people to fail by committing to unrealistic time frames.

Finally, we need to look at the *whom*. Sorry about the lousy grammar. The intent is to differentiate between who is primarily responsible for the action items and who is available to assist. Whom refers to the resources, the people who commit to help the champion in getting the job done. Team members need to commit to helping the champion, and when the action plan is developed it's nice to have two or three people to sign up to help.

Ideally every meeting ends with a thoughtful action plan. If it has three or four specific steps that clearly outline what needs to be done, who will make it happen, when the deliverables are due, and who is available to help, then you are in excellent shape. Doing this invariably increases the likelihood of the team accomplishing the objectives.

We covered a lot of ground here. We explained why meetings are so difficult to manage, and we introduced a generic model that can be used as a guide to make both your internal and external meetings more productive. We made some references to how sales teams can apply these concepts. And we briefly introduced some of the skills that will be discussed in detail later.

This will get us started, but it's only the first step. The overriding objective here is to help sales teams learn new ways to work together effectively and derive innovative solutions for their customers. To do this they must learn about the attitudes they need to embrace, the behaviors they need to demonstrate, and the skills they need to use. That's what we'll explore next. Get ready.

Some Things to Consider

What

Research the effectiveness of your meetings. Learn from that research how to make the meetings more productive. Using the interactive meeting model, explore what you are doing well and what you could do differently. It will result in better efficiency and productivity.

How

Assign a member (or members) of your team to take time to observe one of your meetings. Have them take copious notes and ask them to focus on the process. They should look at the five phases of the interactive meeting model. Ask them to share what they observed without making judgments. Then lead a discussion based on that information that asks the group to determine what they are doing well and what they need to do differently to improve your meetings. Encourage them to address both sides of the ledger.

When

Pick a meeting when many members of your team will be present. And do it soon, like within a few weeks. The sooner you do it, the sooner you will benefit. You will be delighted at how much the team will appreciate it.

3 Easy to Say; Hard to Do . . . Very Hard

When Sam Jamison got home that night from the celebration dinner he was too pumped up to go to sleep. Luckily his wife, Jessica, was waiting for him, as she was interested in hearing how things had gone. She too worked for a large company as a market research specialist, and enjoyed observing how Sam managed the project. Because this was on Sam's mind day and night, she lived through the experience with him, and was very aware of what happened every step of the way.

When they started talking about the evening, Sam was more interested in reviewing what had happened that got them to this place than he was about discussing the dinner. He mentioned it briefly, as he shared how "The dinner was great. Everyone had a good time. They were a bit rambunctious, so I was glad we had the private room. Frank gave me a hard time, but that was fine. It was a terrific night."

But what he really wanted to talk about was the entire experience. Jessica was a willing listener and Sam spoke at length. He knew that he had done many things in his leadership role that optimized the group's contributions. He was aware of what he did well and where he messed up. Some of it he did instinctively as he was extremely sensitive to how people interacted in his meetings. But much of what he did was the result of what he had learned about group dynamics in a course that he took years ago at the local community college. Some of the concepts proved very helpful.

With that in mind, here are some of the basic principles associated with meeting dynamics. These are the kinds of things that our fictitious character might have used to win this piece of business. We could devote this entire book to that subject. Many people have done just that and they have done it well. They explored the subject in much greater depth than we will here, as our intent is to provide basic skills that you can use immediately.

There are interactions, episodes, and events that occur in meetings all the time that keep teams from accomplishing their objectives and reaching their potential. We know that sales teams will be able to do better work if they increase their awareness of these dynamics and apply specific principles when they work together. And as the chapter title suggests, it's not easy; in fact it's quite hard.

The first thing we'll explore deals with the different kinds of meetings we attend and the types of discussions we have in those meetings. Meetings are called for different reasons, and the way we communicate varies depending on the meeting's objectives. Let us explain the different types of meeting discussions.

People typically attend meetings for four reasons:

1. To pass information
2. To seek information
3. To problem-solve
4. To make decisions

You can probably debate whether there are other reasons and we can probably complicate this further, but anything you do in a meeting falls probably into one of these buckets. The interactive meeting model we discussed can be applied to each of these four situations. As you recall, once we position the meeting, there are times to exchange information, generate useful information, and assess what we have developed. That applies to virtually any interactive situation.

When you conduct meetings it is helpful to let your colleagues know specifically what you hope to accomplish. This can apply to the whole meeting or to a particular segment. If you are simply seeking information (What are the target dates for delivering these three items?), you don't need your colleagues to be bombarding you with unwanted ideas. You can avoid a lot of wasted time if you simply explain what you want from them.

You would listen slightly differently to someone who is asking for information than to someone who is asking for help. Problem-solving requires a different mindset than decision-making. It is simply easier to respond if you know what the other people expect of you as different items are discussed. We aren't attempting to complicate things. If you introduce a topic by first saying something like "I am simply updating you on this—no responses are necessary," it makes it easier for everyone in the room to participate. The earlier example can begin with something like "All I need are the answers to the questions on this one." That results in your team members knowing precisely how to listen.

As Sam discussed the initiative with Jessica, he explained that he conducted about eight meetings from the time that he received the RFP until the day the team presented their recommendations to the prospective client. He found himself in each of these four kinds of meetings. Early in the process, Sam was disseminating information so that the respective team members could begin to do their research and formulate their responses to the questions included in the RFP.

Later the team came together to share information. Team members gave presentations to the group summarizing what they had learned and received feedback from their teammates. The intention of these meeting was to make sure everyone knew what everyone else was doing so they could determine how to proceed. Sam took particular pride in how he kept everybody in the loop and went out of his way to submit summaries of what happened so everyone, including those who might have missed a meeting or two, knew how things were progressing.

Of course the team conducted a number of problem solving meetings. Some included everyone; others were smaller in size based on the task at hand. But Sam knew that if he could get talented people together to do some creative problem solving, they would develop innovative ideas and solutions to present to the client in both their proposal and during their formal presentation.

Sam was smart enough to invite people to some of those meetings who were not involved in the project, but were good thinkers and could make meaningful contributions. He realized that in many ways their naiveté was a form of expertise. When people aren't encumbered with too much history, they can think more speculatively and offer creative solutions. Jessica could attest to that. She offered Sam many ideas when he brought up the initiative, and he did in fact use a few of them.

And finally, there were critical times to make decisions. Those meetings were smaller, but Sam actively sought the opinion of everybody before convening the decision makers. Sometimes he made the decisions; other times he deferred to team members. He knew, as stated earlier, that involvement leads to commitment, and he was careful to ensure that everyone's voice was heard. When decisions were made about which recommendations to offer, how to price them, what to prioritize in the RFP, and eventually what to present and who to include in the finalist presentation, everyone on the team felt some ownership. Very powerful stuff, indeed.

The Importance of Establishing an Agenda

The most common answer we get when we ask people why meetings fail is that nobody took the time to set the agenda. Ideally, participants will know what the agenda is prior to the meeting, and they should review it early in the meeting. If you assign time allocations to each agenda item, so much the better.

Can you relate to sitting in a meeting and 10 to 15 minutes into it you turned to the person next to you and asked "why are we here?" It is critical to make sure that everyone knows what the agenda is and buys into it as early in the meeting as possible.

Sam was meticulous about setting agendas. Every time the team got together, regardless of the size of the group or the importance of the subject matter, he sent a memo outlining the agenda. For those who attended remotely, this was particularly helpful. The agenda was sent out at least a week before unless, of course, there was an emergency or something unexpected came up.

Once the group convened he reviewed the agenda and allocated time frames to each item. Often when they began discussing a topic he would let the team know if he wanted ideas or was just seeking specific information. And he always gave the team an opportunity to add to the agenda and express any concerns they might have regarding what he wanted to accomplish.

Agendas are critical in any meeting situation including sales calls. Perhaps we should say *particularly* in sales calls. When you conduct those team meetings, think through what you want to accomplish, set the agenda, and communicate it to your team. Once everyone is together, confirm it and allocate time to each subject. Everyone will appreciate this and it has to improve your meetings.

Setting the Ground Rules

It is helpful for groups to understand the rules of the game. Whenever I facilitate meetings, whether it's for a couple of hours or a couple of days, the ground rules are established early. Different people do it different ways. My friend, Bob Selverstone, who is a PhD psychologist and a wonderful facilitator and teacher, typically tells his groups that "No killer statements are allowed." He has some fun doing it as he asks the group for examples of killer statements and typically gets responses like "that's a dumb idea" or "that will never work" or "let's get real." Then he'll say "Okay, we've got them out of our system, now let's get to work."

Again, there are different ways to do this. It's useful to talk a little bit about roles and responsibilities, how to respect each other's contributions, the importance of listening, and how important it is for everyone to participate. Sometimes you can explain the thinking that led to the agenda and what to expect of each participant. If it's a creative session it helps to talk a bit about the ideation process and why it's important to speculate.

Of course, you should encourage people to avoid using their mobile phones, computers, iPods, and the like, but that depends on your company's culture. I have seen facilitators ask participants to "liberate yourselves from your cell phone for an hour and a quarter until our next break. It can be quite a welcomed relief." Some people actually respect the request.

But what really matters is that you take the time to make sure that everyone understands the ground rules, and more importantly, that they buy in. It has to result in a better meeting.

Intentions

This is a complicated subject and another important one. Team members need to be very careful about their intentions. That's right, their intentions. "They can be quite complex," says Reggie Pearse, co-founder of Organizational Learning Group, a highly respected consulting firm that is located in the Boston area and focuses on organization development and training. Reggie loves to discuss the subject of difficult conversations and has done some excellent work that builds on the revolutionary work that the Harvard Negotiations Project did in this area.

Reggie teaches how intentions can be easily misunderstood. They are often inconsistent with their effect. They don't always align with the impact on others. Often intent and perception have little in common. Think about Sam Jamison's celebration dinner. Even in an upbeat environment like that, his intentions and the intentions of some of his colleagues could have been grossly misinterpreted.

Team members need to do whatever they can to clarify their intentions and prevent them from being misunderstood. And this doesn't fall strictly on the shoulders of the person speaking. When team members do things that seem out of bounds, it never hurts to assume that their intentions are honorable. Most people do not go to meetings to sabotage them, particularly when they are on the same team. The team leader can play an important role by stepping in and asking team members to clarify their intentions when things get uncomfortable.

Reggie tells the story about working with a colleague for years who had gotten into the habit of calling him "Professor." He is an adjunct professor at Boston University's School of Management, where he teaches courses in organizational behavior. Often when he was teaching programs for his corporate clients, this colleague would refer to him that way, and sometimes did it sarcastically. Over time it grated on him, and he eventually confronted her and expressed how this made him uncomfortable and he needed to know why she felt the need to do this.

Her response surprised him as he thought she would get defensive and perhaps overreact. Instead, she could only say, "I am so sorry. I never would have guessed that this was irritating. I thought it was flattering and that it might elevate your role in front of the group." Reggie accepted her apology, let her know he appreciated where she was coming from, and assured her that he did not need for her to try to elevate his image. But more important, it confirmed once again how intentions can be inconsistent with their impact on others. Yes, intentions can be quite complex. It's important to explain them whenever necessary.

Remember Frank Prince, the R&D guy who was a member of Sam's team. He made a few wise cracks when Sam was hosting that celebration dinner. He did this several times. His intent was to have some fun, connect with Sam, and take some of the pressure off. But members of the team could have easily interpreted his actions as having fun at Sam's expense or even putting him down. Fortunately, because the team knew Frank, and the event was festive, nobody misinterpreted what he was trying to do. But in another situation that might not have been the case.

When someone pushes hard to get their idea across, the intent could be to demonstrate to the team how strongly they believe that this will help resolve the problem. But the effect could be turning off the group because the person is coming on too strong and appears recalcitrant or inflexible.

When someone shoots down an idea in a sales team meeting, and states unequivocally that the client will not accept this approach, the intent could be to help the group understand that what they are discussing is inconsistent with the client's strategy. But the impact could be that the person who offered the idea will become very quiet or even shut down. It is not unusual for group members to become reluctant to participate when their ideas are summarily rejected.

Now not everyone is so thin-skinned that you can't say what needs to be said. Nor are we suggesting team members walk on eggshells when they interact or avoid using humor. But there are ways to clarify your intentions both internally and externally and this usually results in more productive interactions.

More than once during the project, Sam found himself asking a member of the team to clarify what they meant or say a bit more about their point of view. He did it in a way that encouraged them to speak freely: "Betty, that's a pretty strong reaction. Can you tell us a bit more about why you feel so passionate about this?" It wasn't something he did all the time, but when he thought it was necessary he stepped in. As a result several potential confrontations were nipped in the bud before things escalated. It's something to think about whenever you participate in meetings.

Treatment of Suggestions

This is as important as any of the meeting dynamics principles that we introduce. How you treat each other's ideas has a major impact on the quality of your work. This applies across the board, whether it's in formal meetings or in everyday conversations. It demands our attention.

When we hear new and different ideas that seem off base, our tendency is to reject them. It's human nature. It has nothing to do with whether we are open minded at one extreme, or skeptical, even cynical at the other. Most of us don't like change very much, even though we have learned how to live with it. Most of us are content with the status quo. Think back to your standing in that corner watching a group interact. We predicted that you would see lots of negative reactions to new ideas. We didn't make that up. It happens all the time. It's a fact of life, as you know well.

This is another one of those things you can blame on your parents. That's right, its their fault, not yours. After all, the first word you probably understood was "no." For those of you who have kids, you are probably doing this to them as well. You have little choice, because in certain situations there aren't many options.

If your two-year-old is standing at the top of the stairs, about to do a trick, you probably wouldn't say something like "This should be an interesting learning experience." Instead you bellow a loud "no," just as you would if the kid got too close to the fireplace or the oven or the pool or that busy street. Yelling "no" in scary situations makes perfect sense. Thus, kids usually have a better understanding of what not to do than what they are encouraged to do. We do that to keep them safe. It's a natural instinct.

The education process also contributes. The child's spelling test comes back with "2 wrong" on top, not "18 right." The composition is returned with the red lines under the mistakes. Our children learn to look for their mistakes, just as we did. It's necessary. That's how we self-correct and learn.

But as children grow up they, like all of us, have been programmed to look at why an idea *might not work* as opposed to *why it could*. That results in the tendency for most people to reject new and different ideas. Use yourself as a way to test this. Think about how you react when you hear new ideas that ask you to do things differently. See what we mean?

But try your best to keep those feelings to yourselves when you participate in meetings. This is particularly important in problem solving sessions. If you can learn to suspend evaluation early, you'll derive better solutions later. That's because the group will speculate more and you'll have richer material to develop.

There are situations, particularly when making key decisions, where you want to first look at the downside risk. It is in your interest to do that and makes good sense. But not when you are problem solving. The biggest detractor to developing innovative solutions is the way participants respond to new and different ideas.

It is every team's responsibility to foster a meeting environment that allows people to comfortably speculate, take risks, and offer undeveloped ideas. When the climate is healthy, and ideas are treated with respect, the group's creative potential increases dramatically.

That doesn't mean you make believe you like ideas that you don't. The last thing you want teams to do is become disingenuous just to be nice. But when your team is in a problem-solving mode, suspend evaluation early. That isn't too much to ask, particularly when you know that you'll diligently evaluate the ideas that you select later in the meeting.

Whenever Sam Jamison conducted problem solving meetings with his team he always reminded them of the ground rules for the session. One of the most important in his opinion was not to evaluate ideas early in the process. "Remember, team," he would typically remark, "let's not evaluate the ideas we generate too soon. Lets just get them up and we'll pick the ones we want to develop later. I promise you that we'll evaluate the ones we select thoroughly. But for now, the objective is to generate as many ideas as we can."

The result was that his team came up with lots of ideas, many of which were quite novel, including the big idea that Lesley offered, which Sam thinks won the job for them.

The Use of Questions

Questioning is an important skill that sales teams have to use. Surprisingly, as important as this is in selling, it can get in the way in internal meetings, particularly when you're problem solving.

Synectics® determined that in problem solving meetings, up to 80 percent of the questions asked were asked for reasons *beyond* seeking information. Most of the questions either had ideas behind them (e.g., "What is the capacity of the elevators?") or they were rejections of ideas ("Do you think we can get that done in time?")

The first example comes from a problem-solving meeting in which someone thought the elevators in a hotel could be used to transport emergency equipment during an evacuation. But rather than just offer the idea, this individual wanted to put his toe in the water first, so he posed it as a question. When he didn't get the answer he wanted, he didn't offer the idea.

That was unfortunate because he learned later that his idea might have worked. The answer he got referred to what capacity was safe for people; the elevator could carry significantly more weight if necessary. So a potentially viable idea was lost.

We suspect that many ideas are lost for that reason. Rather than offer ideas, participants play it safe and ask questions first. If they don't get the answer they wanted, they'll censor their ideas and nobody ever hears them.

The second example about getting that done in time represents a team member saying she didn't think the team could meet the deliverable. It's more polite to reject ideas with questions rather than just come out and say what you really think. When your spouse asks if you really plan to wear that shirt when you are about to go out to dinner, you know that he or she is letting you know that putting on something else is probably a good idea.

Everyone has done this before. We use questions as ways to accomplish other things. The unfortunate result is that our communication is not as authentic as it could be. We need to be sensitive to this whenever we ask our colleagues questions, especially in meetings.

Sam could remember many times when a question came up that sounded like it had an idea behind it. In a gentle way he tried to get below the surface. He would say something like "I sense there's an idea there, Frank. I'd love to hear it." Several times he was able to save an idea that was about to be discarded, and to his delight one or two of those ideas proved helpful. You can do this as well. Don't dissect every question, but if questions are clouding discussions, see what you can do to learn what's behind that question.

Hidden Agendas

You have all heard the term many times. And you have probably experienced this more often than you would like. Hidden agendas are just what the term suggests. People come to meetings with their own agenda and try to force what they want to accomplish upon the group. It's bad form. But it happens often—too often.

I participated in a meeting not long ago that got off to a shaky start. The objective was to determine ways to increase sales for a new product that was doing poorly. The Marketing department initiated the meeting. The VP of sales was one of the participants.

Before the group even started generating ideas, the sales VP angrily said that "Sales isn't the problem—it's the product. Nobody wants it! It's got too many flaws." He was quite upset and everyone knew it.

The room got very quiet. Luckily, the facilitator was a true professional. She calmly asked him to say a bit more about what was on his mind, and when he did, she said "Let's treat that as our first idea," and she captured it on a flip chart. But then she went on to say, "The meeting was initiated by Marketing, so let's stay with the original agenda. We can certainly pursue your idea later." Good for her. Her intervention immediately calmed things down and the meeting continued. The group came up with several creative ways to improve sales, including relooking at the product. It ended on a positive note.

Now we weren't thrilled with that VP's behavior. But at least he was direct about it. He could have easily kept his thoughts to himself and sabotaged the meeting. He could have tried to lead the group to conclude that the problem was strictly the result of the product's deficiencies. But he was open and honest about his thoughts and didn't arrive with a hidden agenda. How he behaved was less than desirable, but you get the gist. At least he wasn't playing games. Too often people do.

Hidden agendas can be detrimental to any interaction. Whether someone attempts to sell an idea, promote a pet project, make themselves look good, or simply impose their will upon the group, they don't add value. Genuine, authentic communication is critical for teams if they hope to reach their potential. When hidden agendas arise it is everyone's responsibility to do what they can to get them on the table. Playing games like these is for losers, not committed team members.

One of the things that Sam liked most about his team was that this never happened. Early in the process when they established ground rules as to how they might work together, and what they could expect of each other, this was one of the values they established. So it never became an issue for the team. Credit Sam for that one.

Control

Even when groups decide not to have leaders, different participants will take control at different times. It's hard to get things done without someone at the helm. It's not a bad thing when people step up and assume leadership. But others may be asking themselves "who appointed you chief?" Meetings do need to have some semblance of order, even when the focus is on developing creative and innovative solutions. The question is who should be in control.

This is a subject we will explore shortly. We mention it here because it's one of those issues that groups need to address early. Sales teams need to define roles and responsibilities. They need to clarify expectations. They need to know the rules of the game. They need to ensure that their meetings are productive and that their client visits are impressive. Understanding who is in control will help them accomplish all these things.

Involving Team Members Remotely

Team selling works even when teams are virtual and all the team members cannot be present for many of the meetings. Technology has helped break down many of the barriers. The most common issue we hear when virtual teams don't do well is poor communication.

All the members of a team need to be involved as often as possible and whenever their contributions are needed. If they can't be there, get them on the speakerphone or conduct a video conference or use webinar technology. But get them involved. If you are in the United States and team members are in Asia, try to schedule meetings at times that cause the least difficulty, like 7:00 if some people are in Boston and others are in Hong Kong. That's early for one group and late for the other, but manageable for both. You'll figure it out.

Seek out the opinions of those who can't attend. Check in regularly. When people contribute on the phone, ask them to mention their name the first few times so everyone knows who is saying what, such as "This is Harry." Use written communications to review everything and keep everyone in the loop. If people complain about receiving too many e-mails, tell them to get over it. You cannot reach your potential if you don't communicate effectively. Just be selective about what people need to know as opposed to copying them on every correspondence.

The bottom line is that you want your geographically challenged colleagues to be active participants in the process. Even if it's challenging, their voices need to be heard.

And Finally

Meetings can be very disappointing and quite frustrating. But they don't have to be. If you agree upon a process, apply specific guidelines, establish ground rules, respect others' contributions, and communicate more authentically, you can avoid the pitfalls that get in the way so often.

Conducting effective meetings is a challenging and difficult task. Like anything else, if you are committed, you can do it well. Sam did, and it paid off big time. For sales teams to reach their potential, and derive innovative recommendations and solutions for their customers, they need to figure this out. We know that they can.

We will constantly refer to these concepts moving forward. Next we investigate roles and responsibilities for everyone on the sales team. When you clarify expectations, determine your mission, and agree on your values, you build the foundation upon which your sales team can flourish. That's where we go next.

Some Things to Consider

What

Take the necessary steps that can turn good meetings into great meetings and great meetings into outstanding meetings. But don't feel the need to do everything at once. Identify areas where you think you can improve and implement changes in a thoughtful, logical way.

How

At each meeting, try to do something different. Perhaps it is sending out the agenda beforehand and confirming it at the meeting. Maybe it is insisting that you start and end on time. Or it could be more sophisticated steps like discussing the importance of clarifying intentions and checking out their impact. It might be establishing specific ground rules like treating ideas with respect or explaining what is behind your question. But again, try one thing at a time.

When

Today. Or if you do not have a meeting scheduled, do it at your next meeting. Think it through, of course, but get started quickly. You will see results immediately.

4 So Who Does What and When?

Years ago I gave a keynote speech about team selling to what was then the American Express Bank. (It has since been acquired by Standard Charter). It was an international sales meeting and the group was very enthusiastic. Harvey Golub, Chairman of the American Express Company at the time, gave a motivating speech the night before and the group was in good spirits.

I was discussing joint sales calls early in my presentation with emphasis on roles and responsibilities. I was preaching about how "the sales department owns the relationship." I gave all the reasons why this was so important. I gave examples and told a few anecdotes and was having a great time making what I thought was a very important point. I probably used the word *own* three or four times. I was on a roll.

Just then, John Ward, who was the president of the bank at that time, raised his hand and said, "Excuse me, Eric." "Of course," I responded, as I was sure John was about to support what I had said. The two of us had a good relationship and he was very supportive of the work we were doing with his sales teams. He had a solid understanding of the sales process, so I eagerly awaited his comments.

Little did I know that he was about to drop a bombshell.

"I agree with you, conceptually, Eric," he said, "but I have to take issue with a very important nuance. The sales team does *not* own the relationship with the client. Sales play a critical role and they are clearly the primary contact with the client. They are the custodians of the relationship. But they do not own it. American Express owns the relationship."

The room got very quiet. I could sense people worrying about how I might react. After all, the top guy in the organization had just contradicted me rather dramatically. But it wasn't a big deal because I couldn't help but agree with him completely. Not because he was the president, but because he was dead right.

For years I believed that the sales team owned the relationship, but instantaneously my opinion changed based on John's perspective. I have never said that sales owns the client relationship since, and I have told that story many times.

The sales function is indeed the custodian of any customer relationship. Sales is the liaison between the customer and the organization. Sales is the client's advocate internally and the company's advocate externally. Organizations have sales functions for that purpose. But I firmly believe John Ward's position that the company owns the relationship.

Robert Christian, who had a brilliant career as a creative instructional designer, strategic planning consultant, and sales process expert, had a very intriguing way of looking at the role of the organization. He often said that "Whenever you meet with a client or whenever you strategize internally, imagine that the company is sitting at the table as a silent partner."

By personifying the company and assuming they were present whenever you interacted, your behavior and approach could change. The company's interests must always play a significant if not a dominant role in every conversation you have and every decision you make.

The Role of the Sales Function

Sales exists to develop, build, and manage relationships with customers. That is by definition what they do. It is very clear to most people what sales is tasked to do. In their marvelous book, *Sales Eats First*, Noel Capon and Gary S. Tubridy explain that " . . . great sales organizations combine world class practices in strategy, organizational structure, and performance management to out-think, out-offer, and out-sell the competition."[1]

In team selling situations, sales takes the lead role. That's their job. Some sales teams will assign a team leader, usually a senior sales professional or even a sales manager, particularly when they work together often. There are

[1] Noel Capon and Gary S. Tubridy, *Sales Eats First* (Bronxville, NY: Wessex, 2011).

exceptions, of course, but there has to be a good reason to ask anyone outside the sales function to play the leadership role on a sales team.

This leadership role applies to both internal and external situations. But before we go any further, we need to think some more about meeting dynamics, because they are inextricably connected to roles and responsibilities.

Content versus Process

Synectics® has developed an incredible body of knowledge that focuses primarily on creative problem solving and innovation. When I was there we introduced participants to a somewhat esoteric formula early in almost every program. I still use it today. It focuses on the probability of success (POS) in interactive situations:

$$POS = f(\text{Quality of Thinking}) \times (\text{Climate})$$

I have written that formula on flipcharts thousands of times. I always apologize when I write it because it seems more complicated than it is. It explains that two key variables impact the likelihood that groups will accomplish their objectives. The obvious variable is what we call the "quality of thinking." There's nothing magical here. If smart people come together with the intent of solving their problems, they will be successful. Rarely do groups fail because they don't have enough brainpower. The lack of quality thinking is rarely a concern.

Climate is the issue. When we talk about climate, we aren't talking about hygiene factors or how comfortable the room is. Climate refers to how it feels to be in that meeting. It refers to things like how safe it is to offer speculative ideas, how willing you are to take risks, and how respectful you are of others. Under the umbrella of climate are issues like how you listen to each other, how tolerant you are, how you share the time, and how much you enjoy working together.

The way to differentiate between the quality of the thinking and the climate is to think in terms of *content versus process*. It's a critically important differentiation. You may recall that one of the first things we said in the Introduction is that this is a book about process. And we briefly introduced this in Chapter 2 and referred to process as the culprit.

Again, in simple terms, content focuses on the "what" and process focuses on the "how." So in a meeting situation content includes things like what was the problem, what were the key issues, what was the primary objective, what were the ideas, what were the reactions to the ideas, and what were the conclusions. One way to look at content is to imagine that you tape recorded a meeting and then turned the recording into a transcript. As you read the transcript, what you would read is the content. The transcript tells you what was discussed, what was presented, what was accomplished, and what was concluded. Groups typically do well with content.

It's the process that usually gets you in trouble. If you return to the exercise we asked you to conduct in Chapter 2 that explored why meetings fail, you'll see that the items listed were process related. If you recall that imaginary meeting you watched from a quiet corner, what caught your attention were the process issues like how people treat each other's ideas, how they listen, how they tend to digress, and how much fun they had.

The list goes on and on. How willing you are to speculate, how safe it is to take risks, how willing you are to accept alternative points of view, and how you try to include everyone are all process issues. Even the logistical issues like how you set up the room, how you capture what was said, and how you assign next steps are process related. If process receives more attention, and groups are more sensitive to process, they will conduct more productive meetings, both internally and externally.

Meeting Roles and Responsibilities

A fair question to ask is why doesn't process receive more attention, particularly if you keep referring to it as the culprit. Take 30 seconds and think about that before you read any further. Come on; 30 seconds is all I ask.

Okay, it's a trick question. The answer is because we simply don't think about it. We are task-oriented individuals looking to get things done, and as a result when we get together with others most of our energy is directed towards the task at hand. Consider the following as shown in Figure 4.1.

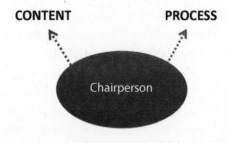

FIGURE 4.1 Content versus Process

When you initiate meetings, you usually become the chairperson for that meeting. Whether you're meeting with a group of colleagues, problem solving with your team, negotiating with the credit guys, or even sitting with some volunteers to explore how to raise money for the little league, if you call the meeting you get stuck with the role of chairperson.

As the diagram suggests, when you find yourselves in this role, whether you like it or not, you are burdened with a dual responsibility. Of course you are very interested in the content, since that is why you called the meeting. You want to hear what others have to say and you want to benefit from their ideas and perspectives. So the content gets lots of your attention.

Process, on the other hand, gets hardly any attention. Because you are so focused on the task, you tend not to even notice whether you are using the time effectively or if you are digressing from the agenda or if everyone is participating. You probably won't even notice that Burt keeps shooting down Andrew's ideas, that Donna is constantly checking her cell phone, or that Mickey hasn't said a word. Many things that keep you from accomplishing your objectives are ignored.

The reality is that most of us just don't spend a whole lot of energy focusing on process. That's an unfortunate fact of life. It's not that you don't care, it's that for most people managing both process and content is simply too much to do and still be effective.

So in an ideal world you take that chairperson role and split it into two distinct roles: the content chair and the process chair, shown in Figure 4.2.

The content chair belongs to the person who called the meeting. This is the person who has asked for help and is responsible and accountable for the issue being discussed. Therefore, this individual makes the key decisions, directs the group and leverages his or her resources. In simplest terms, this is

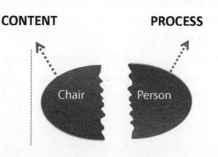

CONTENT   **PROCESS**

Chair   Person

FIGURE 4.2 Dividing the Tasks

their meeting and everyone who attends is there to help that person accomplish his or her objectives.

Enter the Facilitator

The process chair is a little trickier to define. In an ideal setting we would have a *facilitator* present to run the meeting for us. A facilitator's job description is chock full of process responsibilities. At one extreme the facilitator is responsible for the seemingly less important tasks like managing time, taking notes, and keeping the group aware of the agenda. But this person also has many sophisticated tasks like protecting ideas, avoiding digressions, helping people think bigger, and even resolving conflict and minimizing tension.

You can analogize the facilitator to a traffic cop, an orchestra leader, a film director, a quarterback, or a choreographer. This is the person who makes sure that the group works together effectively and accomplishes its' objectives.

Sadly, the in-house facilitator is as obsolete today as the potbelly stove. In the 1960s and 1970s many companies had scores of facilitators trained and available to work with groups when needed. Teams often had members trained in facilitation techniques so they could step in and run meetings when appropriate. General Foods (now part of Kraft) was a wonderful example of this. They had dozens of in-house facilitators trained to work with teams when they conducted creative sessions. This often led to the advent of many new products.

That doesn't happen very often today. With downsizing, mergers and acquisitions, and the need to run leaner in our global economy, most organizations no longer have that luxury. Those resources just aren't available as once they were. But that doesn't mean that every team can't benefit from knowing and applying these concepts every time they work together.

If someone other than the chairperson is the person standing in front of a group with a flip chart handy and a marker in hand, meetings will automatically be better. Just capturing ideas and having someone direct the group results in a more productive meeting. Simple interventions like those in the following list define the role of the facilitator and can have a major impact on any group's output.

- Conduct a round of introductions and/or a warm-up exercise.
- Clarify the agenda and time frame and get the group's buy-in (and stick to it).

- Capture the ideas, recommendations, and next steps on a flip chart, white board, or electronic medium.
- Protect ideas and ensure that people do not evaluate them too early in the process or reject them outright.
- Use the necessary idea generation strategies or exercises to energize the group if needed.
- Conclude the meeting with an action plan and associated responsibilities (those four W's).

Making It Work for the Team

In the ideal situation the facilitator focuses strictly on process. The pure facilitator never offers ideas, as they tend to carry more weight than they deserve and that is not their job. When cross-functional teams come together, they don't have access to an expert facilitator. Nor can they give up one of their resources to focus strictly on process.

But what they can do is allocate the facilitation responsibilities. They can assign different tasks to different team members at different times. One can be the timekeeper, another the scribe, a third can be an idea protector. You could even assign responsibilities like conflict resolver, idea catalyst, and action plan coordinator. The intent is to have different people take responsibility for different process related issues.

As team members become more proficient you may have different people assume the process facilitator role at different times in the meeting. If you have a one-hour meeting scheduled, let three team members each facilitate the session for 20 minutes. That way everyone participates and only one person at a time has to worry about process.

Sam's team realized early that Charlie from Operations was a natural born facilitator. He just had a knack for it so he played that role often, including when they took the big risk at the Finalist presentation. It contributed to the group's productivity throughout the process.

When process does get the attention it deserves, your meetings will be more efficient and more productive, and your ability to develop creative and innovative solutions will increase dramatically. When we relate these three roles to problem solving meetings they appear as shown in Figure 4.3.

As you can see, there are three specific roles in problem solving meetings. The problem owner can be any member of the team who asks for help. The participants are there to contribute and help the problem owner accomplish

FIGURE 4.3 Internal Meetings

his or her objectives. The facilitator manages the process and does the kinds of things listed above. As mentioned previously, if you can't assign a dedicated facilitator, team members can share those responsibilities as outlined above.

The External Meeting

This same concept applies to external meetings. It is a bit trickier since you are in front of the client. A cardinal rule is that the salesperson assumes the role of facilitator. Of course, he or she must devote energy to the content as well, but consistent with the role of the sales function, the salesperson runs the meeting, almost always.

Treat the customer as the problem owner. That makes perfect sense since it's all about them. Whether you are there to help them solve a problem, pursue an opportunity, or satisfy a need, they are the focal point of the meeting. Anyone else who attends the meeting, whether it's on the client side or yours, should be looked at as a resource who is there to help (see Figure 4.4).

If the salesperson's boss is there, if senior managers are there, even if the CEO is there, the salesperson still runs the meeting. This is a fundamental tenet of team selling. After all, sales is the custodian of the account. If anyone else takes over the meeting, they disempower the salesperson in front of the client, resulting in lost credibility. My friend, John Ward, totally agrees with that.

Therefore, whenever you meet with clients, the salesperson leads the introductions and establishes the agenda. He or she decides who from his or her team will speak and when. They decide when to move from one agenda

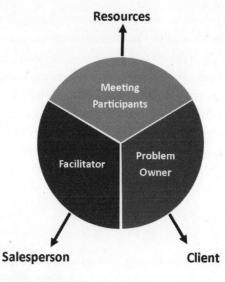

FIGURE 4.4 External Meetings

item to the next. And the salesperson establishes the next steps and develops the action plan. If this sounds a bit dictatorial, that's all right. Someone has to be in charge, and these tasks can all be done gracefully.

That doesn't mean the salesperson does all the talking. In fact, it's quite the opposite. If he or she has invited resources to meet the client they need to actively participate. Clients want to hear from your resources and they want to hear from managers. If you bring in the cavalry, you'd better give them a chance to participate in the battle.

We heard a story in one of our sales training programs from a woman in the mortgage business who had an uncomfortable experience for this very reason. She brought her boss to a meeting with a corporate client with whom she had an excellent relationship. The manager was gracious when he first walked in, and he thanked the client for the business they had given his bank. He was similarly gracious when he left. But he did not say a word throughout the sales call. He just carefully observed and took a lot of notes.

The next morning at 8 : 30 the Sales Rep received a call from that client. He wasn't happy as he barked, "I just want you to know, that if you intend to bring your manager again, and all he plans to do is watch, you can leave him home. Because my impression was that all he wanted to do was assess your selling skills on my time. And I don't appreciate that very much!"

Ouch! Talk about intent versus impact. The manager's intent was to let the salesperson run the meeting and demonstrate his confidence in her. The client didn't quite see it that way. It demonstrates how clients want to hear from the resources who attend their meetings, particularly managers. If you bring members of the sales team to visit clients, include them throughout the call. If not, as that client suggested, leave them home. We will continue to refer to the importance of facilitation, in both internal and external meetings. But for now, let's agree that you'll treat the client as the problem owner, the salesperson as the facilitator, and everyone from the team as resources who participate actively.

Setting the Stage for Success

Sales teams who work together on a consistent basis need to put in some time early to make sure they will be successful. With that in mind we will conclude this chapter by introducing three concepts that every sales team might consider:

1. Clarifying expectations
2. Creating a mission statement
3. Agreeing on values

Clarifying Expectations

One of the key challenges for any team is the need for team members to clarify the expectations that they have for each other. Some of the biggest issues they encounter result from their not taking the time to determine this effectively.

Early in a team's formation, it's a good idea to call a meeting for this purpose alone. Have the team get together and ask each individual to express what they believe their colleagues can expect from them. At the same time, have them share what they expect from each member of the team. If your team is comprised of 10 people, and give each person 15 minutes to do this, you can get it done in less than half a day.

After each person has the opportunity to express their point of view, encourage the other team members to respond. If there are disagreements, discuss and resolve them. The bottom line is that you want everyone to know precisely what to expect of the others.

You can also ask team members to do this on a one-one basis. They can do this on their own without having to call a meeting. A classic exercise is to ask each twosome to spend an hour together. Prior to the meeting each puts together two lists:

1. This is what I expect of you.
2. This is what I think you expect of me.

When these two team members get together, they compare the lists. Typically there are things they agree upon and there are differences as well. Ask them to look at the differences and determine how to resolve them so they agree on what to expect from each other. It takes some time, but it is a marvelous exercise as it clearly confirms what each team member expects of each other. If there are 10 members of your team, they will each invest the equivalent of a day. That's one day to set the stage to work effectively throughout the year. It's time well spent.

Sometimes this can get complicated, even somewhat convoluted, but that can be worth the effort. We worked with a major advertising firm not long ago who was having some major issues in working together well. The four key functions involved were Account Management, Creative, Media, and Planning. We had each group work separately and put together these kinds of lists that summarized what the different functions expected from each other.

It was grueling. When the teams worked alone, collecting the data was easy. They knew the answers to the questions. When it was time to share their individual results, it required some serious problem solving. But they were committed to resolving their differences and they accomplished that objective. They left the offsite with a solid understanding of their expectations across the board. The long-term payout was significant.

With cross-functional teams this has many benefits, including a nice team building component. Everyone learns from one another as they clarify expectations. They get to know each other better and they gain insight into each other's strengths. The long-term impact can be dramatic.

The Mission Statement

Every organization has mission statements, vision statements, and values statements. Just walk into anyone's office and you'll see them plastered on the wall, or on a coffee mug, or at least on the website. They are important as they define the company's overall reason for being. Sales teams can have mission statements as well.

They don't have to be complicated; they just need to define the role of the team. Ideally, they are consistent with the organization's mission statement. The intent is to give everyone on the team an anchor to refer to whenever they question a decision or approach a task.

In their extraordinarily comprehensive book, *Mission Statements*, John W. Graham and Wendy C. Havlick contend, "No clear and easily stated answer exists for this question . . . when asked what a mission statement is."[2] But they go on to reference what others have said, and suggest including things like an enduring "statement of purpose," expressing how they differentiate themselves, and mentioning values or beliefs. For sales teams, the mission statement should in simple terms explain its reason for being.

A proven way to develop them is to break your team into subgroups. Let's assume your team is comprised of eight people. Break into subgroups of two and ask each to develop its own mission statement. It helps if you give them a model that looks something like this:

> Our mission is to work together to develop outstanding innovative solutions that address our clients' needs. We will work collaboratively and demonstrate mutual respect. We will strive to be honest, committed, trustworthy, and cohesive in everything we do, both internally and externally.

Now that's just an example. If you want better ones, go to the *Mission Statements* book. The authors have 622 listed.

Then have each twosome work with another team of two to share their work and take the best of each. So now you have two teams of four and two versions of your future mission statement. Finally, get both statements up, take pieces from each, do some wordsmithing, and you'll come up with a final version.

If the group is 12 people, break it into subgroups of three. You'll figure out that part of it. The beauty of this approach is that everyone participates,

---

[2] John W. Graham and Wendy C. Havlick, *Mission Statements* (New York: Garland, 1994).

everyone owns a piece of it, and often everyone agrees on the final product. Remember, involvement is the prerequisite to commitment.

Agreeing on Values

Finally, every team will benefit if they agree on their values early in the formation of their team. You can think of these as operating principles. You can develop them in the exact same way as we suggested for the mission statement, so that everyone is involved. You can't force values on a team; they have to derive them for themselves.

These values don't necessarily have to look like the Boy Scouts creed. But if team members think about how they want to work together and what values they believe enable them to define themselves, it's a terrific investment of time. Each team will have its own composite of values. Though some, like demonstrating integrity and respecting each other almost always appear, others like encouraging risk taking and stretching the limits may be unique to specific teams. It's up to each team to define them. Our experience tells us that 8 to 10 are more than enough.

There you are. An entire chapter devoted to who does what and when. Every sales team needs to understand this. They need to clarify their roles, responsibilities, expectations, and values. They need to define themselves and figure out how best to work together, internally and externally. If they do they can reach levels of productivity they never imagined possible.

Some Things to Consider

What

There is a lot here about helping teams perform well. We suggest you try to implement several of the concepts we explored. Whether it is agreeing on expectations, creating a mission statement, or clarifying values, these are useful mechanisms to help any team reach its potential.

How

Involve the team members. The exercises are outlined in the chapter. Whether you facilitate the meetings or ask a member of the team to do it, it doesn't matter. But try to involve every member of the team so they feel ownership of the process. They will be more committed to the results if you do.

When

This is something to do when the team is in the formation stage. Once it is done, you will have your guidelines. You may want to tweak these from time to time, but get it done early.

5 Now, Let's Get Creative

That's not a terribly descriptive title for what we are about to explore. We are all creative. Some more than others, of course, but we all have the ability to come up with creative solutions to the problems we encounter every day. Teams have the potential to tap into their creativity and develop innovative ideas every time they meet. They just need to follow some specific guidelines to avoid the traps that get in their way.

George Prince was one of four people who left Arthur D. Little in 1960 to form Synectics® Inc. George served as Chairman of Synectics® for 30 years and is credited with playing a major role in developing many of the concepts that relate to creativity and innovation. Most of them are still very applicable today and Synectics® continues to thrive, now under a new name, Synecticsworld.

Their story is an intriguing one as they were originally part of a group at ADL called the Invention Design Group. Their mission was to invent products and strategies for their clients. They were quite successful at what they did.

One of the things that helped them succeed was that they invested time in researching their meetings. They were curious as to why sometimes they did terrific work and other times they failed miserably. It was that research that led to the original Synectics® body of knowledge. Surprisingly, they became more interested in their research than the inventing they were supposed to do, and as a result they left ADL and formed what is now a 50-year-old firm with an extraordinary legacy.

George had a unique way of taking very complicated subjects and simplifying them. Many of us marveled at his uncanny ability to take a

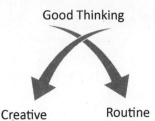

Good Thinking

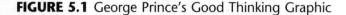

Creative   Routine

FIGURE 5.1 George Prince's Good Thinking Graphic

concept that someone might use to construct a 5,000-word white paper and condense it into one or two paragraphs that clearly made the point.

One of my favorite George Prince graphics is shown in Figure 5.1.

George would scoff at how people believed that creative thinking was good and routine thinking wasn't. That's what his model highlights. Under the headline of what he simply called "Good Thinking" were both the routine and creative channels. As he often said, "Both are good and each has its place."

An example George liked to use was that of an airplane pilot about to take off. George would get groups to smile by telling them that when the pilot was about to become airborne, and he was a passenger, he did not want the pilot to get terribly creative. "Just let him or her do what they have done successfully thousands of times and we'll all do just fine." I remember he used a similar expression when he talked about the gall bladder surgery he had experienced. He mused that he "hoped the surgeon used solid routine thinking in performing the operation." Again, there are times when we do not need to be creative.

But George was quick to say that there were also times he hoped that both of these people would think creatively. If the airplane pilot was participating in a discussion about air safety, for example, that would be a great time to get speculative and generate innovative ideas. If the surgeon was developing less invasive operation techniques, creativity would be welcomed.

The point is crystal clear. There are times when thinking creatively is called for and there are times when routine thinking is more desirable. This is something that sales teams need to incorporate in their day-to-day activities.

Everybody is talking about innovation these days. To compete in this global economy, organizations have no alternative but to develop innovative strategies to address their challenges. Sales teams play a big role here as they are often asked to develop creative solutions to bring to their customers. The ability to conduct successful creative problem solving meetings is a key variable in this equation. Innovative Team Selling demands that you do this often.

We previously introduced you to an interactive meeting model and the guidelines and ground rules that make it work. We discussed roles and responsibilities and explained how important it is to keep an eye on process. That is why we consider the facilitator to be so important in any meeting, and why we encourage sales teams to assign facilitation responsibilities to their members whenever they interact.

Sales teams often spend considerable time in problem solving situations. If they don't, they should. They need to learn how to conduct outstanding creative sessions. This is mandatory if they want to stand out from, their competitors. The good news is that they can.

We'll begin by taking a peek at what a typical problem solving meeting might look like. In honor of George, who I will always consider my mentor, we'll keep it simple. We refer to this as a *skeletal* model; we'll put some meat on the bones and provide you with a more robust model in the next chapter. This will be more conceptual; we'll provide the specific steps later. (See Figure 5.2.)

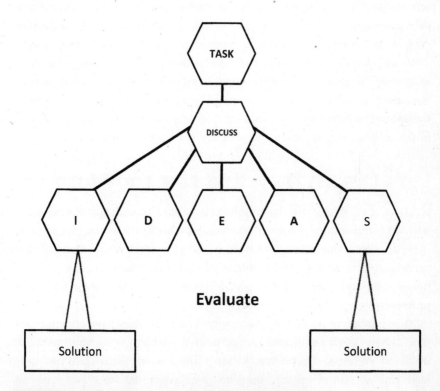

FIGURE 5.2 The Skeletal Problem-Solving Model

The model outlines the steps we take when we attempt to solve problems. It's not very different if you work with others or alone. It starts with a task statement and hopefully concludes with solutions.

The Task

It is important to be very specific about the task statement. Groups need to know immediately what they are being asked to accomplish. This is something that requires thought prior to the meeting. You can't just spring it upon a team without the proper planning.

Task statements can be quite specific ("Explore how we can meet the competitive pricing at this account without impacting profitability") or they can be broad ("Determine ways to improve our hit rate in getting appointments with decision makers at major accounts"). Again, this is determined prior to the session.

The less words you use, the better, but they need to explain what you want to accomplish. Task statements usually start with verbs so they are action oriented, even motivational in nature. (Explore, investigate, determine, clarify, and invent are all good examples of the kinds of words we use to begin our task statements.)

What groups see first is what they will focus on throughout the session. So whenever you craft a task statement you need to be thoughtful. It's helpful to have the task visible to the group on a flipchart or whiteboard throughout the session to help them stay focused. Never underestimate the importance of the task statement. It sets the tone for the entire session.

Let's Discuss It . . . but Not Too Much

Next we need to discuss the problem. It is hard to start generating ideas without acquiring the required information. One of the concepts that may surprise you is that when you want to develop creative solutions, if you spend less time defining the problem, you are more likely to come up with new and different ideas. That's right, *less is more* when you are in a creative problem-solving mode.

Take a moment and think about why. What you may have concluded is that as you learn more and more about a problem, you become more inhibited and less speculative. Really. Those novel ideas that you may have thought about initially may never be suggested once you have all the facts. Nobody likes to offer ideas that are likely to be discarded or rejected. So they don't suggest them. That's unfortunate because quite often these initial ideas lead to breakthroughs.

One of the reasons problem owners ask for help is that they are so engrossed in a problem that they can't free themselves to generate new ideas. That's where the resources come in. You have heard the old term "analysis paralysis." Sometimes we discuss a problem in such depth that we can't come up with ideas to address it.

This doesn't mean you don't provide the participants with the information they need to work on the problem. You don't want your resources to be frustrated as they guess why this is a problem and what you hope to accomplish. We just don't want to overload them with info that will result in their censoring speculative ideas, which could be huge.

That's why Sam cleverly invited a few people to his problem solving meetings who weren't involved in the project. He knew that they would be terrific resources because they could approach the sessions with much less baggage than the team members. And they often made excellent contributions.

Let the Games Begin

Once the group understands the task and has enough information to feel comfortable, it's time to start generating ideas. This is the phase of the meeting that is most energetic, exciting, and even boisterous. It's certainly the part that is most fun, because now you do everything you can to generate new and innovative ideas. This is when you can get creative, even silly. This is when groups stretch themselves to derive new and innovative approaches to address the task.

It helps when ground rules are established. Since the 1920s, when Alex Osborne first coined the term "brainstorming" at BBDO, groups have understood the value of not evaluating ideas too quickly. Brainstorming suggests, as you well know, that if you allow people to generate ideas without having to worry about how they'll be treated, participants are more likely to take risks and speculate.

Knowing that you don't have to defend yourself makes it a lot easier to take risks. Most groups are willing to suspend evaluation early in the process if they know they will have the opportunity to do that later. If they do, you'll get better ideas.

We have all heard hollow clichés that speak to this. I cringe when I hear people say, "There is no such thing as a bad idea." Of course there are bad ideas. Getting in a car and not putting on your seatbelt is a bad idea. Scuba diving without a buddy is a bad idea. Telling your boss to drop dead is a bad idea. Having a couple of drinks at lunch is a bad idea, even if the guys in *Mad Men* got away with it way back when. Let's not kid ourselves. We hear and see and have to deal with bad ideas all the time.

But in problem solving situations, every idea has potential value. If someone has asked for help, and colleagues offer ideas, there is no need for them to be punished or humiliated for having offered a recommendation, no matter how far out it may be. That doesn't mean you make believe you like ideas that you don't. It just means you capture them and suspend evaluation until later.

Similarly, "Every idea is a good idea" is nonsense. Not every idea is a good idea. If that destroys a myth you believe, please accept my apology. When ideas are requested they deserve fair treatment. But don't make believe that they're all good. They're not. You know that.

Experience tells us that if a group finds that one out of every five ideas they develop is worth pursuing, they are doing great work. That's right; one out of five is terrific. If a team generates 25 ideas in a one-hour session, and can select 5 of them to develop, they are cooking. A more likely hit rate is one out of eight. But even then you'll have 3 ideas to develop and that makes the work you did in generating those 25 ideas very worthwhile.

What Osborne proposed almost a century ago asks you to fight your tendency to evaluate ideas too quickly. It was probably suggested long before then. It can be hard, but if you do this, the results will speak for themselves.

As you know, groups get stuck. They run out of gas. The well runs dry. They get tapped out. Every group does hit the wall, and when they do they can use idea-generating strategies. These can energize the group, they can be fun, and they often lead to new ideas. Stay tuned. We will explore this soon.

A Time to Judge

You have probably walked out of brainstorming meetings feeling frustrated, even unfulfilled. Sure, you had fun and the group was inspiring and you felt good about your contributions. You may recall that one idea you came up with had real potential. But sometimes you have left these meetings feeling a bit disheartened.

That was because all you had was this bushel basket full of ideas. You did not have any solutions. There was no sense of closure. And that is the rap on brainstorming. As much as people enjoy the ideation process, and as much as they appreciate the opportunity to contribute, they often leave asking themselves if they really accomplished anything and worry about what will be implemented. No wonder they are frustrated.

That's why the fourth step in this skeletal model talks about evaluation. The approach suggests that whenever you problem solve, it makes good sense to spend part of the meeting generating ideas, and then devote time to develop those that are selected. Ideally you were able to resist your tendency to evaluate up to this point; now it is time to select the ideas that intrigue you and try to transform them into solutions.

Most meeting participants are willing to hold off evaluation if they know they will do this later. That can apply to one meeting or several meetings. You can work on a problem for an hour and generate as many ideas as possible in that time frame. Then you can call another meeting to develop the ideas that you liked the most.

If you need closure now, spend the first half of the meeting generating ideas and the second half evaluating them. Both are viable approaches. It's up to the problem owner to make those kinds of decisions.

There are many ways to look at the evaluation process. Our favorite is derived from the approach work that Synectics® developed. It suggests that ideas are dynamic, not static. They can be treated as *work in progress*. Ideas are only ideas. They are not yet solutions. Teams can work together to transform these ideas into acceptable solutions.

Once again the problem owner takes the lead as he or she selects the idea to develop. That can happen with or without input from the group. It's the problem owner's call. It's their problem and they asked for help, so it's up to them to determine how to proceed.

When sales teams work on problems, different players can assume the problem owner role at different times. It relates to their responsibility and their role on the team. If the team is working on a marketing problem, they wouldn't want someone from manufacturing to decide which idea to develop, just as if it was production related, they wouldn't want their distribution expert to make the call. The problem owner makes many decisions throughout the problem solving process, one of which is selecting which ideas to develop.

Once an idea is selected, you need to give it every chance to survive. Ideas, particularly speculative ideas, need lots of tender loving care. One proven way to help ideas evolve is to begin by identifying their appealing parts. It is important for the problem owner to first share with the group what they like about the idea.

You don't do this to be nice although it is a nice thing to do. The problem owner does this so that the team understands what parts of the idea are intriguing and need to be preserved. Simply put, the team needs to know which parts of the idea appeal to the problem owner. If he can identify two or three positive aspects of the idea, that is sufficient. If she can't come up with at least a couple of pluses, there is probably little hope for the idea.

Once the positives are captured, it's time to express the concerns about the idea. As with the pluses, you need to hear from the problem owner first. The other members of the team will certainly have their own opinions, as they were actively involved in the meeting. But in spite of how useful their comments may be, what matters most is what the person responsible thinks. All team members are equal, but when it comes to selection and evaluation, problem owners are more equal than anyone else. (An apology to George Orwell is certainly in order.)

Starting with the biggest concern first is encouraged because if you can resolve that one, the others appear less formidable. A critically important tenet in idea development is to express concerns in "invitational language." That was a huge breakthrough for Synectics®. If you can express concerns as *invitations*, you encourage your team members to jump in and help.

For example, if the idea is too costly and you say, "It costs too much," whether you meant to or not, you just killed the idea. An option is to ask "How can we do it for less," or "How can we get our budget increased," or simply, "How can we justify the cost." These invitational questions ask the group to come up with ways and means to resolve the concerns, as opposed to accepting them as reasons not to move forward. "It will take too long" becomes "How can we get it done in less time?" or "How do we get the time line extended?" "The client will never accept it" becomes "Let's figure out how to get the client to see the value." Get the gist?

We call this "reframing" and you will see later how sales teams can use a similar approach when resolving client objections. But for now we want you to see that if you express your concerns about ideas as invitations, you dramatically increase the likelihood of resolving them.

Expressing concerns this way helps the group resolve them because they are expressed as tasks, not deal breakers. They can take one concern at a time and address it. If they do this successfully, the idea will eventually become a solution. Often the results are innovative solutions that will enable you to differentiate yourselves.

The late Bill Cope was a personal friend and an outstanding facilitator. He did some marvelous work with groups in helping them derive creative solutions to their business problems. He had particular expertise in new product development and technology utilization.

In his early days Bill was a wonderful architect. When he explained this method of evaluating ideas, he compared it to when he was an architect designing a building. "When the first draft was done," Bill would explain, "I knew I was a long way from the finished product. But I didn't throw away the first draft. I took a piece of tracing paper and kept the parts that I liked. Then I'd modify the parts that I didn't like. I continued to do this until I had a plan that worked."

Bill explained that this is the way groups could develop ideas; hold on to the parts you like and modify those you don't. With that twinkle in his eye, which anyone who knew him remembers well, he'd conclude his lecturette by encouraging the group to approach idea development that way. Continuing his architectural analogy he would often encourage groups to "build upon your ideas and great things will happen."

My former business partner, David Hauer, used to compare idea evaluation with the way a copywriter crafted a print ad. "Chances were pretty good that the first draft wasn't satisfactory," he would explain, "but that didn't mean the writer would throw it away. She kept the parts she liked and modified the parts she didn't. Eventually she had something she was comfortable submitting. But it was a distant cousin from that first attempt that almost ended up in the wastebasket."

Again, the same applies to ideas. If you work hard to generate them and then select several to develop, give them every chance to become solutions. By holding on to the appealing parts and problem solving to overcome the concerns, you may just end up with some exciting and innovative solutions. And isn't that what creative problem solving is all about?

Finally, the Solution

Once the idea crosses the threshold, you can call it a solution. Again, there is a big difference between ideas and solutions. Ideas are only ideas. You'll find us saying that often. It's important to understand the difference. You don't get in trouble for your ideas. You can get in lots of trouble with your solutions.

Sales teams need to consistently remind themselves about the significant difference between ideas and solutions. If they keep this on top of their minds they will invariably do better work and they will consistently develop innovative solutions to the problems and opportunities they encounter.

Most teams establish criteria for solutions. If the idea meets the criteria, call it a solution. If you still have doubts, you can call it a tentative solution. But now it's time to assign next steps. That's when you apply the four W's we discussed earlier. Carefully assign people to take the next steps. You need to determine who will do what by when and with help from whom. Without at least three next steps the likelihood of implementation diminishes significantly.

There will certainly be times that you don't reach closure. Sometimes the idea does not cross the threshold. It happens. There are concerns that you have yet to resolve. But that doesn't mean you have to discard the idea. If the group is excited about it, do what you can to keep it alive.

If there are issues to resolve, assign that responsibility to specific team members as one of your next steps. We like to refer to these as "ideas to pursue." It helps to include in the record what it was about the idea that intrigued the problem owner. Also include the concerns that need attention. And in the heat of battle decide who will continue to work on developing that idea.

With respect to the criteria for acceptability, Synectics® believed that if an idea was both new and feasible and developed to the point of implementation, they could call it a solution. But every team needs to determine that for themselves. The key is to work together to transform the idea to a solution and assign specific next steps. If you have done that, you probably have yourselves a solution.

So that is our simplified, conceptual model to apply when problem solving. You may think it's too simple. You're right. You need more, since most people feel more comfortable when they have road maps to reference as they navigate through the process. So let's move on and add more structure to the process of creative problem solving.

Some Things to Consider

What

When you conduct your next creative session, we encourage you to use a specific process. It does not have to be the skeletal model we introduced earlier. But having a specific approach will always help your team work more effectively when they find themselves in creative sessions.

How

Review the model that you will use with your team before you begin. Use a facilitator to assist. Let your team know that you would like to use this approach at this meeting and that you will discuss it afterward to see how it worked. Make sure you use it throughout the meeting. Reference each of the phases as you apply them so the team sees the value. Stay focused and have some fun.

When

Try this at your next creative session. The intent is to provide your team with a "road map" to help them navigate through the process. Again, do it sooner, not later.

6 Adding Structure to the Process

There are five key phases in the problem-solving process. We introduced a simple skeletal problem-solving model in the previous chapter as a way to illustrate that. It's a good way to begin, but what we introduced was conceptual. We explained that you begin by introducing and discussing the problem. Then you generate ideas. Next you develop the ideas that you like most. Finally, you determine if you have a solution and put together an action plan.

We have determined that groups need a more structured process. Just knowing about these five phases isn't enough to make anyone become a better problem solver. The same applies to teams. With that in mind, we will introduce you to a more structured approach.

Now, structure does not inhibit creative thinking. No one can tell you how to think when you encounter problems. But any group needs to know where they are in the process—are they discussing the problem, generating ideas, developing them, or changing direction? Even when you ask the most creative people you know how they work in groups, they'll tell you it helps to know where they are in the process.

This model is a specific variation of the interactive meeting sequence we introduced previously, since it includes the key components of the problem-solving sessions. It has the five phases, but they are each more detailed (see Figure 6.1).

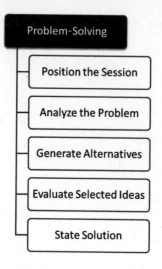

FIGURE 6.1 The Problem-Solving Model

Position the Session

We discussed the importance of positioning previously. In problem-solving meetings, it typically includes four key steps:

1. Set the climate.
2. Review the ground rules.
3. State the task.
4. Check for questions.

It is good to start with a warm-up exercise to get the group comfortable. It's not mandatory, and not everybody likes these kinds of exercises, but it can help create a healthy climate.

Even when groups work together often, warm-ups help. You can vary the exercises and relate them to the task at hand. If the focus is on managing the project, ask the participants to talk about a project they managed outside the workplace. If it's creative session, get them talking about a new idea they embraced recently.

These exercises don't have to relate to the meeting. Warm-ups can ask people to talk about what they did last weekend, what their plans are for the holidays, or even what they had for breakfast. They can be serious or frivolous. The intent is to have some fun and give each person the chance to hear the sound of his or her voice before the meeting starts. That often results in participants participating more freely.

I was attending a board meeting one morning that started early. When I arrived I greeted the board members I knew, but noticed there were several newcomers in the room. The configuration of the room made it hard to connect.

The chairman started the meeting by thanking everyone for attending, which was nice. He distributed the agenda, which was helpful, but he made no attempt to conduct a round of introductions. We had no idea who these newcomers were. That made it uncomfortable for us to seek their opinions, and it probably inhibited their participation.

Later in the meeting these two guests had the chance to speak. It was then that we learned they were both physicians from a prestigious hospital and were there to share their latest research. We didn't know that for the first 45 minutes. If we did, we could have tapped into their expertise and learned more from them.

A round of introductions and, when appropriate, a warm-up exercise, will always lead to a healthier climate and a better meeting. That is the facilitator's job. If you don't have a facilitator, the person who called the meeting has that responsibility.

We have already discussed the importance of reviewing the ground rules so everybody knows what is expected of them and how you'd like them to behave. Even if the group works together all the time, it's a good thing to do.

Clarifying the agenda and establishing round rules when appropriate are important, and this varies depending on the agenda. It's also a good time to establish a "time contract." If the meeting is scheduled to end at 11 : 00, then that's when it should end. It is disrespectful to do otherwise, and it makes it uncomfortable for those who planned to leave at that time.

The task statement is extremely important. Give it the time it deserves, both before and during the meeting. Make sure it is clear and specific. Nobody wants to see a convoluted three-sentence task when they begin to problem solve. Remember to use action-oriented words, ideally verbs like "develop" or " explore." And whenever possible avoid task statements that are questions (e.g., what is the best way to win the business?). Questions suggest there is only one approach. Task statements like "explore what we need to do to win the business" suggest many options.

Finally, answer whatever questions participants may have. Just make sure that the questions don't get you into problem analysis too soon. That's what you'll do in the next phase. And be sensitive to the questions that come up. Often they are ideas in disguise and you don't want to jump the gun.

Analyze the Problem

Whenever you define a problem, remember, "less is more." Groups need to know certain things like what events led to the meeting, why it's a problem or opportunity, and what has been done prior to the meeting. And of course they need to know the desired outcome. These are important pieces of information. But if the group turns the problem analysis into a long drawn out Q & A session, you'll lose ideas. That is a certainty. As people learn more and more about a problem they censor their ideas.

Give the team enough information to work on the problem without overloading them. In many ways this is a trust issue. The problem owner knows an awful lot about the problem. After all, it's his or hers. In the spirit of teamwork, you want participants to feel comfortable offering ideas without knowing every single detail. You want them to be confident that the problem owner is not there to criticize them, and will treat their ideas with respect. This dramatically increases the likelihood of speculation, which often leads to more creative thinking.

Generate Alternatives

This is the most exciting part of any problem-solving meeting. Notice our choice of words. We call this *generating alternatives* because you want more than just ideas. Pragmatic and realistic ideas are welcome, of course, but you can do more. Ideas fall into many categories including beginning ideas, speculative ideas, fragmented ideas, absurd ideas, silly ideas, and downright crazy ideas. All are fair game. You can go beyond ideas and offer perspectives, insights, suggestions, and perceptions. You can even offer totally different ways to approach the problem.

Anything goes during this phase, and if you establish the "no evaluation" ground rule, lots of creative thinking will happen. Even the way you express ideas can help shake off some inhibitions. Hewlett Packard had a memorable ad campaign years ago known as the "what if" campaign. It showed salespeople meeting with clients and calling the office afterwards asking "what if . . . ." The intent was to show that their people were thinking creatively in an effort to help their customers. Their approach caught attention. If you put a "what if . . . " or "how about . . . " or "I wish we could . . . " before you offer an idea, it gives you permission to think bigger.

These are also called *directional ideas*. These open up the door to new lines of thinking that fall under a specific umbrella or direction. An example that we like to use is based on a true story and demonstrates this. Please read the next two paragraphs. Then put the book down. Then generate three or four ideas ranging from realistic to silly. Make at least one of your ideas directional and offer one that's a perception. Here we go:

My house is secluded from my neighbors. We live in a rural community and there are trees on both sides of the house. We like it that way as I travel a lot and when home we enjoy being together as a family without distractions. It works for us.

Unfortunately, one day one of my neighbors decided to cut down the trees that separated our homes. Before I knew what was happening he had taken down four 50-foot trees. As a result, I could now see his generator, garbage pails, garden tools, and kitchen window. Needless to say I was not happy. I went to see him a few times that weekend but never connected. End of story.

So my problem is "determine what I can do to stop the neighbor from cutting down any more trees." Generate a few ideas to help me solve my problem.

For those who chose not to play, it's not too late. Here are some of the answers we have heard over the years.

Realistic Ideas

- Find out if you have legal recourse.
- Invite the neighbor to dinner and explain how you feel.
- Send him a note.

Silly Ideas

- Steal his chain saw.
- Tie yourself to the tree.
- Put notes on the tree saying "please spare me."

Perceptions

* Plant your own trees and quit complaining.
* Move to a more rural location.
* Assume there's a good reason he's cutting the trees.

Directional Ideas

* Do something to your property so he won't want to cut down trees.
* See if you can get your neighbors involved.
* Find a way to make him feel guilty about this.

You probably came up with some of the above as well as your own ideas. I'm sure that you saw the range that is available. You can get silly or absurd ("threaten him"). You can get wishful ("I wish he knew how much this is troubling me"). You could offer a "what if" (what if you could educate him on the harm he's doing to the property value). And the list goes on and on.

The point is, when you have a task, if you want to get creative and derive innovative solutions, you have to go beyond the obvious. Giving yourself permission to think bigger invariably helps. Albert Einstein said: "If an idea has no element of absurdity, I have no hope for it."

He also said, "The same thinking that caused these problems cannot possibly be used to solve them." This is great advice from someone we might want to pay attention to.

Idea generation is fun. When you think in terms of generating alternatives, and don't limit yourself just to ideas, it's even more fun. Building on others' ideas takes this to still a higher level. When team members let the thoughts of others trigger new ideas for them, the ideas get even better. That is why silly ideas can be so valuable. When someone says "steal the chainsaw," someone else might come up with "borrow it until you figure out what to do." When someone says "tie yourself to a tree," a colleague might suggest putting pictures of yourself on the trees with clever notes.

The most creative teams know how to leverage off each other's expertise. That's why when different functions work together they can be so creative. A marketing person might say something that triggers an idea in the technical person's mind.

Or an R&D guy can offer an idea that results in the customer service rep thinking differently about how to approach a customer. It's all about

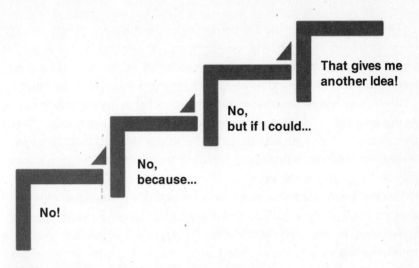

FIGURE 6.2 Four Levels of Idea Response

working together, finding value in what each person says, and then generating the most exciting ideas you can.

Listen to your teammates in a way that encourages you to build on what they say and to enhance their contributions, as opposed to falling into the trap of looking for the flaws. If you suspend evaluation and build on others' ideas, great things can happen.

One way to look at this is what we refer to as the four levels of idea response. It's a concept that I learned from my good friend, Rick Harriman, who was the managing director of Synectics® for almost 30 years. The model looks like the one shown in Figure 6.2.

The model explains the different ways that people respond to ideas they don't like. You hear ideas all the time that don't appeal to you. The challenge is in how you choose to respond.

Level One, which obviously is the lowest level, refers to situations in which your response to the idea is to simply say "no." It doesn't require a great deal of life experience to do this. Have you been around a two-year-old lately?

Level Two is somewhat better. At this level you focus strictly on the concerns. You don't attempt to find value in the idea. You focus on what's wrong with it. That's where most people are. Your parents are a bit responsible, as we explained earlier. The education process also plays a role. The spelling test comes back with "two wrong" on top.

The composition has the red marks under the mistakes. When children learn, they need to understand what they are doing wrong. It makes perfect sense. But these learned behaviors stay with you as you mature, and as a result you tend to respond to ideas by focusing primarily on the flaws.

Level Three represents what we introduced earlier as invitational thinking. At this level the difference is that the "no" is followed by a phrase like "but if we could . . . ." You attempt to find value in the idea and look for ways to resolve the concerns, rather than simply expressing them. It's a great place to play and a great place to be.

At *Level Four*, you try to make the ideas you don't like trigger new ideas that are more acceptable. You find value in the ideas you hear and think about ways to improve upon them. "That gives me another idea" is a wonderful way to respond to ideas you don't appreciate. It's not something you can do all the time, but when you can it brings collaboration to a higher level.

Let's return to the neighbor and the trees. If someone suggests that I steal the chain saw I can respond at each level. I could simply say "no" (level one) or I could find myself at level two and say something like, "No, because stealing is something I just won't do. It sets a terrible example for my kids, and what if I get caught"? If I was having a good day, I might offer a level three response: "No, I won't steal the chain saw, but I wonder if there is a way to get it out of his possession until I figure out how to deal with this." And finally, some gifted person might find him or herself at level four and let the idea trigger a new one: "What if you were to borrow it instead of stealing it and don't return it until you come up with a way to stop him from cutting down any more trees."

So there you have it—four different ways to respond to the same idea. That's something every team member can do. If team members consistently challenge themselves to respond to ideas at higher levels, they will elevate their creativity and develop exciting solutions for their clients.

Evaluate the Selected Ideas

Okay, so now you think the fun is over. No way. Sure, generating ideas and developing the raw material you need to address problems and opportunities is energizing and exciting. But so is the process of transforming ideas into solutions. It's hard work, but when teams get together they can often turn that sow's ear into a silk purse.

We talked about the idea evaluation process at length in the preceding chapter so we won't repeat that here. What we do want to explore is how teams evaluate ideas.

The problem owner selects the ideas to develop. He or she can do that with or without the group's help. Most like to hear the team members express which ideas they like the best, so they can benefit from their opinions, but the final decision is theirs. After all, it's their problem and they will implement the solution. You don't want the group to force their will upon the person who has asked for help.

Once the ideas are selected the problem owner will explain what he likes about the idea and what appeals to him. Next he shares his concerns. With the help of the facilitator, if available, he'll express his concerns in invitational language. And then the group does whatever it can to address those concerns. So if a salesperson expressed a concern like "we need to figure out how to make the customer feel comfortable with the systems change," the group would do whatever it could to figure out ways to resolve that issue.

So, even though the problem owner does the selecting and evaluating, the group is locked and loaded, ready to help address those concerns and transform the idea into a solution. That's what teamwork is all about.

So what about that team member who sees a concern that the problem owner missed? Assume that there is a good reason why he or she didn't address that point. Trust their decision. If you think it's important, raise the issue. But wait. You don't want to throw a monkey wrench into the system too early. You'll have your turn later in the meeting. We're not saying, "speak now or forever hold your peace." It's just that quite often resources worry about concerns that the problem owner has already resolved in their own mind.

Ideation Techniques

There are times when you'll get stuck. It happens and when it does you can apply specific ideation techniques.

Sometimes you can ask participants to offer absurd ideas, which the group can use to trigger new ideas. This can be very effective, as you saw in the examples we gave earlier. When things get quiet you can break your team into twosomes and have them look at the problem from their partner's point of view. You can ask the problem owner to discuss the problem at a very basic level and see if that gets you a new perception or two.

Synectics® loved to use metaphors and analogies to explore the problem from different perspectives. For example, if you were working on a packaging problem you could ask the group to look at packaging from the world of nature. Or if that was too obvious, look at it from the world of psychology. The group comes up with examples first and then uses that information to trigger new ideas. Even role playing can help when you are out of ideas.

Another technique is to ask participants to assume they were different kinds of people—a retired teacher or an ambitious politician or a police officer. Ask each to muse about what they would want the solution to do for them. This too can get the group thinking differently.

The point is that when you find yourselves out of ideas, sometimes a quick exercise to rejuvenate the group can help. This is usually up to the facilitator. Sometimes they help, other times they don't. But at minimum these kinds of interventions can energize the group and ask them to approach the problem differently.

The big idea, which Sam believes won them the job, started off as a pretty risky suggestion from an unlikely contributor. But as the group worked together to develop it they came up with something that definitely differentiated them from their competitors. It never could have happened if someone didn't take a risk and the team didn't work together to invent an approach that was truly remarkable. That's the beauty of teams.

State the Solution

Solutions are ideas that have been developed to the point of implementation. Remember, it's important to establish criteria to use to measure the idea to determine if you have a solution. If you don't reach a solution but have an exciting idea, you want to keep alive and follow the guidelines we established previously.

Never lose sight of the importance of assigning next steps with deliverables to ensure that the solutions are implemented. If you don't get the commitment in the heat of battle, chances are good that that the fruits of your labor will never be realized.

Too often groups leave meetings very excited, only to be disappointed when nothing happens several months later. This is often because they did not take the time to develop specific next steps. It's no more complicated than that.

With that in mind, we introduce the concept of the "champion." You have heard the word used often in business. We define the champion as the person who assumes both the responsibility and the accountability for the next steps. The champion is the person who makes it happen.

George Prince spoke often of champions. Having been involved in so much new product development work, both as an inventor and facilitator, he had a good handle on why some new products make it and others don't. He often talked passionately about the role of the champion. "This is the person who lives, breathes, and sleeps with the project in mind," George would say with a smile. "This person wakes up thinking about the product and does the same before going to bed. It is on their mind all the time. They live through every phase from conception to implementation."

George believed in work/life balance, so I don't want to give the impression that he believed champions should be mono-dimensional when they get involved in a project. But he learned from his experience that when the champion was involved in all aspects of implementation, the likelihood of success increased. When they participated in all aspects of the roll out, whether it was the research, production, market test, or training, products were more likely to end up on shelves in the store. "Champions were the primary difference," I heard George say time and time again.

This concept relates well to sales teams. Assign champions to different parts of every project. Don't inhibit yourselves by only assigning people tasks that fall in their areas of expertise. Stretch your team members when appropriate. Determine who will champion the RFP. Decide who has responsibility for research or the literature search.

Assign someone to coordinate the presentation. Figure out who will do the benchmarking. Someone needs to explore what the competition is up to. Assign a colleague to keep track of the calendar. And, of course, you'd better make sure that someone or several people on the team do what is necessary to make your meetings productive.

You can probably make a case that all these responsibilities can be handled by Sales. In many organizations that's precisely what happens. But if you're the leader who delegates specific tasks to others, and makes them responsible for the outcome, you will outperform your competition over and over again.

Ensure that those champions leverage their resources to get the most out of the team, of course, but make it theirs. Let them own it. Tap into your collective expertise. Once again, *teams outperform individuals*. We never tire of saying that.

The "rugged individualist," a term often used at Lehman Brothers in the 1990s, is as obsolete as rabbit-ear antennas on TVs. The world is just too complex for anyone to go at it alone. You need to reach out to others. Remember what the Sloan study we referenced in Chapter 1 said: "Intuitively we still attribute too much to individuals and not enough to groups."

So that's our structured approach to creative problem-solving. The phrase sounds like an oxymoron. But the steps are all necessary and helpful.

Position your problem-solving meetings crisply and carefully. Analyze the problem, but keep it brief without overloading the participants. Generate as many alternatives as you can and think creatively and speculatively. Hold off evaluation and give your colleagues permission to get silly or even nutty and build upon others' ideas. Select the ideas you are most excited about and evaluate them diligently, involving as many team members as you can. And, finally, when you cross that threshold and have a solution, put together a comprehensive action plan with associated champions.

Innovative team selling has several components. The internal part may be most important. We are confident that if you apply what we have introduced here, you will be well prepared to pursue those opportunities that you and your sales teams encounter regularly. As a result, you'll be excited to present to your clients the innovative solutions that your team develops. That's what comes next.

Some Things to Consider

What

Do whatever you can to protect the ideas that your team members offer. Ideas need tender, loving care. Transforming ideas into solutions takes effort. It begins with treating them with respect. You will be doing your team, your company, and, most important, your customers a great service if you do what you can to protect ideas when you work together.

How

Whenever the team meets, remind them of how important it is to suspend evaluation when ideas are generated. Explain that the tendency is to look at why ideas might not work, but that they need to control that. Assure them that you will evaluate ideas diligently later in the meeting, but for now you are just collecting them. You might even introduce the four levels of idea response and ask them to aim for level four.

When

Any time two or more people meet, the team leader needs to do what he or she can to protect ideas. Remind your colleagues of that before any meeting that incudes idea generation as part of the agenda. And if some of them do not play by the rules, a gentle reminder is in order.

7 Getting Our Acts Together

I co-authored an article on planning years ago with my former business partner, Kate Reilly, one of the co-founders of Consultative Resources Corp. (CRC). CRC has been training sales professionals for more than 30 years. Just before the article was formally submitted, Kate inserted a new opening line: "Mention the word planning and salespeople start to yawn."

The fact is that most salespeople would rather be doing than planning. They want to be out there. We have heard countless sales mangers lament about what a lousy job of planning their salespeople do all the time. Yes, *all* the time. We have also heard of many lost opportunities that could be attributed primarily to the lack of planning prior to the client meeting.

Sales teams often fall into the same trap. They work diligently in putting together their presentation. They develop some wonderful innovative recommendations to present to their customers. They do the necessary research and market analysis so that they have a solid understanding of the opportunity. They often feel gratified about what they did to be ready to tell their great story.

But after putting all this time and effort and energy into developing their presentation, they don't take the necessary steps to plan *how* they will present to the client. They just don't do it. It's another example of the *content versus process* conundrum. They know pretty much what they want to do, they just haven't figured out how to do it. And that can lead to disaster.

The time you put into planning your presentation is critically important. Whether it's simple stuff like what your slides look like at one extreme, or sophisticated concepts like how you segue from one team member to another, or what to do if you get derailed, you need to go to every client meeting well prepared. There simply is no option.

Roles and Responsibilities

Let's start with exploring who does what. Someone has to play the lead role in every client meeting and we know it will help if someone facilitates. That is usually the salesperson or the team leader. There are exceptions to the rule, but that's what they are—exceptions. There has to be a good reason for someone outside the sales function to run the meeting.

Geoff von Kuhn has spent his entire career in the financial services industry and has successfully transformed sales cultures at Bankers Trust, Bank One, Citigroup, and AmSouth. I have observed firsthand what he has done to significantly impact these cultures. Several times the groups he managed doubled their sales within a year. He understands what it takes to make change happen in organizations.

Geoff always made a practice of visiting major accounts annually. He believes that "the most senior sales executives should visit every major customer at least once a year." He also believes that "the person who is closest to the relationship manages the sales call." When pressed on this point, he responds, "If any manager at my level takes over the sales call, it sends a terrible message to the customer. It gives the impression that we don't trust this person and the impact has to be a dent in their credibility."

Now that doesn't mean that a manager just watches what's going on. Remember the mortgage rep and her boss who simply observed and irritated their client? Geoff explains, "I want to contribute. Customers expect that and hopefully they find value in my perspectives. But I am there to help the customer and support the salesperson. I am not there to run the meeting." That's great advice from someone who has been there and has enjoyed much success in managing sales organizations.

So rule number one when you visit clients is that someone plays the role of the facilitator, and this is usually the salesperson. This applies not just to the client meetings, but to internal meetings as well. When you work internally, the sales professional might assign a facilitator or distribute those responsibilities to others. But process has to get the attention it deserves, and that starts with the facilitator. This is particularly important when you conduct planning meetings.

But what about everyone else? Where do they fit in?

For starters, if you bring resources to meet clients, they had better participate. We can't emphasize that enough. We have a client who used to bring as many as 10 people to their finalist presentations. Only four or five participated and the rest simply observed. Their clients didn't like that very much. Our client finally got the message when his client said: "No wonder your prices are so high. You have to compensate all these people who don't have much to say." Oops!

If you bring people with you on your sales calls, give each one a specific role. Everyone needs to contribute. If it's simply two of you on a joint call, or eight of you for a major presentation, whoever is there must participate.

We have been teaching a specific pre-call planning model for years. We call it our "reporter's approach to planning," because we encourage team members to ask themselves the same questions that a reporter would ask before writing an article—who, what, where, when, why, and how. Each question deserves attention.

Who

The roles and responsibilities piece is huge. We'll hold off on reviewing the importance of facilitation for now. Instead, let's explore the importance of leveraging resources. One way to approach this is to assign different team members specific responsibilities prior to the meeting so you'll know who does what.

It is obvious who will kick off the meeting, review the agenda and lead the introductions. That is the salesperson's or team leader's job. But the team needs to define everyone else's role. Who will ask the key questions, particularly the challenging ones? Who will present the different components of the recommendation? Who will we turn to when objections arise? Who will take notes? Who will make sure we watch the time? If people are participating remotely, who will make sure they have the chance to participate?

These issues and others need to be thought through prior to the meeting. That doesn't mean you'll write a script, but you will know what to expect of each other. There is no excuse for any team to meet a client and not know beforehand the role that each person will play.

What

This may be the most important of the six questions. Before meeting with clients, a team must know what their objectives are. They need to be clear about the agenda. They must think seriously about the questions they will ask and how they will ask them. They need to think long and hard about what they want to present—what products, what services, what ideas, and what support systems.

There's never enough time to explain every detail so they need to know what to include and what to omit. They need to anticipate the objections that the client may raise and think about how to resolve them. In simple terms, they need to be very clear about what they will do to make this a great meeting.

Where

This is one of the two logistical questions you need to ask. Of course everyone on the team needs to be well informed as to where to meet and to get to that location early. Everyone has at least one sad experience when you showed up at the wrong location or at the wrong time. And although it's so obvious, when you meet at the client's location, dress appropriately. Sometimes overdressing is as bad as underdressing. Ask the client about the dress code, and follow their guidelines. If necessary, err on the side of overdressing.

See what you can do to impact the room configuration so it supports your presentation. We once were asked to include in our presentation a demonstration of how we teach a specific skill. But when we arrived the room was set up in classroom arrangement, what we call "theater style." We typically work with groups in a "U" format.

I explained to the training director that we needed to change the format. She resisted, but I took a strong position. I explained that if she wanted to see how we teach a module, then we needed to do it consistent with the way we teach programs. She reluctantly agreed. We did win the job, but I learned later that the vote was 6-1. Who do you think voted against us? In fairness I should have arranged for the room setup prior to the meeting.

When

This is the other logistical question. And we don't always have a say as to when the meeting will take place. But you know from your experience that morning meetings are better than afternoon meetings and that meetings after lunch are extremely challenging. One of our team members, Tom French, used to refer to the "food coma" when observing groups after lunch, particularly those hearty lunches.

If there are several people presenting in a finalist situation, most teams prefer to go first or last. If you go first, you set the standard that everyone has to meet. That's a nice position to be in. If you go last they remember you best. That's not too shabby either. So ideally you'll get to present first or last, even though you rarely know when you will go in advance of your presentation.

Having said that, one of the biggest jobs we ever won happened in spite of our presenting third in a group of five immediately after lunch. Conversely, we have lost jobs when we went first or last. So when you get to present might have an impact, but it is usually dwarfed by what you have to say.

Why

Why is what we often refer to as the soul searching question. The person in charge has to ask him or herself why these people are attending. There needs to be a good business reason to bring them, so the client isn't skeptical as in the example above. Quite often, people who would like to attend just can't. These are tough decisions and you can ruffle a few feathers along the way, but you need to do what's best for the client and what's best for the team, in that order.

I attended a rehearsal for one of my clients recently. It took place about two weeks before a major finalist presentation. The vice chairman of this major corporation was planning on attending. He was there primarily to show support. They asked him to speak briefly in the beginning of the meeting about the vision of the company and how it paralleled the vision of the client. His entire contribution would last about three or four minutes.

He asked during the rehearsal if he should attend. We could see that he was reluctant to do so, primarily because he didn't think he should be there "if all I am doing is speaking at 30,000 feet." I also sensed that he was concerned that he was so far removed from the day-to-day activities of the business that he wouldn't have much to add.

I pushed back, gently of course. His presence would send a very powerful message to the client about both their commitment and interest in working together. Bringing him was an excellent business decision. And we were confident that, if he was asked questions that he couldn't answer, he would defer them to the people who could. He did attend, he did a great job, and was glad he did.

Who you bring to a client meeting is less dependent on the quantity of what they say than the quality. Substance rules. Ask yourself what you'll miss if this person is not there. Bring the people with you who will impress the client the most by demonstrating your understanding of their business and how you can help. And remember, less is more . . . again.

How

This, of course, is the magical question. A good chunk of the balance of this book deals with that particular question. Remember, *how* refers to *process*. Any sales team worth its salt has to think through how they will make their meetings successful.

This can refer to things as basic as where you sit and how you arrange the group, to things as complicated as how you deal with unanticipated objections and how you get back on track if you get derailed. You need to anticipate what you will do to get the meeting off to a great start, how you will quickly connect with the clients, and how you review the agenda. You'll need to think about how you obtain the information that you do not yet have and how you'll demonstrate your understanding of the clients' needs

You need to give significant attention to how you will offer your recommendations and how you will include your team members. You need to know how you will transition from one part of the process to the next and how you will hand off the discussion to the designated presenters. And of course you need to know how you will resolve whatever conflict arises and how you will comfortably attempt to reach closure.

That's a lot of important information to be thinking about and, yes, it can seem daunting. And this isn't even a complete list of all the things that can go wrong. But it is all very manageable. If you respect the concept of process and trust your colleagues, you can approach any client meeting confidently and so well prepared that you'll knock them dead.

But no matter how well prepared you are, surprises happen. Recently we were one of three finalists for a big job and had only 45 minutes to give our presentation. We were well prepared and knew precisely what we wanted to accomplish. But before we even finished introductions, one member of the client team started asking question after question about our capabilities internationally.

When these kinds of things happen we recommend that you defer to your primary contact and ask him or her how to proceed. We did that: *"Susan, we certainly can continue in this direction, but I need guidance from you as to how to proceed."* More often than not, the sponsor will bail you out. Not this time, unfortunately. Susan was as interested in learning about what we could do in Asia and South America as the individual who was bombarding us with those questions. We stayed on that topic for over 15 minutes—one third of our allotted time. And it unnerved us to the point that we weren't at the top of our game when we finally got back on track.

We did not win the business. I don't know if that is why. I do know that even when you do everything the way you planned, and you feel you're on track, stuff happens. You do the best you can, but there are always those unanticipated issues. Going to your sponsor is a way to get out of the jam, but as you saw in this example, that doesn't always work out the way you hoped.

So Let's Rehearse

Most of us don't like to rehearse. Rehearsing isn't cool. Practicing beforehand isn't a whole lot of fun. We're good on our feet, we know what we want to do and what we want to say, so we typically discuss what the game plan is and we're off to the races. Too often we do what is commonly called "elevator planning." We plan the meeting in the elevator on the way to the client's offices. Not a good idea. In fact it's a lousy idea. We could add it to the list of bad ideas in Chapter 5. It belongs right up there with not wearing a seat belt. That old saying, *a great dress rehearsal leads to a lousy opening night*, may well apply to the theater, but it doesn't apply to team calls.

So rehearse, several times if necessary. If it's a finalist presentation there is a lot on the line. Try a few different approaches. Experiment. Discuss what you might try that's new and different. That's what Sam's team did and they believe to this day that this is what won them the business.

During their rehearsal they realized that they weren't really doing any-thing to dramatically differentiate themselves. Yes, they had a solid under-standing of their prospective customers' needs. They had an outstanding state of the art recommendation. They knew exactly what each person would do. They even had a few contingency plans in place. But as they debriefed rehearsal number two, they were still concerned about how to stand apart from the their competitors.

That's when Lesley spoke up. She was from Customer Service and had spent hours reading and rereading the RFP. *"One of the things they kept saying, even though it isn't expressed overtly in this document, is how important innovation is to them and how they want to partner with a company who values teamwork,"* she remarked. *"What if we could demonstrate our creativity and how well we work as a team during the presentation?"*

The group instantly jumped into problem solving mode. Sam let it go because he saw the value, but the first few ideas weren't exciting. But then out of the blue, Lesley offered a speculative beginning idea; *"I wish they could see how we work together. I wish there was someone from the client team observing us right now."*

The group picked up on that notion and came up with a unique albeit risky idea. If the client mentioned a problem that was important to them during the meeting, the team would ask the client if they could work on it right there and then. They were told they had an hour and a half for their presentation. If they could take 15 minutes and use that time to discuss the problem and generate a bunch of ideas in real time, they would clearly do something the competitors wouldn't dare to try. They would demonstrate not only their ability to collaborate and develop innovative solutions, but would show just how effective a partner they could be.

Sure enough, that's what happened during the finalist presentation. The client raised the issue that their people would be reluctant to change. Sam asked the client if it was all right to spend a few minutes addressing that issue. The client said, *"Sure, it's your time,"* so Sam asked one of his team members to assume the facilitator role. This was well planned before the meeting, of course. The facilitator asked the client a few questions, got the group to generate a dozen ideas, two of which came from the client team, and got a couple of next steps. He did all this in 15 minutes. Needless to say, the clients were blown away and Sam thinks that's what won them the business.

These aren't the kinds of risks we usually take in key situations like finalist presentations. But innovation and risk taking are inextricably connected. Lesley took a risk in making the suggestion. Sam took a risk in going with it. And the team took a risk in deciding to try this if the situation presented itself.

Someone said that team selling is like wallpapering a bathroom. The hard part is the prep work. Once the old paper is removed, the walls are sanded, the paper is cut to size, the fixtures are protected, the drop cloths are down, and the glue is ready, putting up the paper is relatively easy. If you ever wallpapered a bathroom, you might take issue with this, but the point is a good one. Do the prep work and do it well and everything else will fall into place. A sales team that has its act together can do great things. Planning may not be the most fun part of the job, but it may well be the most important.

Kip Testwuide is the Co-Head of Fixed Income for BNP Paribas, Americas. He has been with the firm for more than 25 years and is an outstanding sales leader. He genuinely understands the value of team selling and has sponsored programs to introduce it to the firm for both homogenous and heterogeneous groups.

Kip believes that there are three key elements to team selling—planning, executing, and debriefing. He is a big advocate of the planning process. Take note of his wise words: "We are much more likely to provide our clients with outstanding solutions if we plan effectively as a group. We are more focused, we are more confident, and we simply do a better job when we take the time to determine what to offer the client and how to do this effectively. We need to clarify our objectives and understand what we hope to accomplish. We are in a world that is changing rapidly and since what we sell is 'content,' we need to be well prepared to help our clients solve their problems."

You can't say it any better.

There isn't much to say after that, so let's move on to the next chapter and investigate how you can reap the fruits of your labor and present yourselves brilliantly to your clients and prospects.

Some Things to Consider

What

Planning is critical; rehearsing is mandatory. As much as people push back when they are asked to plan for client meetings, leaders are encouraged to insist upon it. And though not everyone thinks rehearsing is cool, if you have important client meetings coming up, particularly finalist presentations, rehearsing is something you have to do. No excuses. Just do it.

How

Explain the value of planning to the team. Share an anecdote in which planning helped and one where not planning hurt. Try the reporter's approach—the who, what, where, when, why, and how—and determine the value. When it is time to rehearse, remind your colleagues that the best in the world rehearse—whether they are actors, singers, dancers, athletes, politicians, or even public speakers. Rehearsing only helps in the big picture.

When

Before your next important client meeting, get the team together and apply both concepts. Thoroughly plan for the meeting and conduct a rehearsal or two. After you visit the client, ask the team to share how planning helped. Do that quickly.

8 It's All About Connecting

I would love to have a nickel for every study that has been done to determine why customers buy. I'd be a very wealthy person. Everyone in business is very interested in learning as much as possible about what drives buyer behavior, whether they are buying computers or toothpaste or anything in between. The more sellers know about buyers, the more successful they will be. You can't argue with that.

We find it particularly interesting that the results of recent surveys are similar to those that were conducted decades ago. People in the buying role consistently demand these key behaviors from their salespeople:

- Credibility
- Empathy
- Sensitivity
- Trustworthiness

Credibility, empathy, and trust have always been front and center. Sensitivity, which many people believe is a subset of empathy, is a more recent entry to the scene. But they are all important, and all members of every sales team must do everything they can to demonstrate these behaviors to their prospects and customers.

Your customers want to feel as comfortable with the team as a whole as they might about the individuals who comprise the team. Chances are pretty good that a customer will not be enamored with every member of the team. It happens. But you do want them to feel very positive about the team overall. The whole is often greater than the sum of its parts, and we think this applies well to sales teams.

Credibility

You know that this is an important behavior for anyone involved in sales. Think of yourself in the buying role. If you're buying something as simple as a toaster, you want your salespeople to know what they are talking about. If they don't, you'll feel uncomfortable. As the ticket price goes up for any item, credibility becomes more and more important. The good news is that most sales teams have the ability to demonstrate credibility. The not-so-good news is that the competition is probably equally as capable. They know it and you know it.

If you do your homework, know what's going on in the marketplace, are aware of your competition, and know your products cold, you'll come across as credible. If you're honest, resist the tendency to exaggerate, let the customer know you have their interests in mind, and deliver on your commitments; those things contribute as well.

Both what you know and who you are impact your credibility. One without the other isn't good enough. Many people in business who are extremely knowledgeable do not come across as credible because of their behavior. Every team member has to demonstrate their credibility both in what they know and who they are.

Sensitivity

This is a funny one. It's less obvious, and in the past we weren't hearing much about its importance. That's changed. When we talk about sensitivity, we're not suggesting you tell your customer that you cried the first time you saw *Bambi*, or that you like to take long walks on the beach. But we can't treat it lightly either. Buyers like to buy from people who are sensitive to their situations.

That means being sensitive to the pressure they are feeling, how over-worked they may be, how insecure they may feel about their jobs, or how risky it is to make significant changes. Just letting customers know that you are aware of their situation can demonstrate sensitivity. Not mentioning a touchy subject can do the same. Covering for them when they slip up without telling anyone also demonstrates this behavior. Demonstrating sensitivity is something anyone involved in customer contact has to take seriously.

Jim Schwarz, founder of Compass Management Group and a member of our team, tells a story from his sales days. He had traveled for over an hour to see an important customer. He was kept waiting for 20 minutes, which was unusual. When he finally got into the customer's office, Jim could see how frazzled he was. Jim suggested that if this wasn't a good time, they could reschedule the meeting, even though he had traveled so far to get there.

The customer was most appreciative, and he assured Jim they could get done what was most important. Though the meeting was shorter than anticipated, it was still productive and the customer was grateful that Jim was sensitive to his situation. He mentioned that several times at future meetings. Often giving up something in the short run can lead to long-term benefits.

Empathy

This behavior is critically important to many aspects of our lives. Complete books have been dedicated to this subject. We hear empathy referred to every day, whether we are talking about teachers or policemen or politicians or our significant others. It applies to almost any interactive situation.

Our definition simply suggests that empathy is the ability to see things from someone else's perspective. Empathy reflects your ability to feel what someone else feels. To use the vernacular, empathy is the result of your walking a mile in the other guy's shoes.

If you want a definition that has a bit more substance, go to *The American Heritage Dictionary of the English Language*. They define empathy as "identification with and understanding of another's situation, feelings and motives." Most impressive. I wish we had come up with that.

You might ask why are we making such a big deal about empathy. It's because virtually every survey we have seen says it is the primary reason why buyers buy. Number one. The ability to connect with the people with whom you do business is paramount. And it has withstood the test of time. There are surveys out there that are over 50 years old that make the same point.

But it isn't just what appears in surveys. If customers can't connect with you, if they don't think you understand them, or if you can't relate to them, the chances of doing business with them are quite remote. You can add any number of elements to the sales process, but ultimately people buy from people they like.

So an immense challenge for any sales team is to do whatever they can to connect with the customer, both individually and collectively. The customer must feel that they can relate well to the team as a whole, as well as with the individual members of the team. And this has to happen comfortably and naturally.

Connecting with people is a hard thing to fake. You have to be genuine. Just think about how you found yourself reacting when someone approached you and acted like you were good friends when you weren't. Kate Reilly calls that "unwanted familiarity." Connecting and relating comfortably with others doesn't happen instantaneously. It takes time and effort.

As an example, we work with a client whose sales force is extremely seasoned, particularly those who call on major clients. One member of their team has such a large book of business that if he were a company, he would be among the top 20 producers of their product. That's big! He is extremely committed to his customers and is obviously very successful.

He participated in one of our programs and was delightful. He shared with the group how he begins every sales call by asking his client about something personal that was discussed at the previous meeting. ("How was the graduation"? or "Tell me about the trip to Lake Tahoe," or "Is your mom feeling better?") He told us how he even goes so far as to write himself a note after each client meeting to remind him to do that. He said he does this for every client meeting.

Now before you go any further, ask yourself how you are reacting to that story.

Do you think that what he does seems to be a bit contrived, even manipulative? It sounds like his interest isn't being authentic, but rather that it's part of a ritual he uses. But he actually is quite sincere. He cares about his clients enormously and is genuinely interested in them as people. Taking the notes is done to avoid confusion on his part. And it works. I for one would never want to second-guess someone with his track record.

What he does to start these calls shows interest in the client and demonstrates empathy. David Maister, who has done some marvelous writing on building meaningful client relationships and selling professional services, uses a line that John Maxwell derived and we hear people use all the time: "*Clients don't care how much you know until they know how much you care.*" It's a great phrase. It says both simply and profoundly that empathy trumps credibility. And it does, every time.

We need to explore how teams demonstrate empathy. For starters, consider the possibility that groups can better understand their client's situation more effectively than individuals. Think about sales calls you have experienced with others. When you left the call and shared results, did you notice how different people had different perceptions? That happens all the time. We all see things differently, and if we share our individual impressions after a meeting we have to derive a deeper understanding of the situation.

I remember making a call with Tom French on a large prospect. When we debriefed the meeting, I felt much better about how the clients responded than he did. He pointed out how several of their comments and questions implied they did not agree with our point of view. As it turned out he was right. We did not win that job for the exact reasons he suspected. Simply put, he saw things that I didn't.

Had I taken his comments more seriously and sent the client a memo afterwards clarifying our position, it might have turned things around. We'll never know. What we do know is that listening to your colleagues after a client visit can yield some awfully good insights if you are willing to pay attention. In certain situations one person might be more empathetic than another.

My wife, Lois Baron, has worked as a parent educator and preschool director. She has been fascinated with the subject of empathy since she first studied it at Sarah Lawrence College. She applies much of what she learned when working with parents and educators. She talks passionately about the importance of empathy when raising children or working with kids.

She doesn't take credit for this definition but describes empathy as "an internal tool that can make us more effective at connecting and understanding externally." Think about that. Empathy is an internal tool. She believes that when groups share their perceptions, they can use what they learn to respond effectively to the issues they face.

The Ariel Group, located just outside of Boston, is one of the most prestigious training and coaching firms in the world. They are known primarily for their work in "leadership presence," since their book by that name was a business best seller. They teach participants in their courses to authentically connect, communicate, and build relationships.

They believe that empathy "involves finding the humanity in someone else, even in their weaknesses, and connecting that humanity with your own." They also believe that "What (leaders) do is communicate and act upon empathy. (It's) what links leaders' emotional skills with hard results." Most enlightening.

This certainly applies well to sales teams. If the product manager picks up on the customer's confusion, or if the Customer Service Rep notices how everyone seemed bored during the review of a procedure, they need to share that information with the team. Even if it's just a feeling or a speculative guess, if any member observes something in a client meeting, good or bad, they will help everyone if they share it.

I remember preparing for an upcoming presentation not long ago. After the rehearsal, one of my colleagues suggested that I was overly enthusiastic when discussing the importance of coaching. She thought that several of the clients attending the meeting might not coach their people very often, and for me to be preaching about its importance so passionately could be overkill. She was right. My approach had to be toned down so that's what I did. See how teams can do great things?

Sales team members, like anyone on a team will do everyone a great service if they use that internal tool that Lois describes in trying to better understand the client. They can do this before, during, and after any client interaction.

Before the Meeting

Even before you meet with the client, each team member can express his or her take on the situation. Team members need to listen carefully to their colleagues' observations, whether they are based on what they read, what they heard, or what they saw in previous meetings.

Teams need to discuss these perceptions since they can impact the way they will approach the meeting. Groups have this ability to see a bigger picture than the individuals in the group, and it would be foolish not to take advantage of that.

I think it was Sir Thomas Newton who said: "If I have seen further than others, it's only because I stood on the shoulders of giants." We all know what a brilliant thinker he was, one of the greatest ever. So if Newton saw value in learning from others, so can we, particularly as it relates to understanding our clients.

Sam Jamison understood that. In the planning meeting prior to the formal presentation, he asked each team member to share their perceptions about the opportunity. He encouraged them to say what was on their mind, even if it differed from the conventional wisdom of the group. That's what encouraged Lesley to offer her big idea, which was such an important part of their presentation. Had he not opened that door for the team, things might have turned out differently.

Trust your teammates. Trust their intuitions. Trust their feelings. Listen to what they say. You don't have to agree with them, nor do you have to accept their ideas. But you'll be the beneficiary of some very useful information if you give them the chance to be heard.

During the Meeting

Once you are in the client meeting, you can do several things to connect, particularly early in the process. The round of introductions always helps. During introductions listen carefully and take notes about each person. And start memorizing their names. That's right, get those names memorized. Do it early in the meeting.

Almost everybody says they have a hard time with names. Often they share this with us during our training programs because our facilitators have usually locked in everybody's names by the time introductions are completed. Participants are often impressed. What they don't know is that our team is no better with names than anybody else. They just learned how to memorize them. Like anything else it's a skill you can learn.

If there are three people in the meeting, or more, you can learn their names immediately. Just write them down and repeat them to yourself. Let the list build. Do it over and over. Here's what it might sound like in your mind: "Bill." "Bill, Doris." "Bill, Doris." "Bill, Doris." "Okay." "Bill, Doris, Frank." "Bill, Doris, Frank." "Bill, Doris, Frank." "Got it." "Bill, Doris, Frank, Barbara." "Bill, Doris, Frank, Barbara." "Bill, Doris, Frank, Barbara."

Okay, you get the gist. If you do this you will know most of their names by the time intros are done. That allows you to refer to everyone by name throughout the conversation. "Excellent question, Barbara" has a nice ring to it. "Let me build upon what you just said, Bill" carries some weight. "Frank, I need to push back just a bit on that point" sounds sincere.

Whenever you can use your clients' names, good things can happen. And if you miss one or two along the way, people can be very forgiving and appreciative of the effort. It's a nice way to connect during a meeting. And it's a marvelous way to differentiate your team.

There are other ways to remember names. Sometimes an individual looks like someone you know or even someone famous. Make that connection. Sometimes there is something about their appearance that might relate to their name ("Tom is tall" or "Gloria is gracious"). Other times, even what someone is wearing helps (Betty is in blue or Bryan has a bright tie). The challenge is to get the names. You'll figure out ways to do it and you'll be glad you did.

Another skill that helps is paraphrasing. A wonderful way to connect is to let your counterparts know that you heard what they said. "Fernando, I'd like to go back to that point you made earlier about the conversion issue. Could you tell us more about those concerns you experienced previously?" Or "Janet, you mentioned how the budget cuts might not affect this initiative. I'm curious to learn more about the thinking behind that."

Just like in written correspondence, if you punctuate your sentences and questions with the other person's name, and let them know you heard them, it will have a positive impact and help you connect. And, again, it will show how you're different.

One key component of team selling is demonstrating your understanding of the clients' needs. This may be the single most important step in the sales process. Knowing what they are isn't good enough. Your customers need to *know* that you understand them. There are several times you can do this throughout the sales process and it's a wonderful way to connect with your customers. When you demonstrate that you understand what they are trying to accomplish, you will connect at many levels.

As Tim Seifert, who has had a remarkable career managing sales professionals at places like The Hartford, Prudential, and PLANCO says, "It's not what you know, it's what you do with what you know."

After the Meeting

Of course, sales teams will share their perceptions and insights with each other when they debrief their meetings. That's obvious. What's not are the ways to connect with clients after the meeting.

Sales professionals usually take the lead here. They typically send the primary contact a note reviewing what was discussed and what the next steps are. Thanking the client for their time and appearing gracious is always encouraged. But the team can go further, and they should.

We like the idea of surprising the customer after the call. Sending them a white paper or article or even a book that focuses on something of interest to them is a nice touch. It can be business related or not. If that client mentioned the fly-fishing trip he's going on next week, sending an article or book about fly fishing is a thoughtful thing to do.

If it's a major presentation, perhaps key members of the team can send brief notes to their counterparts. For example, your R&D specialist might reach out to the new product development manager with a note saying he enjoyed the time they spent together and would welcome the opportunity to work together. That can't hurt. And if your customer service rep does something similar with their distribution manager, so much the better.

Not everyone has to do this, of course, and it's always situational. But these are nice ways to connect after the meeting. Any time something happens during client meetings that gives your team members a chance to be visible, go for it. Too often we think of connecting only during client interactions. Your ability to demonstrate empathy can go further, and sales teams who think in these terms can build long and mutually beneficial relationships.

Trust

We save trust for last, not because it's most important, but because of all the behaviors it's the most challenging one to develop and demonstrate. You don't just walk into a prospective customer's office and say, "trust me." It's much more complicated than that.

What makes building trust so difficult is that it's dependent upon other behaviors, some of which are beyond our control. The following concept was developed by John Philipp and Bill Cope at Synectics.® It's called the "Trust Formula." Many people have taken the formula and enhanced it, but we still like the original version:

$$\text{Trust} = \frac{\text{Credibility} \times \text{Intimacy}}{\text{Risk}}$$

This is not a mathematical equation. Nor is it quantitative. It says that trust between people is dependent upon three variables. The more credibility you demonstrate, the easier it is to trust you. The more intimate the relationship, the same. But trust is inversely proportional to the level of risk (or perceived risk) in working together.

The formula is extremely well suited for sales teams, though when it was first developed it referred to groups in problem solving situations. John and Bill became intrigued with how teams within the same organization demonstrated different levels of trust among them. It impacted their ability to derive creative solutions. So after exploring this and giving it significant thought, they unveiled the formula, which has probably been introduced to hundreds of thousands of business people throughout the world.

This applies very well to sales teams, both internally and externally. As we mentioned earlier, if you do not demonstrate *credibility*, it's hard for people to do business with you. Remember the toaster example. You need to know everything about what you are selling and you need to understand your business. Very few companies let salespeople represent them without providing them with the technical knowledge they need to do their jobs.

Intimacy requires a bit more explanation. It's not a word we use in business very often. Many people have replaced this word with alternatives like *empathy* or *familiarity*. But whether we just feel the need to honor the past, or because other words feel like a compromise, we stick with it.

Kent Reilly, a long-term colleague, founder of Kidder Reilly, and an outstanding trainer, suggests that we look at the roots of the word. They translate to *not timid* or *not afraid*. An intimate relationship is a safe relationship. That's why the term works for us. Our clients need to know we have their interests in mind. Our clients need to know we are empathetic, sensitive, and concerned about them. Our clients need to know we care. And our clients need to know that we're not out to get them.

The numerator of the equation has two variables that are within our control. Any member of a sales team can demonstrate to a client over time that they know what they are talking about and that they have the clients' interests in mind. It may take time, but teams can prove this to their customers.

Risk is the challenging variable. Often we have to deal with the customer's perceived risk that is impacting his or her decision. Every sales team needs to figure out what they can do to minimize the risk in the client's mind, whether it is real or perceived. Often this determines whether or not they do business together.

The formula suggests that, as the risk increases, the level of trust decreases. That's why buying a toaster is a heck of a lot less complicated than buying a new software package, or changing a 401K plan, or buying an injection molding machine. This is the variable that is hardest for us to control.

So let's do one of our exercises. Think about one of your customers who just can't seem to pull the trigger. Everything is in place, they seem ready to buy, but they won't commit. Assume that risk is the issue. Think of several things you can do to reduce that risk. Take a minute or two and do this.

What you concluded might address what's in the numerator. Providing the customer with referrals, testimonials, third party examples, and parallel situations will in fact make their decision less risky, but those tend to fall in the credibility bucket. Similarly, demonstrating your concern about them, and letting them know how committed you are to their success will make them feel more comfortable, but those may be ways to demonstrate intimacy.

You can approach this challenge by first understanding the customer's perception of the risk. Maybe you have to start small and do a pilot run. You might have to provide some kind of incentive or guarantee. Perhaps you need to explain how you are dealing with some of the risk as well and that you also have skin in the game.

The bottom line is you need to build trust. It's important to pay attention to all three variables in the formula. Realize that the numerator is more about you, and the denominator is more about them. If you pay attention to their concerns it will accelerate your developing trust. And that will result in stronger relationships.

Visibility

Before we conclude this discussion about connecting with clients we need to discuss the importance of being visible. Ted Levitt, the late marketing guru from Harvard Business School, published a classic article in *Harvard Business Review*, "After the Sale Is Over." It was written years ago but is still perfectly relevant today. One of my favorite lines from the article says it all: "*The sale . . . merely consummates the courtship, at which point the marriage begins.*"[1] Or said another way, "The real selling starts after you get the business." You want to be more visible the day after you close the deal than you were the day before. If you don't you'll pay a price.

You've all heard the expressions "buyer's remorse," "cognitive dissonance," even "severe second guessing." You know how that feels. You just bought a big-ticket item, and before you get to your car in the parking lot you begin asking yourself if you made the right decision. We've all been there. It's part of the buying process.

---

[1] Theodore Levitt, "After the Sale Is Over," *Harvard Business Review*, September 1, 1983.

That's why the advertising folks will tell you that a consumer is more likely to read the ad for a car the day *after* they buy it than the day *before*. They are looking for confirmation. They feel uncomfortable. They are doubting themselves. So you need to be visible in order to assure them they made a good decision.

I have had the pleasure of working with Dave Renke of First Data. He has significantly impacted several sales cultures. Dave uses a term he calls "transfer of power." He knows that when customers are in the buying mode they hold all the cards. As potential suppliers pursue their business, they are pretty much in control. But once they decide on who will get the business, things change. Because now they are dependent on that supplier. If they fail to produce, the person who made the decision is responsible. A *transfer of power* has occurred.

Now the customer is still the customer, which gives them advantages. But this transfer of power must not be ignored. That's why we need to be visible throughout the process and more visible once they are on board. I had a sales manager in my early days who said, "Anyone can get the first order. I put my money on the guy who gets the second, third, and fourth. They are the winners." Being visible helps.

Sam Jamison may or may not have known all this. But after he learned that they had won the business, he had each team member call his or her closest counterpart to thank them for the business and let them know how thrilled they were to be working together. It was well orchestrated by one of Sam's designees. Two of the clients heard from more than one member of Sam's team, but that made sense. The right people heard from their counterparts at the right time with the right message. It was an important thing to do.

Within two days Sam sent his client an action plan outlining what needed to be done in the next 30 days to ensure a comfortable transition. He set up a meeting a week later. The key players from his team who would be involved in the first phase of the project attended. Sam did what needed to be done, not only to get the project off to a great start, but to assure the client team that they had made the right decision. Good for him.

We'll end where we began. People buy from people they like, they respect, they enjoy, and they trust. Connecting with clients is critical. Every sales team needs to take this into consideration in every decision they make, every action they take, and every conversation they have. If they do, great things can happen.

Some Things to Consider

What

Sales teams need to be visible. They need to see their clients. The occasional visit isn't good enough. You simply can't develop meaningful relationships and demonstrate key behaviors like empathy, credibility, sensitivity, and trustworthiness without interacting with your client on a regular basis.

How

Determine how often to see each major client and which team members need to be involved. Of course you have to be sensitive to the costs involved, but visibility is something that has to be considered whenever you put together a sales plan. Let your team know they have to stay in contact with their clients and prospects—if not face to face, at least by telephone. If they aren't in touch, you will regret it because chances are good that their competitors will be.

When

When sales teams convene it is important to determine together how often to see your clients and who should be involved. If it is a temporary team, establish this during the formation stage. If it is a permanent team, review your client list quarterly and determine whether you are seeing them often enough.

9

You Mean We Have to Sell, Too?

So far we have focused on the internal component of innovative team selling, which is one of the three components to team selling. The other two are making outstanding team presentations and coordinating everybody's contributions.

We explained how your ability to conduct productive meetings, facilitate exciting creative sessions, leverage your resources, and plan effectively can all contribute to your success. Putting together mission statements, clarifying expectations, and agreeing on values are all critically important activities.

But once that is done, it's time to meet with your customers and present your recommendations. The team's challenge is to demonstrate their understanding of the client's situation and explain how the team can help them accomplish their objectives. That's where the external component takes center stage.

Most of the time sales calls are conducted by the sales professional and that is usually done alone. The team can help in the planning process, but the salesperson has the responsibility of meeting with the customer. But when sales teams visit customers, whether it's to help assess a situation at one extreme, or to make a formal recommendation at the other, so much is on the line. That's why it is mandatory for every member of the sales team to understand the sales process and know how to feel comfortable making meaningful and relevant contributions.

In my first book, *Selling Is a Team Sport*, we devoted significant time to dissecting the consultative selling process and the associated skills. There is some recent research that challenges sales leaders to move beyond this approach. But the way we define consultative selling suggests that the skills, techniques, and approaches that comprise it are very well suited for sales teams. In fairness, the term has been used for decades, but the methodology as we define it isn't used nearly as often as you might think.

So for starters, here is our definition:

> Consultative selling is a customer-focused approach that encourages sales professionals to employ a problem solving mindset in order to thoroughly understand their client's situation and provide products, services, and *ideas* that address their business challenges, problems, and opportunities.

Yes, that's a lot of words. You should see what was edited out. Let's get more specific. The definition focuses on the *sales professional*, but the methodology applies to sales teams as well. The salesperson is the key figure in any sales process, and we don't want to give the impression that this only applies to teams.

The sales process is a *problem solving* process. That's an important statement. The problem solving and consultative sales processes are very similar, as are the skills that make them work. The highest level of selling is when salespeople transform sales calls into problem solving opportunities.

The heart and soul of consultative selling revolves around responding very specifically to what clients want to accomplish. Sales professionals must demonstrate an insatiable desire to completely and thoroughly *understand the client's situation*. This goes beyond simply understanding clients' needs. It means learning about the client's goals, problems, concerns, objectives, fears, aspirations, and more.

It requires the use of skills like questioning, listening, interpreting, inferring, paraphrasing, reframing, and understanding nonverbal signals. Those who understand the client better than anyone else usually win the business.

And finally, consultative selling suggests that sales professionals think bigger and go beyond just recommending their products and services. They also offer their ideas, their perspectives, their insights, their suggestions, and even their warnings based their experience. An expression that I first heard in an executive business program at Columbia Business School has stayed with me for years: "It's not just what's in the bag, it's what's in your head."

Of course, consultative selling includes concepts like effective planning, building mutually beneficial relationships, resolving issues, gaining commitment, and following through effectively. But the essence of consultative selling is all about using problem solving skills to thoroughly understand clients in order to bring them outstanding solutions that address their business needs.

Before we introduce the consultative selling model and demonstrate its similarity to problem solving, there is one anecdote that illustrates the process better than any words, graphs, charts, models, or sequences ever could.

We previously introduced you to Jim Schwarz of Compass Management. He was the guy who let the customer off the hook when he was jammed and asked if this was still a good time to have the meeting. Jim spent most of his sales career in the packaged goods industry. One of his most exciting jobs was when he was a national sales manager for Pepsi. Shortly after he joined the company he was asked to manage selling Pepsi products to the airlines industry, which Coca-Cola dominated. Pepsi was trying frantically to break into that market and Jim was asked to make that happen.

Jim often tells the story of when he was about to call on Eastern Airlines. (Anybody remember Eastern? Frank Borman, the former astronaut, ran the company. "We have to earn our wings every day" was their memorable tag line.) They were a great airline in their day. Jim was preparing for his first sales call and had put together his sales presentation. They called them "decks" in those days. He had never even heard the term consultative selling at that time.

His presentation was impressive. It spoke about the *Pepsi Challenge*. It reviewed all the data about how customers preferred the taste of Pepsi. It explained how Pepsi had outsold Coke in most grocery stores. It had some impressive comparative data. It told a wonderful story about Pepsi, but it said little if anything about Eastern Airlines.

The only strategy that Pepsi had initiated was to try to offer Eastern pricing incentives. But anything they tried was met and enhanced by Coke. There was no way they could buy the business. Coca-Cola had deeper pockets than they did. They knew that.

Shortly before the presentation, Jim received a call from one of their marketing consultants, who suggested that Jim approach the call quite differently. He suggested that he not bring the deck. In fact, he suggested that Jim go into that initial meeting with Eastern with nothing but a pad and a pen. Jim smiles when he tells groups how shocked he was at such an off-the-wall recommendation. "Going into a sales meeting without a formal presentation would be unprofessional and unprepared. Like trying to sail without a rudder," Jim recalls. This was something he had never done and even thinking about this approach made him uneasy.

But the marketing consultant was quite persuasive and convinced Jim to do it. He offered to join Jim on the call. They flew to Miami (on an Eastern airplane, of course) and went to the meeting at Eastern's headquarters. The meeting was scheduled to last an hour. Present in the meeting were the VPs of Catering, Operations, Hospitality, Marketing, Inflight Services, and Procurement (called Purchasing in those days).

Jim and the consultant set the stage and said they were there to learn what they could about Eastern's situation. And then they started to ask questions. Lots of questions. Some they had prepared beforehand and others came up spontaneously as they went along. They learned about the company's challenges, their goals, their objectives, their customer base, and their opportunities. The hour meeting became a two-hour meeting, and Jim was blown away at how receptive the audience was and how eager they were to answer the questions. And he was thrilled at how positively the meeting had concluded. After the two hours Jim had dozens of pages of notes.

It was a great meeting and it felt productive, but when Jim returned to Pepsi headquarters the big question was "now what?" He had learned an awful lot about Eastern's situation, and was struck by the fact that their single biggest need was to fill the seats in the airplane. They made it clear that this was unequivocally the biggest business issue they faced. If an airplane took off with 12 empty seats, that meant lost revenue that could not be reclaimed.

As Jim tells the story, "So Eastern needs to sell more plane tickets and I'm selling sugared, artificially flavored carbonated water. And I'm here to provide a solution. Uh-oh!"

But that's where the story gets interesting.

Jim called a meeting with his team to figure out if there was a way to help Eastern sell tickets. Pepsi had many talented creative people—they always have—and when they attacked that task they generated many interesting ideas. One particularly intriguing suggestion was to tap into their bottling network. They had over 400 bottlers across the country. Consistent with the industry, when bottlers promoted their products they would often include giveaways, which they called "dealer loaders." Typical gifts ranged from television sets to bicycles to cameras. It was common practice. But it was getting a bit repetitive and didn't generate a whole lot of excitement. That provided the team with the opening.

They concluded that in the future, instead of offering another tired promotional item, their bottlers could buy coupons from Eastern to allow people to fly on Eastern at a discount. There were restrictions, of course, as there are today, but the idea enabled people to fly anywhere in the United States that Eastern flew at a lower cost. They thought this could be a new way to help the bottlers promote their products and help Eastern fill airline seats.

The bottlers loved it, and when the idea was presented to Eastern, they could not wait to sign up. It was a totally new and different approach and the airline was happy to switch from Coke to Pepsi if this would help sell tickets and reduce the number of empty seats on the airplanes.

Pepsi anticipated annual coupon sales of $700,000 from the promotion in the first year. Sales actually reached $2 million. More importantly, Pepsi won the business at Eastern. It was a classic win/win. Coke had nothing to match it. It changed the game. Pepsi took the concept and used it with other airlines and grew that channel of their business dramatically. They used similar programs with other industries. It became a new way to enhance relationships with their customers.

This made Jim a true believer in the consultative selling process, which he teaches to thousands of people every year around the world. Jim is a wonderful storyteller and never tires of sharing that particular experience with his groups. It certainly proves the point.

Doesn't Everybody Know This?

While most professional salespeople talk about how they believe in consultative selling, surprisingly few actually use this approach. This is not a condemnation of sales professionals; it is our observation. We realize that applying the principles of consultative selling is not nearly as easy as it appears.

This can actually be exacerbated when teams come into play. That's because subject matter experts too often believe that their role is to discuss what they know, as opposed to first learning what they must about the customer. So with that in mind, let's explore how to make this approach work for sales teams.

First let's take a look at the model (see Figure 9.1). If it looks familiar, it's because it is in many ways a mirror image of the problem solving model that we introduced earlier. It also includes much of what we presented in the interactive meeting model.

As you can see, there are five phases and each is critically important. We will explore each phase in detail in subsequent chapters. But to put everything in perspective, let's take a cursory look now.

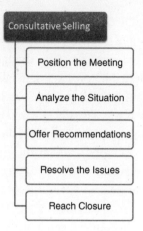

FIGURE 9.1 Consultative Selling Model

Position the Meeting

There's that word again. We rarely turn down an opportunity to discuss what sales teams need to do to get every client meeting off to a good start. They are much more likely to accomplish their objectives if they make their clients comfortable, connect with everyone, review the agenda, confirm the time frame, and set the stage for what's about to happen.

You'll notice that we refer to the client *meeting*. There is nothing wrong with terms like sales calls or sales contacts or sales interactions. But we like to think of these client visits as client meetings, and like any meeting, in order to achieve your goals, you need to pay attention to the process. That means involving everybody, ensuring that they are on the same page, following specific guidelines, playing by the rules, and reaching meaningful conclusions. Positioning helps make all this happen.

Analyze the Situation

Situation analysis is the epicenter of this approach. When we teach courses for our clients, we make the point that if we only had a few hours with them as opposed to a few days, all we would discuss is this phase of the process. We go further to say that if all we had was only one hour, we would focus only on questioning. Situation analysis is by far the most important phase of the selling process, and many salespeople believe that questioning is the most important skill.

The better the job a salesperson or sales team does in understanding the client's situation, the better relationships they build, the better recommendations they make, the less resistance they encounter, and the more deals they close. It's all about the client, and the best way to stand out is to know more about them than anyone else. Ask Jim Schwarz about that if you are skeptical.

Offer Recommendations

This is the part of the process that most sales professionals like best. This is when you get to tell your story, share what you prepared, and demonstrate what you know. And that's just fine as long as you do all this after you have successfully demonstrated to your customers that you understand their situation.

One way to look at this part of the process is to realize that when you talk about your products and services, you are talking about how you earn your livelihood. Whether you have your own small business or work for a multinational corporation, your products and services and your ability to demonstrate their value are the driving force behind what you do. Offering recommendations in a client focused way is an exciting moment in the sales process. Once you have earned the right to present, go for it and do it articulately, persuasively, and enthusiastically.

Resolve the Issues

If offering recommendations is the part of the process salespeople like most, then dealing with resistance is the part they like least. When clients push back, too many salespeople have the tendency to behave more like a stereotypical peddler, and less like a consultant who has the clients' best interests in mind. Too often sales professionals undo much of what they have accomplished when they encounter resistance.

That's why we refer to this phase as *resolving* issues. We avoid terms like "overcoming" or "handling" or "minimizing" objections. None of those feel very client focused. You don't *overcome* an objection, you *resolve* it, and work with customers, not against them. This step in the process presents every sales professional and every sales team with a marvelous opportunity to work together and use their problem solving skills to manage the client's resistance.

Reach Closure

Finally, we need to talk about closing, and we will. But we'll probably surprise you, since we tend to play this down. Closing is an extension of the resolving objection process. Asking for the business is difficult for most of us, but as you will see, it is the natural thing to do once you have resolved the issues that arise.

We will not present dozens of closing techniques. We'll look at a few for the fun of it, but like everything else in consultative selling, you want to take the high road, and this applies to the closing process in particular. "Coffee is for closers" was a great line in the marvelous play and movie, *Glengarry Glen Ross*, but that isn't the approach we recommend.

Comparing the Sequences

When we introduced the consultative selling model, we suggested that it might look familiar. That's because it did. It is a mirror image of the problem-solving model we introduced in Chapter 6. Take a peek at Figure 9.2.

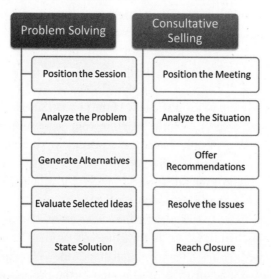

FIGURE 9.2 A Comparison of Problem Solving and Consultative Selling

The comparison demonstrates the similarity of the models we use in problem solving and consultative selling. It helps explain why we contend that the sales process is a problem solving process. That is why it is so well suited for sales teams and why we think they will do better work if they understand and apply the concepts.

The majority of the sales professionals we work with tell us they never thought they would find themselves in sales. But the same skills, techniques and approaches that make them good problem solvers can make them successful in the selling role. The reason so many people do very well in sales, in spite of what they thought earlier in their careers, is that they are good problem solvers, they like the excitement associated with the job, and they interact well with their colleagues and customers. They are also motivated by results, and careers in sales provide them with many opportunities.

With that as a backdrop, look at the comparison of the sequences. If you are problem solving or selling you need to do some *positioning* and get a good start, ensure that the participants are comfortable, and that everyone knows the agenda, the approach, and the time commitment.

Analysis is a critical piece of each process. The amount of information that is shared varies, but when you are problem solving, you need to know the answers to specific questions, and if you are selling you need to learn much about the customer. In both scenarios the key person, whether it's the problem owner or the customer, does most of the talking as the group listens for connections.

Making recommendations is fun. Offering ideas in a problem-solving meeting can be exciting, even exhilarating. It's your turn. You listened conscientiously as the problem owner introduced the task; now you get to offer ideas, which is exactly what happens in consultative selling. You ask the important questions and listen intently and make connections. Then you offer recommendations to show how you can help. In both processes you do a lot of listening early and get a return later when you make your contributions.

In both models there is a time to *confront the resistance* required to reach conclusions. Idea evaluation is all about preserving the parts of the idea you like and modifying the parts you don't. (Remember the architect analogy?) The intent is to transform the idea into a solution.

That is exactly what you do when you resolve objections. The intent is to work with the client to address their concerns in order to derive a mutually acceptable solution. Using your creativity is essential in both phases, which again are quite similar.

And finally, you need to reach *closure* in both. Hopefully you conclude your problem solving meetings with solutions and next steps so you can take your efforts to the next level. In selling the ultimate goal, of course, is to close the sale and develop an action plan.

You don't always get there, of course. In problem solving, if you can't reach a solution, and you think the idea has promise, you develop an action plan to keep it moving forward. Similarly, you don't close on every sales call; in fact that's the exception, not the rule. But you conclude by getting the next steps to make progress with the intent of eventually closing the deal.

Yes, the two processes are very similar, and your ability to use problem solving skills and techniques when interacting with your clients brings the sales process to a much higher level. That is how we define consultative selling. The ability to leverage your resources is a critical component in making this happen.

Sam Jamison and his team used this model to contribute to their success. Sam had had several needs determination meetings with his clients, sometimes alone and other times with team members. Some were on the telephone; at least two were face to face.

He was ultra-careful to ensure that the primary objective of those initial meetings was to learn as much as he could about the client's situation. He did everything he could to avoid falling into the trap of presenting too early in the process. Positioning those meetings clearly and clarifying the objectives helped considerably.

That helped him in his planning efforts and led to the fabulous presentation that won them the business. They encountered a few objections along the way, both in person and in memos. Whenever he could, Sam used his resources to resolve the objections using a specific objection resolution model.

And, as you know, they eventually won the business and closed the deal. The consultative selling approach worked for them, as it will work for you and your resources as you internalize it and make it an integral part of your sales process.

The Value Pyramid

We conclude by introducing you to what we call the *value pyramid*. My colleague and friend, Nadine Keller, author of *Make It All About Them*, a marvelous book about sales presentations, helped us develop this model. She had used a similar model known then as the value chain when she was

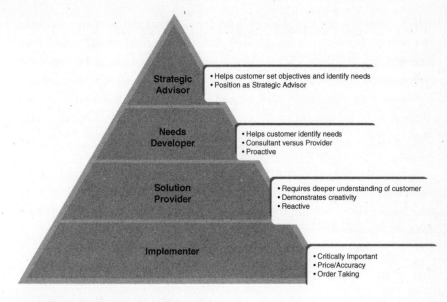

FIGURE 9.3 The Value Pyramid

Director of Learning and Development at Chase Bank prior to its merger with JPMorgan. We were fortunate to have her assist us in developing the model that appears in Figure 9.3.

The model explains the different kinds of relationships you develop with your clients. Each of you can find yourselves at every level depending on the client and the depth of the relationship. The challenge, of course, is to do what you can to "get up the pyramid'" and become strategic advisors to your clients.

Implementation

Sometimes we call this *Execution*, but in too many businesses, like advertising for example, execution is so important we don't want in any way to denigrate this responsibility. When we think of implementers, we think of order takers. The customer tells you what to do and you do it. You do it as professionally, impeccably, and efficiently as possible, but you are only doing what you were asked (or told) to do. Unfortunately, you don't add much value to the relationship when you play at this level.

You find yourselves here more often than you would like. We had a client for years in the pharmaceutical industry who deliberately kept us at this level. They liked our body of knowledge and used us often to participate in their two-week programs. We were asked to show up and teach our concepts in the time frames they established. But they developed the cases, they arranged for the groups, they decided what was to be taught and when. They even insisted on who on our team was best suited to teach certain modules.

We never compromised what we had to offer. We made sure that we had adequate time to incorporate the appropriate training methodologies, which they accepted. They liked our stuff, and appreciated what we did, but we had virtually no input on anything else.

It was extremely frustrating. We knew we had a positive impact on the participants and contributed to the program. That felt good. We just didn't add much value beyond that. We were classic implementers. Everyone endures those kinds of relationships.

Solution Providers

This level sounds impressive, as it should. Solutions are good things. But we believe that when you are at level two, even though the name has a nice ring to it, you are still in a reactive mode as you were at level one. Solution providers bring customers solutions that address needs they already know they have. When you play at this level you are responding only to what you were told, not what you learned, even though your response may be thoughtful solutions.

Think about receiving an RFP. When it arrives, you and your team put your heads together, do some terrific work, and develop outstanding recommendations. But you are responding only to what was included in the RFP. Little else. Your competitors did the same thing, and with all due respect, probably came up with solutions every bit as good as yours. (Sorry about that, but that's what happens.) Your response doesn't add as much value as it could because you don't know the whole story. You only know what is in the RFP, and as a result you could miss some big opportunities.

Needs Developer

When you first look at the model, you may think that levels two and three are in the reverse order. I did. Level three focuses on uncovering needs that were not only unknown to you, but perhaps to the client as well. Too often salespeople make the assumption that their customers know what they need. That's not always the case.

We conducted a focus group with senior level buyers of professional services years ago that I will never forget. That is because when asked what they demand from the people who call on them, a CFO said rather boldly: *"I want my salespeople to bring me solutions to problems I don't even know I have."* I found that to be a great compliment for anyone in sales. He realized that sales professionals know things about the application of their products and services that he didn't. He was smart enough to know that outside resources might know more about his needs in certain areas than he did. That CFO was asking you to play at this level. He wanted the people who called on him to be true needs developers.

Sales teams can use their resources to differentiate themselves. If they are asking the questions that others aren't, and learning about needs that others miss, they can outperform the competition every time. Let's stay with the RFP example. If you receive an RFP, rather than just responding, call a meeting with the prospective client. Once you connect, whether it's in person or on the telephone, if you ask thoughtful, provocative questions, you can learn so much more than what appeared in the document. The result is you'll provide better solutions and differentiate yourselves.

When you play at this level you find yourselves in a proactive mode. You're in a more secure place. Your relationships are stronger and your recommendations are better. This is the level on the pyramid that we encourage all of you to aspire to reach. Everyone finds themselves playing at lower levels more often than they would like. The objective, of course, is to do what you can to get a higher level.

Sales teams can become true needs developers. When they work productively to thoroughly understand their customer's needs, their recommendations have the potential to be unique. And they'll beat the competitor who is working alone every time.

Strategic Advisors

This is the ultimate goal. Strategic advisors are perceived as if they were members of the client's team. This doesn't happen as often as you'd like. But every sales team can aspire to get there. Imagine a sales team in which every member is perceived as an advisor to their counterparts within the customer's organization. Nobody could compete effectively with such a team.

When you are playing at this level, your clients look to you for guidance, even in areas beyond your expertise. When you develop these kinds of relationships, your clients will call you to ask an opinion or seek an idea when they need help. Strategic advisors are invited to their clients' internal meetings when appropriate, and sometimes are even invited to their clients' off-sites and events.

If we use that RFP example one last time, when you are playing at this level, a client will ask you to look at an RFP before it is distributed. They don't do this to give you an unfair advantage; they just want your opinion as to whether they are asking the right questions or if they omitted something of importance.

Nobody gets to this level with all of their clients. Even the most successful and seasoned sales professionals will say they get there with 25 or 30 percent of their clients. But they try to get there with all of them.

The concepts associated with consultative selling significantly contribute to making innovative team selling viable. This methodology will certainly help you get up the pyramid. Connecting with your clients is a big part of it, but it's only one piece of the puzzle. As we dissect the team selling approach, we will investigate what it takes to get there and what you can do to make it work for you.

Some Things to Consider

What

Whether you call it needs-driven selling, relationship selling, solution selling, or consultative selling, a sales process that focuses on the customer is mandatory today. There is simply no option in this competitive global economy. Your team must know that it is all about the client. They must realize that to be successful they have to build strong relationships that add value. They must understand their client's needs completely, which will allow them to make recommendations that address those needs—and that will usually yield positive results.

How

Explain to your team that this is the approach you will use. But do more than just say it—live it. The principles need to apply to all aspects of the job whether you are planning, implementing, or debriefing client meetings. Your collateral material, spec sheets, and promotional material should reinforce this process. Your mission, vision, and values must reflect this. Ideally, the same skills you use with clients will be used internally when interacting with colleagues. The sales process drives everything you do that impacts the client.

When

The most successful sales organizations agree on their sales approach and internalize it throughout the organization. It becomes their way of representing themselves to the world. It is something that is applied every day, regardless of the situation.

10 Positioning . . . A Key Ingredient in Understanding Needs

I f you dissect the consultative selling model, shown in Figure 10.1, you can see that there are two key components: the diverging part and the converging part.

The diverging component focuses on positioning the meeting and analyzing the client's situation. The diverging part is all about the client, since they do most of the talking. After all, it's hard to learn about your clients if you are the one dominating the conversation.

The converging part is devoted to your explaining what you can do to address the client's needs and opportunities. When you make your presentation, resolve the client's issues and conclude with a commitment—the focus is on you. Of course all this is done in a client centered way, but if the diverging part is more about *them*, the converging part is more about *you*.

What surprises many people is that the way you begin your sales interactions—what happens in those first few minutes—usually has a major impact on your ability to truly understand your client's situation. But before we get too specific, let's look at why it's so hard to determine needs and what *you* can do early to enhance that process.

You can't do it all at once

Many organizations today use a two- or even three-call approach. The initial call is devoted primarily to learning as much about the customer as possible. Other than the occasional credentials presentation, the objective of that first meeting is to connect with the prospective client and begin the process of

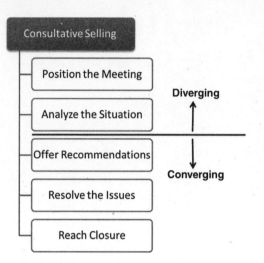

FIGURE 10.1 Consultative Selling Model

analyzing their situation. Simply put, the desired outcome of that initial meeting is to learn as many of the client's needs as possible.

Today many organizations don't want their salespeople to make recommendations on that first or even second call. They want them to do what Jim Schwarz did when he was at Pepsi; ask as many questions as you can and learn as much as you can. After conducting that initial meeting, salespeople can review what they learned with their teams in order to develop outstanding recommendations (See Figure 10.1.).

The thinking in many quarters is that only when you have a solid understanding of your customer's needs do you have the "right to present." Some believe that this is a privilege that you earn. That makes tons of sense, and you'll recall it's the way we define consultative selling.

Is It Happening Out There?

Our research confirms what you have already guessed. While some companies have been doing this for years, and many more talk about it often, most do not. Most sales professionals make their recommendations much too early in the process. They present before they truly understand the customer's needs. They usually present their products and services without tapping into the expertise of their resources. As a result they miss opportunities all the time.

One of the most significant benefits of using a team selling approach is that it significantly increases the likelihood of truly understanding the client's situation. If you do that before making recommendations, you have to be more successful. That's what the Pepsi story clarifies for all of us.

Many sales professionals truly believe that they employ a consultative approach, when in fact they don't. That's not a derogatory statement about sales professionals. It's just that many things prevent this from happening.

They think that they understand their customers' needs, but their customers rarely agree. They understand the value of teamwork, but few truly leverage their resources. They understand the importance of differentiating themselves, but don't accomplish that as often as they'd like. They see the value of a consultative approach and aren't trying to kid anybody when they say these things. They truly believe in what they are saying.

But as we interview customers, see the results of focus groups, observe sales professionals in the performance of their jobs, and work with client facing professionals in our training programs, we are convinced that most client facing professionals do not use this approach. It's not that they don't want to, or that they don't make the attempt. It's just that there are complicated dynamics that make this difficult. What looks very manageable on paper can be extremely challenging in the heat of battle.

Salespeople as Problem Solvers

We made a strong case in *Selling Is a Team Sport* that sales professionals tend to be excellent problem solvers. We explained how salespeople demonstrate the same behaviors that we observe in successful problem solvers. Whether it's their curiosity, their ability to quickly make connections, their tenacity, their ability to handle rejection, their people skills, their cleverness, or simply their desire to succeed, we know that successful salespeople and effective problem solvers demonstrate the same behaviors in group situations.

But, surprisingly, those wonderful skill sets and behaviors can contribute to their missing needs that they could have uncovered. That's right; the same thing that makes them good problem solvers often makes them less proficient at determining needs. The two skill sets, ironically, can work against each other at certain times in the sales process.

Let's prove that. We'll do it with a quick exercise that we include on many of our training programs. Here are five very simple situations. Read each one and ask yourself what the need is behind the statement.

1. My office is disorganized.
2. I want to take my spouse on a memorable vacation.
3. My lawn is burned out halfway through the summer.
4. My bookkeeper is making me nervous.
5. My basement is flooded.

When I tell people that my office is disorganized, their tendency is to suggest that I need better furniture or more filing cabinets or storage bins. If I tell them I want to take my spouse on a memorable vacation, before I finish my sentence, there's a good chance that they will think of two or three places we need to consider visiting. If I complain about my lawn burning out too early in the summer, they typically come up with a few suggestions about how to restore it immediately or perhaps preventing it from happening again. When I complain about my bookkeeper, they are likely to come up with ways for me to turn things around before I even get to the heart of the issue. And when I mention my basement is flooded, they'll suggest I install a sump pump or get a wet vac.

Every response above is a *solution*, not a *need*. If your answers were similar, don't take it too seriously, or personally. It just means that you think pretty much like everybody else. When you hear someone mention a problem or opportunity, the tendency is to immediately start thinking about solutions. That's the problem solver part of your brain going to work.

Notice that in each of these cases there was a request for help, whether it was about the office, vacation, lawn, bookkeeper, or basement. The most common responses we hear are actually solutions, which make perfect sense. Someone asks for help and the natural response is to offer a solution. It's perfectly logical.

But in selling situations you will do so much better if you determine the *needs* first and worry about solutions later. That's what consultative selling is all about. There is a big difference between needs and solutions. Make that a *huge* difference. No, make that an *enormous* difference. Sales teams that figure this out stand apart from everyone else.

Let's first realize that all this is coming from a good place. Our ability to make connections immediately and generate ideas rapidly is a wonderful skill. It helps us every day as we tackle the inevitable problems that we encounter. The conundrum is that when you do this in selling situations, and offer solutions too soon, you miss the opportunity to truly uncover the customer's needs.

It happens all the time. With the best of intentions sales professionals sabotage their efforts to be consultative. When they hear an opportunity, their tendency is to stop listening and offer recommendations. They are programmed to think this way. Everybody is. It's not a bad thing. It enables you to manage the issues you encounter every day.

But, again, it works against you in the selling role. In an effort to help the customer, you offer solutions too quickly. You fall into this trap without even knowing it. Sales teams will stand out if they embrace the principles of consultative selling and learn how to avoid these pitfalls. The good news is that they can.

Turning Sales Teams into "Needs Development Teams"

For just a few minutes reconsider the way you think about sales teams. Let's think of them as *needs development teams*. That's what we'd like to call them for now. Here's why.

Remember the value pyramid? Needs developers were at the next to highest level, just short of strategic advisors. Sales teams can make it their collective responsibility to get there. In fact, sales teams can make it their primary reason for being. If they accomplish nothing else, and of course they will, they would see immediate results.

Even when sales professionals visit their clients alone, the team can help them determine needs. They can do it before and after the meeting. Think about a situation in which a salesperson visits an important prospect for the first time by herself. If she collects lots of useful information, she can share that with the team. They can then help transform that information into needs. What the product manager or operations director hears will invariably result in different perspectives about the client's situation.

Just think about any meeting you attended recently. When you discussed the meeting afterwards, you may have noticed how different people had reached very different conclusions as to what happened. Sometimes those different points of view were quite striking.

The same thing applies to sales calls. Everyone will see things from their own unique perspective, and if they share those observations, the result will be a broader, richer, more comprehensive understanding of the client's situation. Then all they need to do is collaborate and share results.

Ideally, salespeople will regularly bring resources with them to their client meetings. But that can't happen all the time or even the majority of the time. It isn't cost effective and their colleagues have other things to do. So it is incumbent upon salespeople to debrief their sales calls with their teams so they can better quantify the needs of the client

Of course there are times that different team members do join sales professionals on calls beyond the formal presentations. That is a big part of team selling, and when the resources are there, they can help make those calls much more effective and productive. Thinking of sales teams as needs development teams, in our opinion, elevates their stature, because you are including your resources in the most important part of the sales process.

It All Starts with Positioning

You knew we'd eventually get here. Don't get nervous. Remember that we discussed this concept previously when we introduced the interactive meeting model and when we discussed creative problem solving. And we referenced it in our broad overview of consultative selling. So we are not going to rehash what was presented earlier. Take a sigh of relief.

But we would do you a disservice if we didn't discuss the importance of positioning as it relates specifically to sales interactions. This is particularly important when several members of the team are present. It seems strange at first glance, but positioning plays a major role in your ability to understand your clients' needs.

Figure 10.2 highlights the three steps that comprise this phase. We believe that these are part of every sales call, whether you are flying solo or have a number of colleagues there for a major presentation.

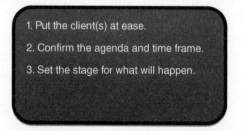

1. Put the client(s) at ease.

2. Confirm the agenda and time frame.

3. Set the stage for what will happen.

FIGURE 10.2 The Three Steps of Positioning

Put the Client(s) at Ease

We have spent a lot of time talking about connecting with clients and demonstrating empathy. Once you are there, you need to do whatever you can to make your clients comfortable early in the meeting.

You'll notice that we avoid the term (the cliché, actually) of *developing rapport*. It's not that you shouldn't; it's just that it seems so contrived. Not every client wants to chitchat. One of the best ways to make a client comfortable is to get right to work. It's situational like everything else in sales. Remember that frazzled customer from earlier. My guess is he didn't want to discuss last Sunday's football game.

On the other hand, there are those customers who feel the need to spend time discussing non-business related subjects before the meeting starts. They want to get to know you and want you to know them. They need to know that it's not just about business. Think about that successful sales-person we discussed earlier who started every meeting by talking about something personal that the customer mentioned previously.

Every customer is different, and part of the salesperson's job description is to know their customers and know what it takes to put them at ease. We can never underestimate the importance of establishing a healthy climate. Every member of the sales team has to take responsibility for this.

Getting off to a great start isn't complicated. If there are several people there, conduct a round of introductions. Give each participant the opportunity to tell you who they are and what their role is in the company. It's also very important to ask each person from the customer side to explain what they want to accomplish. Whether there are three people in the meeting or a dozen, give each one the opportunity to hear the sound of their own voice. Do the same with your team members. It's always a good way to kick off the meeting.

Confirm the Agenda and Time Frame

You simply cannot conduct a professional sales call without confirming the agenda upfront. You need to set the agenda before the meeting and confirm it once you are there. Make sure that you get both your agenda and the client's. The single most common mistake that we observe salespeople make is forgetting to ask the client for their agenda. That's right. It happens all the time. Most are pretty good at getting their agenda on the table; they just forget to get the client's. And that often results in missed opportunities.

We had the pleasure of working with a group of seasoned commercial lenders from a large regional bank. They were very experienced and knowledgeable. After the program concluded, one of the most accomplished members of the team sent us an e-mail. He told us that, shortly after the session, he visited one of his largest clients. As he always did, he sent them the agenda prior to the meeting and reviewed it when he arrived. That was his standard approach.

But this time he decided to use one of the principles he learned in the course. He asked his client if there was anything he wanted to add to the agenda. He had never done that in the past as the agenda had been communicated and confirmed. He never considered that necessary; in fact, he thought it was overkill.

You can imagine how he felt when in response to his question the client brought up three new opportunities that he was not aware of previously. Two were in his area and the third was in personal trust. He was shocked and asked the client why he hadn't raised these before. The answer was predictable: "You never asked."

It doesn't seem like a big step but it is. Be sure to confirm your agenda in every meeting and give your clients the opportunity to express theirs. A question we are often asked is whose agenda goes up first. We believe that if you initiate the meeting, your agenda should be expressed first. Since you asked for the meeting, you could look silly if you ask them what they want to accomplish. I did that once and the customer looked at me quizzingly and said, "What are you asking me for? You called the meeting!" Oops.

Conversely, if they call the meeting, it makes sense to ask them first. They invited you there for a reason. You should have established the agenda before you arrived, but once you're there, review it and make sure nothing has changed. As you guessed, it is the facilitator's job to make that happen. And if there are many people there, do what you can to learn what each individual wants to accomplish.

Who's Who?   When several people are present, ask each to explain their *role* in the company as opposed to their title. Titles can be confusing. An AVP in a bank can be a teller. An AVP at an insurance company can be a very senior manager. A managing director at an investment bank is usually a member of the club. A managing director in a smaller company could be anyone holding an exempt position. Titles mean different things to different people. Ask customers to tell you their roles, not their titles.

Try to connect as you conduct the introductions. Repeat the names and write them down. As we mentioned previously, try to memorize them. That may not be possible with a dozen people, but you can certainly do it with five or six, and that number will increase as you do it more often.

The Time Contract   Don't forget the importance of confirming what we call the "time contract." Clients are quite resentful of salespeople who don't respect their time. Early in every meeting you need to confirm precisely how much time you have and then do whatever you can to stick to it. From time to time you can remind everyone how much time remains. It's even okay to look at your watch, as long as you let them know why.

Setting the Stage for What Will Happen

Positioning the meeting concludes with setting the stage for what will happen next. Again, this is situational and varies depending on the meeting's objectives. This step also serves as a transition to the next phase. It becomes a bridge from phase one to phase two of the consultative selling approach.

If the objective of the meeting is to analyze the client's situation and learn as much as possible about them, set the stage by preparing them for questioning. You simply let the client know that you would like to ask some questions and relate it to their agenda. You can make it even more comfortable if you can let the customers know how this will benefit them: *"Since this is our first meeting, I'd like to spend most of the time asking questions to learn about your situation. This will enable us to focus on areas of interest to you when we make our recommendations. Is that okay?"*

If the objective of the meeting is to present your recommendation, you would set the stage by explaining how you will proceed: *"What we would like to do is first review our understanding of your situation, confirm that we have it right, and then offer our recommendations and explain how we can help you accomplish those objectives. Seem reasonable?"*

If you are there to address an objection that came up at the last meeting or during a phone call, you would set the stage differently: *"The last time we were together you raised a concern that we would like to address today. We have given it serious thought and feel good about how we can work with you to resolve that issue. First we'd like to review our understanding of that concern and then review our thinking. Okay?"*

Finally, if you are there to negotiate a point of difference you might set the stage like this: "*We respect your position and you were very clear in explaining what you expect from us. This relationship is very important to us. We have approached this meeting with the intention of deriving a solution that works for both of us. And with that in mind we would like to begin by reviewing our respective positions.*" This example includes what is known as a "positioning statement," which can help get negotiations off to a good start.

Setting the stage is an excellent example of the power of facilitation. It lets everyone know where you are and where you are going. It gives the meeting the structure it needs. And it makes sure that you stay on task and accomplish the objectives for the meeting—yours and the client's.

Understanding your clients' needs and analyzing their situation thoroughly is a challenging assignment. Most of us run into trouble trying to do this. That's one of the many reasons that we like to see sales teams think of themselves as needs development teams. Every member of the team can bring unique perspectives when analyzing the client's situation.

If you take the time to carefully position the meeting, particularly when you do this in teams, you will establish a climate that is more conducive to learning about the client. If you know who is there, how they fit into the organization, understand what they want to accomplish, and clarify how the meeting will proceed, the likelihood of your effectively analyzing the client's situation will increase significantly. Investing a few minutes early pays big dividends later. Stay tuned. We're about to explain ways to do this that will knock the clients' socks off.

Some Things to Consider

What

Everyone knows how important it is to get your meetings off to a great start. Anyone who ever sold anything will tell you how they establish rapport and establish agendas and all the niceties that go with that. But positioning is bigger than that—it is the first step in learning about clients. So from the minute your client meetings begin, think about how you will uncover their needs.

How

When you begin your meetings with clients, avoid thinking about solutions. If they occur to you, write them down but focus on needs. Think of your sales team as a needs development team. Let them know that unless you are there to present, they must do what they can to avoid presenting too soon. There will be plenty of time to do this later, in the meeting or later in the process.

When

Whenever you plan for a meeting, put in the time you must in thinking of how best to position it. But also put some time into determining how you will do what is necessary to focus on the needs of the client as opposed to the solutions you can provide.

11

Just One More Question (or Ten), If You Will, Please

n the previous chapter we explored the first few steps in the consultative selling process. We explained how having excellent problem solving skills can actually work against your ability to uncover customer needs. And we addressed the importance of positioning your meetings in order to set the stage for analyzing the client's situation.

But now it's time to investigate what is involved in truly understanding the customer's needs. Sales teams can leverage their resources very effectively when they attempt to understand their client's situation. When they work in sync and have their acts together, they can learn more than just their needs. They can uncover their customers' problems, aspirations, concerns, goals, objectives, issues, worries, and even their deepest fears. Sales teams must make it their mission to know as much about their customers as possible. That is a key component to their success.

When Sam Jamison's team was smack in the middle of pursuing that big job they later won, they had two memorable meetings. The first one was with the customer when Sam invited Heather, his product manager, and Jerry, his manufacturing specialist, to join him while he visited the customer shortly after receiving the RFP. It was early in the process and the meeting was positioned as exploratory in nature. While there, all three asked a ton of questions. They had prepared the customer for that, of course, so the meeting didn't turn into an interrogation.

But the questions they asked were serious, ranging from factual to big picture. They collected lots of information. What they did wasn't very different from what Jim Schwarz did when he visited Eastern Airlines for Pepsi. That was the first meeting with the prospective customer, and they planned it very carefully.

The second big meeting, was when they debriefed the team on what had happened during that initial customer meeting. Sam set it up and asked Lesley to facilitate. The three members met with the customer and shared what they had learned. Perhaps not surprisingly, they did not all interpret what the customer said in exactly the same way. Each had his or her own perspective.

But as they shared their findings, the group was asked to interpret what was said and transform what they heard into needs. Everyone was encouraged to participate. Each person shared their take on what they thought the key needs were. All this was captured on flipcharts and later typed and distributed to the team to review. The list was impressive; more than 25 needs were listed. This information was reviewed over and over as the team continued on their journey towards winning the business. One of the needs that appeared on that list led to the idea about demonstrating how effectively they worked together in front of the customer. That, you may recall, is what Sam believed led to their winning the business.

What Sam's team did was to live and breathe what is the heart and soul of the consultative selling process. If teams are going to truly differentiate themselves by presenting innovative solutions to their customers, they need to know more about those customers than anyone else on the planet. Phase two, situation analysis, is by far the most important part of the consultative selling process.

The better job you do in understanding the client's situation, the better relationships you build, the better recommendations you make, the fewer objections you encounter and the more business you win. Situation analysis drives everything. And as you start to explore this phase you'll quickly realize that questioning is at its core. Sales team can play a unique and critical role throughout this phase.

Every member of the sales team brings a fresh perspective to the sales process and can play an important role in understanding the client's situation. We weren't kidding when we suggested that sales teams can think of themselves as needs development teams. Their potential for understanding the client in depth is remarkable. They just need to understand how to channel their energy and make it happen. That's what phase two is all about.

Situation analysis consists of four key steps, shown in Figure 11.1.

1. Prepare the client for questioning.

2. Ask the appropriate questions.

3. Listen for the needs and opportunities.

4. Review your understanding of the needs.

FIGURE 11.1 The Four Steps of Situation Analysis

Preparing the Client for Questioning

Questioning is an important skill but, as we mentioned earlier, sometimes questions can be misinterpreted. So it's important to be sensitive, even somewhat cautious when you enter into the questioning mode.

We explained that it is important to transition comfortably from one phase to the next, thus the last step in positioning is to set the stage so the client knows precisely what to expect at the next meeting.

When you visit a client to learn about them, you must set the stage by preparing them for questioning. You simply explain to the client that as a way to get started you would like to ask some questions to better understand their situation. Ideally, you can relate your need to ask questions to the agenda, and better yet, let the customers know what's in it for them.

On Sam's initial visit to his customer, he kept it simple. After putting the customer at ease, introducing his colleagues, and clarifying the agenda and time frame, he said something like this:

"Since this is our first meeting, and our intent is to understand precisely what you hope to accomplish in this initiative, we'd like to ask a number of questions. The RFP was quite specific, but there are some areas we'd like to explore further. This will help us develop a recommendation that clearly addresses what is most important to you. Is that okay?"

It doesn't have to be that wordy, but on the first visit a bit of caution is encouraged. Remember, people are suspicious of questions. We explained that when we discussed how parents use questions as ways to make their points with their children (*would you like to take a bath?*).

If you're not convinced, just imagine you are sitting at your desk at 11 : 45 on a Wednesday morning. In walks your boss. The first words out of his or her mouth are: *"What are you doing for lunch?"* Now ask yourself what you might think if that happened.

If you are like most people we asked that question, you immediately said something like "uh-oh." The boss may have had an assignment for you. Or he was wondering why you weren't with a customer. Or perhaps she had good news to share. Or bad. Maybe the boss just wanted to have lunch with you.

The list could go on and on, all because a manager asked a perfectly appropriate six-word question. Everyone is suspicious of questions. Customers are, too. And since questioning is such an important skill, you need to set the stage for it. This even applies to long-term relationships. If you visit a customer you know well, you might say something as simple as, *"It has been a while since our last meeting. I'd like to catch up by asking a few questions, okay?"* Or as I like to say to those who know me well, *"You know the drill. I need to ask a few questions before we get into our discussion."*

You'll figure out what works for you, whether you're flying solo or with your team. But this is one of those subtle facilitation skills that help get the meeting off to a good start while ensuring you'll be able learn about the customer's situation.

Asking the Appropriate Questions

You have all had situations in which you walked into a client's office and they talked and talked and talked and provided you with all the information you needed without your having to do anything other than steer the conversation from time to time. We love those kinds of sales calls. You learn precisely what you need to know without asking many questions. Unfortunately, that doesn't happen very often. If you are going to learn about the client, you have to get in the trenches and ask questions.

Firms like ours have classified many types of questions, but you can narrow this vast amount of material into a few buckets. Almost any question you ask falls into one of these categories:

- Transactional questions
- Needs clarification questions
- Strategic questions

We'll take a look at each category. But first, we want to point out again the difference between content and process. This concept is something to apply when asking questions. How you do this can dramatically impact how the client responds. It not just the questions you ask (the content); it's how you ask them (the process). That is something you must take into account. We will briefly discuss the content, even though most sales professionals and their colleagues know what they want to ask. But like most interactive skills, process deserves more attention.

The Content Perspective

Transactional questions are those fact finding, information-seeking questions that everybody asks. They aren't terribly imaginative but they are extremely important. You cannot scope out an initiative or qualify a prospect or understand the opportunity if you don't ask these kinds of questions. They tend to be closed and they have right answers.

Theoretically, if you ask several members of the customer's team a transactional question, you'll get the same answer (*How many locations are involved?*). Surprisingly, they can be quite provocative (*What is your budget?*). But they are absolutely necessary, and though they won't do much to get you up the value pyramid, you and you teammates have to ask them all the time. Here are some examples.

- What are your annual sales?
- Who else is participating in the project?
- How do you inventory the material?
- What are the customer demographics?
- What is the target date for the roll out?
- What software are you using now?"

Obviously, we need to ask these kinds of questions to understand our customers. They provide useful information. But we can go deeper.

Needs clarification questions are quite different. As the name suggests, they are asked with the intent of uncovering needs. When we say needs, and you've noticed we do that often, we really mean more than just needs. We refer to problems, opportunities, issues, concerns, and so on. We keep it simple by putting all these under the needs umbrella.

These kinds of questions encourage the client to talk. They are more open-ended. They can be quite imaginative and provocative. But unlike their cousins, the transactional questions, they do not have right answers. If you ask those same several customers a needs clarification question, you would probably get three different answers (*What are the key challenges you are facing right now?*). Needs clarification questions help get you up the value pyramid. If you want to be perceived as a needs developer, you had better ask these kinds of questions. If sales teams are to become needs development teams these questions are extremely important. Again, a few examples:

- How do you differentiate yourselves?
- What are your customers asking for now that they weren't asking for in the past?
- What do you expect from providers like us?
- What led to the decision to go to RFP?
- How has morale been affected by that decision?
- What would be the ideal outcome?

You have the opportunity to get creative and imaginative when asking these kinds of questions. Obviously, you need to know your customer, and what you might ask one customer you'd never consider asking another. We have heard many clever questions from participants in our training programs over the years. Here are a few examples.

- If you could change one thing in the way you do business today, what would that be?
- Assume you decided to do business with us today. A year from now you couldn't be happier. What happened?
- What is the best thing a provider ever did for you? The worst?
- What will make this a tremendous win for you personally?
- When all is said and done, what do you want your colleagues to think when they reflect upon the initiative?

Of course, you need to know your client. But sometimes adding a little spice to the questioning process can make it more interesting and less tedious. This is also a great time to use team members. If Charlie from Operations asks a question that may seem unusual, the customer would be more forgiving than if it came from the salesperson. On the other hand, using team members in this way allows you to ask questions you might otherwise avoid. For example, the salesperson should know who the competition is. But if the R&D manager asks the question it may land on friendlier ears.

One of the big questions that Sam asked on the initial call that led to the big idea was: *"Of all the criteria you are considering when deciding who will be your provider of choice, which is most important to you?"* The client's answer focused on a team that would collaborate and bring creativity to the relationship. Sam and his team recalled this in their internal meetings, and it led to Lesley's idea of demonstrating to the customer in real time how well they work together. Again, that may be what won them a job that they did not think they could win.

Strategic questions are the big picture questions. As the name suggests, they focus on the long term. They are not the easiest questions to ask, nor are they easy to answer. But if you aspire to reach the strategic advisor level of the value pyramid, it helps to ask these kinds of questions.

They require planning. You can't just think of these on the spot. You need to be very careful in the way you ask these, since clients can find themselves on the defensive if they don't have the answers. They will often uncover less obvious needs. Different members of the team can ask strategic questions more comfortably. Think about that as you review the following examples.

- Where do you want the business to be in five years? What might prevent that from happening?
- What do you anticipate as the biggest changes in technology that you need to address moving forward?
- How will you leverage your success in the past to ensure continued success in the future?
- How do you expect to maintain customer loyalty in the long term?
- As you look to the future, what will you do to ensure that you have the right talent to perform their jobs?

These are not the kinds of questions that most people could answer easily or comfortably. But think about how logical it is for the strategic planning person to ask about growth of the business, or the market research specialist to ask about customer loyalty. It is easier for customers to enter into those kinds of discussions when they know that the person asking the question has expertise that they can share. This is a marvelous way to leverage your resources.

The Process Component

Knowing what questions to ask is obviously very important. As you reviewed the examples, much of what you saw may have been familiar. Maybe a few were new, but for the most part sales professionals and their colleagues know what questions to ask. What they don't always know is how to ask them. Enter the process component.

Setting the Stage

At the risk of sounding redundant, the first step to making the questioning process more comfortable is to explain that you will be asking questions and that the meeting is in your mutual interest. Preparing the customer is the first step and it's a big one.

Early in my career when I was selling for Union Carbide, I found myself asking a potential customer many questions. I didn't pick up on how annoyed he was. Finally, he looked at me and said, *"What are you writing, a book or something?"* The best answer I could come up with was a pathetic *"No, sir, I'm just trying to learn about your business."* The sales call ended shortly thereafter.

Had I explained how Carbide liked to work with small businesses and could assist with capitalization programs and extended credit, he may have been more willing to answer my questions. Like anything else, if you eliminate the element of surprise it leads to more authentic communication.

Make the Process Conversational

The questioning process is not an interrogation. It isn't like you're taking a survey. This isn't a press conference. It's part of a conversation. You need to treat it as such.

You don't just start firing questions after you position the meeting. You want your questions to become part of a conversation. You might ask a few questions and then digress based on the answers you get. For example, if you are asking about market conditions and something relevant comes up that relates to what you recently observed, it is perfectly fine to discuss that for a few minutes. That's what makes the process conversational.

What you don't want to do is mention your products or services. That will happen later. That doesn't mean you can't ever make reference to your products. The occasional "commercial" is just fine, in our opinion.

A commercial is a 10- to 15-second reference to something you do that might come up during questioning. *("One of the products we will be discussing later addresses that issue head on. But we'll discuss that after I learn a bit more.")*

The occasional commercial can create some interest and add a bit of color to the conversation, but don't fall into the trap of allowing that to lead to a premature presentation. It's just another way to avoid the "Q&A trap" and to ensure that the questioning process is conversational.

Asking the Difficult Question

Too many sales professionals avoid asking the difficult or uncomfortable questions. They can range from *"what's your budget?"* to *"who makes the decisions?"* to *"what led to that unfortunate outcome?"* Just for the fun of it, take a minute and put yourself in the customer's shoes and pretend that you were asked a question like one of those. What would you think was the reason the salesperson asked the question?

When people ask budget-related questions, customers assume they want to see how high they can price their recommendation. When they are asked who makes the decision, they can be insulted in assuming you don't respect them or want to go over their head. When they ask what led to an unfortunate outcome, they might think you will exploit what happened.

This questioning stuff can get convoluted. But that's where your process sensitivity can help. You don't want to be misinterpreted. Nor do you want to insult the customer. There are ways to avoid that.

The Pre-Question Statement

Most of us are suspicious of questions. We encourage you to address this directly. The concept of the *pre-question statement* suggests that if you have a controversial question to ask, first begin with a preamble. That's right— before you ask the question, explain why you are asking it and/or why you think it is in the customer's interest to answer it. (See Figure 11.2.)

The Reason You Are Asking

As the graphic suggests, before you ask the question give the customer a good reason for asking it. You'll not only demonstrate credibility, but also eliminate the guesswork that can result from it. If the marketing manager

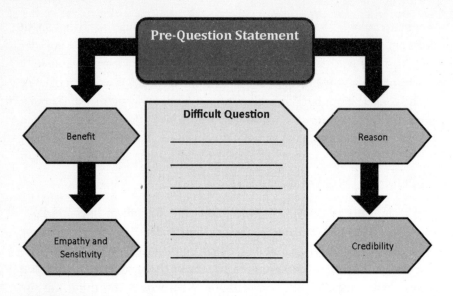

FIGURE 11.2 The Pre-Question Statement

mentions the research she has done about the growth of the business before asking the client about what they anticipate, it removes some of the skepticism. Similarly, if the sales professional explains how every company has their own decision making process, it justifies his need to ask how decisions are made. Letting the customer know why you need the information before you ask a question demonstrates your credibility and makes it easier for them to respond.

Why They Should Answer

The flip side of this is letting customers know what's in it for them to answer the question; that is, you give them a benefit to answering your question. If you want to ask them about their budget, it helps if you explain that you want to get them the best possible return on their investment.

If the R&D specialist explains how he can help the customer adapt to the changing technology, they'll feel better about discussing how they feel about the new approach. If the market research manager shares a bit about her understanding about what consumers are thinking, and the importance of assessing customer loyalty, she has a better chance of learning about the customer's long term thinking. The point is that when there is a difficult, challenging, or confidential question to ask, explaining why you are asking, and why you think the customer should answer, makes the process more comfortable for everyone.

The Pre-Cluster Statement

Questions can fall in groupings or what we like to call *clusters*. You might want to ask a series of questions about the customer's strategy, their competition, their customer base, their product line, or even their philosophy. Each cluster can include a series of questions including all three types.

One way to keep your questioning focused, and to avoid confusion, is to stay within a specific cluster. The last thing a customer wants to endure is a convoluted questioning process. Asking a question about the marketplace, followed by a question about their new CEO, followed by a question about their plans for next year, simply isn't effective. And it won't sit well with the customer.

To ensure that you stay within a cluster, we encourage you to use what we call a *pre-cluster statement* (see Figure 11.3.)

This is similar to the pre-question statement, except that it sets up a cluster of questions. Explaining the reason you're asking and providing the associated benefit is still in order: " . . . *that was helpful. Thank you. Now I'd like to learn a bit about your current strategy. The more we know about your current thinking, the better prepared we will be to explain how we can assist,"* This would be followed by a series of questions that focus on strategy.

The pre-cluster statement can help involve your team members. If you brought in Sarah, a technical expert, defer to her and let her ask the necessary questions: *"Sarah is our expert in this area so I am going to turn the meeting over to her. As we mentioned earlier, we would like to learn more about these technical issues you are encountering."* Then you hand the ball to Sarah and let her do her thing. Pre-cluster statements will keep you focused, will make the customer feel more comfortable, and will allow you to better use your resources. It's another example of the power of facilitation.

Those Appreciative Phrases

We discussed making the questioning process conversational. We also explained how people don't like to be questioned, particularly when they

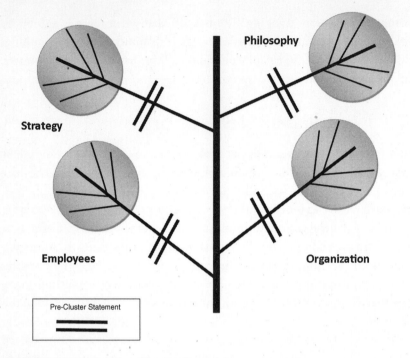

FIGURE 11.3 The Pre-Cluster Statement

don't know where the questioning process is headed. With that in mind, we encourage you to show your appreciation every now and again. You can use simple phrases like "*that was helpful . . .*" or "*thank you, that was very insightful . . .*" or "*this is extremely useful. I appreciate your providing that information. . . .*" Phrases like these, inserted in the process every so often, can make questioning much more comfortable for everyone involved.

Avoid Manipulation

We'll finish where we started. The questions we ask, and what purpose they serve, can often be misconstrued. Often they are really ideas (*Can we meet with the committee?*). Other times they are polite rejections of ideas (*Do you really think you can be ready in two weeks?*). Still other times they are downright insulting (*What were you thinking?*). And sometimes they express someone's opinion in no uncertain terms (*You're not really going to wear that shirt to dinner, are you?*).

And that's why you have to be ultra-careful when asking your customers questions. It is such a critical time in the sales process you need to do it professionally. Asking manipulative questions like the ones that start with *"if I could show you a way . . . "* don't sit well with most clients. They feel like they are getting set up. The "if I could" is a tentative statement. But it's asking the customer to commit to something that is definitive.

If a salesperson asks you something like: *"If I could show you how we could save you money and improve your bottom line, would you be interested in working with us?"* nobody would say no to that. But it's not authentic. It's painting the customer into a corner. Compare that with *"We believe that what we offer can save you money and improve your bottom line. I'd like to explain how, if that's all right."* In both cases the message is the same. But one sounds like a stereotypical salesperson. The other sounds more like a consultant or partner.

You have probably heard that the more questions you ask the more success you enjoy. That's logical because questions get you important information, and buried in that information are needs. And whoever determines the most needs usually wins. Asking questions is something you have to do. One of the reasons that many salespeople lose business over time is that they get complacent and stop asking questions. Their competitors seize the opportunity and chip away their share. It happens all the time.

So ask questions every time you meet with your customers. Do it authentically with sensitivity. Use questions as a way to demonstrate credibility. Make sure that your customers are comfortable and avoid the guesswork. Leverage your team members throughout the questioning process. It is the most important skill, and if you and your colleagues do it well, you'll outshine your competition every single time.

Some Things to Consider

What

We try hard to avoid absolutes, but our team is convinced that questioning is the most important skill of all. It is also perhaps the most insidious skill. It can help you assess a client's situation, but it can also get you in trouble with clients. The better you understand a client's situation, the stronger the relationship, the more focused the recommendation, the less daunting the objection and the more likely the success. Ask those questions—all the time.

How

Teams can contribute successfully to the questioning process. Before every meeting, devote time to thinking about the questions you would like to ask. Decide who will ask what questions. If the questions are challenging, think about the pre-question statement you will use. Don't lose sight of keeping questions in clusters. And remember the different types of questions you learned, as each is important.

When

Before every client meeting, put some serious time into thinking about the questions you will ask, how you will ask them, and who will ask them. Do this for every client meeting.

12 Are They Sales Teams or Needs Development Teams?

The previous chapter focused primarily on one skill—questioning. Entire books have been devoted to this subject. That is because so many people, yours truly included, believe it's the most important skill of all. Success in sales is all about understanding the customer's needs, and there is no way to do that if you don't ask the appropriate questions.

But questioning is only one variable in a complicated equation. You can ask brilliant questions, but if you aren't listening effectively it is all for naught. It's quite obvious that you'll never learn what you need to know if you aren't listening.

Anyone who has been in the game knows that understanding the customer's situation better than anyone else is what leads to building meaningful relationships. You have to hear what the customer says and you also have to hear what they don't say. You'll never give yourself a chance to hear what matters if you don't ask the right questions and listen to the answers. It's all about questioning and listening.

We just investigated questioning and we'll discuss listening with equal passion in the next chapter. But before we explore listening, it's important to explain what *to listen for*. Sales teams must learn as much as possible about their customers. They have to go beyond just determining needs; they have *to analyze the client's situation*. Those words were not chosen lightly. There is so much to learn beyond the needs, and when sales teams work together they can do this brilliantly. When they do, they will distinguish themselves.

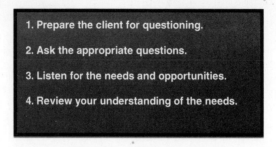

1. Prepare the client for questioning.

2. Ask the appropriate questions.

3. Listen for the needs and opportunities.

4. Review your understanding of the needs.

FIGURE 12.1 The Four Steps of Situation Analysis

When we introduced situation analysis, we discussed the steps that comprise this critical phase. Here they are again, shown in Figure 12.1.

Notice the three key words: listening, questioning, and needs. They may be the three most important words in the consultative selling process. *Listening, questioning, and needs.* They can become a mantra. Salespeople and sales teams who stand out from the pack find themselves not just giving lip service to these words; they understand how to apply them day after day.

We explored the first two steps in situation analysis in the previous chapter. Now we'll explore the next two steps.

Listen for the Needs and Opportunities

If you know what to listen for, it will make you a better listener. So we'll begin by looking at needs. Every time we mention the word need, remember that it is a convenient shorthand way to refer to needs, problems, opportunities, issues, concerns, goals, objectives, fears, aspirations, and anything else that relates to the customer's situation.

Recall that exercise we did around my disorganized office and flooded basement and troublesome bookkeeper. Our objective was to crystallize the difference between needs and solutions. The exercise illustrated how in spite of our best intentions our tendency is to jump to solutions too quickly. That is why most customers contend that the majority of the sales professionals they see don't understand all of their needs. They'll affirm that salespeople determine some of their needs; they just don't get all of them. And too often they miss the ones that are most important.

The most successful salespeople are the ones who get it. They are the ones who work diligently to understand their clients' needs. In a world in which most of us are selling commodities, the best way to differentiate yourself is to understand the client better than anyone else. A wonderful way to leverage the resources of a sales team is to collect their perspectives on the customers' needs before, during, and after meeting with clients. It all comes down to effectively analyzing the customer's situation.

It helps to define what a need is. Again we refer to *The American Heritage Dictionary of the English Language*. They define "need" this way: "*a condition or situation in which something is required or wanted.*"

That works for us. We like to simplify things, and this is a nice, concise, simple definition. Again: *a condition or situation in which something is required or wanted.* Pretty cool, huh?

Needs are also motivational statements. If indeed something is required or wanted, there is a motivational component. If you don't want it, and if it's not a requirement, you probably don't need it. That's why the expression "creating needs" is troublesome. You can uncover needs. You can develop needs. You can clarify needs. But you can't create them. Either the client has them or hasn't. Clients may not know they have them, and you may enlighten the clients as to what they are, but you do not have the power to create them for the client. People who think otherwise are kidding themselves.

One basic guideline that helps differentiate between needs and solutions is that needs are usually expressed as *verbs*. Solutions, on the other hand, tend to be expressed as *nouns*. There are exceptions, of course, but the rule applies almost all the time.

Let's go back to those five examples we used previously.

1. My office is disorganized.
2. I want to take my spouse on a memorable vacation.
3. My lawn is burned out halfway through the summer.
4. My bookkeeper is making me nervous.
5. My basement is flooded.

In each example we can identify a need and corresponding solutions. We are guessing here, of course, because we don't have as much information as we'd like, but we'll use these examples anyway. Think of them as educated guesses.

If my office is disorganized, my need is to bring order to my office. The solutions could be new filing cabinets, a professional organizer, or a more user-friendly desk.

If I want to take my spouse on a vacation, my need could be to spend quality time with my wife. The solutions could be to book a trip to Paris at one extreme, or to rent an RV and explore places in the U.S. that we never saw before. (Just for the record, the trip to Paris is a better solution.)

Just one more. If my bookkeeper is making me nervous, the need could be to feel more comfortable about that individual. The solution could be a heart-to-heart talk, or agreeing to some ground rules, or even replacing the bookkeeper.

See the differences? The solutions are nouns. "Trip" is a noun, whether it's going to Paris, the Grand Canyon, or Evansville, Indiana. But the need is *to spend quality time with my wife*. "Spend" is a verb.

If you turn to your client and say *"you need ____,"* and the blank is a noun, it's probably not a need. If you tell someone they need a new inventory system, or a more effective e-mail marketing strategy, or a more sophisticated asset allocation plan, or even a sump pump for the basement, you are offering solutions. They aren't needs.

Those examples may be perfectly viable solutions. But again, you are guessing what the solution is if you don't understand the need. If you figure out the needs first, you'll come up with better solutions, more focused solutions, more creative solutions, and quite frankly, more acceptable solutions. If you can express your understanding of the needs first and get confirmation from the client, when it is time to offer your solutions they will fall on friendlier ears. That's not debatable; if you are skeptical, just ask your customers.

Are you getting the impression that we're extremely focused on customer needs? You're right. We are. The team that does the best job of uncovering needs is inevitably the one who wins. That's why we like to think of sales teams as *needs development teams*.

Teams outperform individuals. Consistent with that, sales teams can do a better job of understanding needs than any salesperson can by him- or herself. Much better. Put that one in the bank.

When we observed Sam's team we learned that they focused on the customer's need to work with a provider who believed in teamwork, was different from the others, and would bring innovation to the process. They understood precisely what the customer's most important needs were. And their demonstration of how they worked as a team during the finalist presentation sealed the deal. Had they never uncovered that need, which they reviewed when the team was rehearsing, they would never have taken that risk. And they may not have won the business.

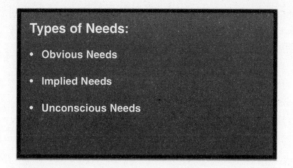

Types of Needs:

- Obvious Needs
- Implied Needs
- Unconscious Needs

FIGURE 12.2 Types of Needs

The first thing you need to do is understand what these things we call needs are and how to be sensitive about how your customers express them. They come in different shapes and sizes. Customers tend to verbalize them in three ways, each of which is quite different, as illustrated in Figure 12.2.

The Obvious Need

These are the ones that the customers come right out and tell you. They literally explain to you what their needs are. If you miss them, which is unlikely, it's for one of three reasons: you weren't listening, you don't care, or you're brain dead. I'm not being a wise guy here; it's pretty straightforward. When a customer goes out of their way to tell you what his or her needs are, you'd better listen up and hear them.

Here are a few examples:

- We need to cut costs.
- We need to reduce cycle time.
- We need to improve quality.
- We need to grow our business.
- We need to reduce inventory.
- We need to work with people on the cutting edge.

The customer tells you specifically what they need; your job is to listen effectively and make sure you understand them. It's no more complicated than that.

The Implied Need

These needs are a bit more challenging. As the name suggests, these are the needs that the client doesn't share with you directly. They are hinted at. You have to read between the lines. You need to infer what was behind what the client said. There is some guesswork on your part, and you may not always guess correctly. But sales professionals and sales teams who are able to uncover implied needs will clearly differentiate themselves.

You may recall that Sam's team did that. The RFP never spoke directly to the teamwork issue. And not once did the word "innovation" appear in the text. They concluded that these needs were important based on what they heard the customer say. These were clearly implied needs. The team identified them, jumped on them, and addressed them. You know the result.

Time for an exercise. What appears below are two statements from a customer. See if you can uncover the implied needs that are buried in these statements.

"We have never done this before."

"I like it, but my boss second guesses all my recommendations."

Come on. Do the exercise. Take a minute or two and ask yourself what the implied needs may be.

Let's go in the order they appear. If someone says they've never done something before, here are a few possible implied needs:

- To understand how it works.
- To be assured it's a good decision.
- To minimize the risk.
- To learn how to use it.
- To make the transition easy.

The second one is a little trickier. If the guy is concerned about being second-guessed by the boss, here are a few possibilities regarding his needs:

- To feel confident when he explains this to his boss.
- To have the backup he needs when he talks to his boss.
- To anticipate what the boss might ask and be ready to respond.
- To have the courage to stand up to his boss.

Again, these are guesses. You'll need to confirm them with your client. But based on what the customer says, you can infer what the needs are. This is a real differentiator. Sales teams can challenge themselves to find the needs that aren't obvious—the ones that don't jump out at them. After every client interaction they can compare notes and discuss their different perspectives. (By the way, if you said he needs a new boss, that's not a bad recommendation. But it's not a need; it's a solution.)

In the first case, where something was new for the customer, your tendency might have been to offer to give a demonstration of how it worked or arrange for a tour of another customer's facility. Those are excellent solutions, but once again, they're not needs. In the second case, if you said you'd be delighted to meet with his boss, that might have appealed to your customer, but that, too, is a solution. Early in the process the focus has to be on needs, and if you avoid coming up with solutions too quickly you won't miss those implied needs. You'll always be able to come up with superb solutions later.

The Unconscious Need

These are the really tricky ones. These are the needs that clients do not know they have. You have to be very careful in the way you capture and review these because there is a big risk of being perceived as presumptuous. But the teams who uncover these will clearly give themselves a huge advantage when it's time to present. If you want to get to the top of the value pyramid and become a strategic advisor, you need to be quite proficient at uncovering these unconscious needs.

Let's look at an example of an unconscious need that a salesperson raised in one of our programs. She shared a situation that she experienced in which a prospect said something quite insulting: "You guys are all the same." You may have heard that one yourself. It doesn't feel very good. In fact it's downright impolite, even nasty. Your likely tendency is to jump all over it and talk about the things you do that make you different.

This is an example of an unconscious need. The truth is we're not all alike. Each sales professional, each sales team, and each company is unique in its own way. For a customer to say that you're all the same illustrates how he doesn't understand this and how misguided he is.

Instead of coming across as defensive and explaining how you're different, a more professional response might be to first express your understanding of the potential need. It could be to understand how you are different, or maybe it's to see what you can do that others can't, or perhaps it's to know what they will get from you that they aren't getting now. You won't know for sure until you review your understanding. But if you review the unconscious needs, without overreacting, your response has to be better.

Here's another example, again thanks to a course participant. He talked about how a customer who knew little about his product foolishly said, "it simply will not work." The salesperson was frustrated because he knew it would. He had seen the product do precisely what the customer said it couldn't. Again, the tendency is to let the customer know they're wrong and offer to give testimonials, references, and the like. But these would be solutions. An alternative approach is to treat what they said as an unconscious need.

The need could be to learn about the product, or to see how his concerns are resolvable, or to understand how the product can work for him. Again, we're guessing. But sometimes your customers do not know what their needs are and that's when you can really help. As we mentioned earlier, this is a wonderful way to leverage sales teams. Different members of the team will hear needs that others may have missed completely. And often they are unconscious needs.

So needs can be expressed in different ways. Sometimes they are explicit; sometimes they are implicit. Sometimes they are obvious and other times they aren't. Most sales professionals hear the obvious needs; some pick up the implied needs; few get the unconscious needs. With the help of the team, we know you will increase your ability to get them all. If you do, you'll see results.

Another Way to Look at Needs

What appears above are the different ways our customers express their needs. But they can be broken down further into three categories, as shown in Figure 12.3.

Categories of Needs

- Organizational

- Personal

- Job Related

FIGURE 12.3 Categories of Needs

Business Needs

True professionals make their decisions based on their business needs. Some people refer to these as organizational needs. They focus primarily on the return on investment. The business need focuses on one thing and one thing only—what is best for the organization. If you owned your own business, and people on your staff were making purchasing decisions, you would clearly want those decisions to be based on the needs of the organization.

As you may recall, Bob Christian said that whenever you make decisions you should assume that the company is seated at the table. Think in terms of their needs as well. Personifying the organization drives this point home rather effectively.

Here are several examples of business or organizational needs.

- To reduce costs.
- To increase profits.
- To differentiate us from our competition.
- To enhance our product line.
- To establish a presence in Asia.
- To keep employee morale high.

Notice how, if these needs are addressed, the organization will benefit. Each need focuses on the business.

Job-Related Needs

These are a little more subtle. Job-related needs are more focused on the individuals who are making the decisions. Job-related needs are somewhat bifurcated, since they address two key areas of interest to the buyer—how they can do their jobs more effectively and how they can feel more secure about their jobs. The job security component has become much more significant in recent times.

The ability to do one's job more effectively can range from acquiring tools to assist the worker, to what the product offers that simplifies the process, to the role of the supplier in helping them accomplish their objectives. Of course, if any individual performs better than before, the company will benefit, so there is a business component here, but the buyer who is driven by job-related needs is thinking about his or her own performance first.

Again some examples:

- To save time in execution.
- To reduce the amount of paperwork.
- To expedite the process.
- To require fewer touch points.
- To minimize the risk involved.
- To receive the required training.

These are all important. But as you can see, they lean more toward the individual performing his or her job well than on the return on investment, even if one may result in the other.

Personal Needs

These are the ones that can be somewhat maddening for salespeople. That's because these are the needs that apply primarily to the buyer. Again, they can impact other needs, but here the individuals involved are focusing primarily on what is good for them.

Many people believe that too many decisions in business are driven by personal needs. That's not good. Individuals shouldn't make important buying decisions for their company based on how those decisions impact themselves. You would hope that they think about the company first.

Whether buyers are driven by their insecurities, their need to be liked, their desire to be in control, or how powerful they feel, these kinds of personal needs often cloud sound judgment. We hope that the professional buyer will avoid the tendency to make buying decisions based on who they like the most or who makes them most comfortable. Unfortunately, they do make such decisions, and too often. Every sales professional needs to take this into consideration.

One more time, here are some examples.

- To look good in front of the boss.
- To justify the bonus they expect.
- To know that they are respected.
- To avoid making major mistakes.
- To know their opinions are valued.
- To feel like it's more than just business.

Anyone who has ever interacted with a customer knows how personal needs impact decisions. How buyers feel about the individuals calling on them, and how buyers feel about themselves, play a major role in most buying decisions. Don't lose sight of this.

Sales Teams and Needs

Sales teams who think of themselves as *needs development teams* can accomplish great things. The phrase speaks volumes. There are so many ways that sales teams can raise the bar in working with existing and prospective clients. Nothing exceeds the importance of needs development.

Every member of the sales team must attempt to understand the customers' needs before, during, and after sales calls. From the time the customer says something of interest or the initial inquiry arrives, the team's top priority is to start delving into the process of uncovering needs. The individual team members can do this by themselves and share results later, or they can meet and discuss what they know collectively. The key is to learn what everyone thinks regarding the needs of the customer.

Different perspectives are so helpful here. Each team member has a particular area of expertise, and as a result what one person sees so vividly another might not even notice. Sometimes the person who you would least expect to hear from might get a sense of something that everyone else missed. But it will never happen if the team doesn't convene and discuss this.

In the previous chapter we mentioned how Sam's team met to discuss the opportunity. It was in that meeting that they determined how important teamwork, collaboration, and innovation were to this customer. Those words never appeared in their naked form in the RFP. It was only from the discussions that they had with the customer that they concluded these values were so important. One team member shared those perspectives in the meeting, and that led to the presentation that won them the business. Had they not taken the time to hear from everybody, they never would have considered putting on that amazing demonstration.

So How Do You Do This?

It isn't difficult to leverage this expertise. Teams can accomplish what they need to do in a one- or two-hour meeting. Ideally, the entire team will be present, either in person or remotely if necessary. The suggested approach is to first review the information and data that the team has acquired. All the relevant information is shared. Then each member of the team will be asked to share his or her perspectives on the needs of the customer. It helps if they state their needs as verbs so they don't inadvertently offer solutions. Speculation and risk taking should be encouraged.

With the help of a facilitator, all the ideas are captured, ideally on white boards or flipcharts so they are visible to everyone. Again, the participants are encouraged to speculate, which must be tolerated. Even participants who did not attend the customer meetings can be valuable resources.

As in any creative session, the participants need to avoid judging or evaluating what is offered prematurely. There is no need to do that yet. The intent is to capture the information as it is generated without worrying about what's right and wrong. There will be plenty of time to evaluate later.

Then the group can determine which needs are most viable. They need to be very thoughtful here. As previously mentioned, sometimes those implied or unconscious needs are the big ones. But the objective is to conclude what the customer's top-priority needs are so that the team can address them in their recommendation. If ever a team can shine, it's now, and not taking advantage of their potential is a big miss.

The selection process is important. Different teams select the priority needs in different ways. Each person can pick the ones that they think are most important and explain why. Or they can rate each need "high," "medium," or "low." Another approach is to have each participant rate each need "1 to 5," and then tabulate the results. The intent is to give each team member the chance to be heard. Remember, involvement leads to commitment.

Once that is done, the sales professional or team leader would make the final decision. They will, of course, pay very close attention to what everyone said, but the final decision is theirs. Remember, we're talking about sales teams, and by definition Sales assumes the leadership role. The group is involved, but the decision is made by Sales. And once that is done, the needs are confirmed and the team is ready to proceed.

It's all about the customer. That means that sales teams have to work together to know more about their customers than anyone else on the planet. By understanding how clients express their needs, and paying attention to the different kinds of needs, they can direct their efforts toward the customer. If they meet regularly, collaborate effectively, and reach thoughtful conclusions, they will be well positioned to make marvelous recommendations. That is what team selling is all about.

By the way, we haven't inadvertently avoided the subject of listening. That's what the next chapter will explore in depth. But it's all about *knowing what to listen for*. Yes, the grammar could be better, but the importance of the message could not.

If sales teams understand the difference between needs and solutions, know how needs are expressed, and understand the different categories, they can approach client meetings with a very powerful, confident mindset. That will make them extremely effective and help them stand out when they attempt to analyze their customer's situation.

Some Things to Consider

What

Sales teams can do lots of great things. But bringing their clients innovative solutions begins with a solid understanding of the clients' needs. If they understand needs that their competitors don't, if they learn things that the client doesn't even know him or herself, they will inevitably derive innovative solutions to help that client. That is why sales teams can think of themselves as *needs development teams*.

How

Identify a big client opportunity. Get the team together before the meeting and have them speculate what the client's needs are based on what they know at that point. When they are at the client meeting, they can ask questions to clarify their understanding and learn of additional needs. And of course, after the meeting they can debrief what happened—even with those who weren't there can participate—to make sure they have a precise understanding of the client's needs. It's all good.

When

You may not do this thorough an investigation of needs in every client situation, but if the stakes are high we would encourage you to do this and do it well. Remember, needs come in all shapes and sizes. Whoever learns the most needs usually wins.

13 Is Anybody Listening?

In Chapter 12 we discussed needs. We defined what a need is, we looked at different kinds of needs, we discussed the different ways customers express their needs, and we distinguished between needs and solutions. We also made a few suggestions about how sales teams can collaborate to clearly capture the needs of the customer.

Needs, needs, needs. You are probably tiring of hearing the word. Well it's not over yet. Not by a long shot. Understanding them is the key to consultative selling and is a major component of innovative team selling. You can ask the best questions in the history of the world, resulting in the customer talking at length about their needs, but if you don't hear what they say, it's a big waste of time.

Let's look at Figure 13.1, which shows the four steps in situation analysis one more time.

The first two steps focus on questioning. The next two are all about listening. We preached about the importance of questioning and the role sales teams can play in asking questions. But many people will say that listening is every bit as important. And they have a point. Why put the time and energy into questioning if you don't hear the answers? And, sadly, everyone misses much of what clients say all the time.

If questioning is the *ying*, listening is the *yang*. You can't have one without the other. Or put another way, perhaps more seriously, if sales teams are going to evolve into needs development teams, they had better do both, and do them well. Needs development builds a bridge between the

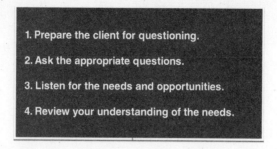

1. Prepare the client for questioning.

2. Ask the appropriate questions.

3. Listen for the needs and opportunities.

4. Review your understanding of the needs.

FIGURE 13.1 The Four Steps of Situation Analysis

seller and the buyer. Questioning and listening are the pillars that support that bridge.

Now that we know what to listen for, let's look at listening, which as you know is a complicated, challenging, and critically important skill. We have never met anyone who could not benefit from being a better listener.

The Problem

Nobody ever meets with clients with the intention of not hearing everything they say. Anyone who has ever carried a bag will talk at length about how important it is to listen. It's part of the job description. Those who excel will hear not only what their customers say, but also what they don't say. But they are the exception and not the rule. Most people in the selling role miss much of what is said and they don't even know it.

The question, of course, is why.

Exercise time. This is important. Think about why it's so difficult to listen. Think about what you do, not what the other guy does. Distractions, interruptions, and other external annoyances clearly impact your listening. But for now focus on what you do; that is, what's going on internally. Give it a shot.

You probably came up with several good reasons for not listening well. We have been asking salespeople that same question for decades. Here are some of the most common responses:

- Thinking ahead.
- Anticipating what the customer will say.
- Planning your response.
- Worrying about your last comment.
- Thinking about your next question.

There are many other reasons. Dozens, in fact. They include things like lack of respect for the speaker, not being interested, confusion, personal issues, and even boredom. You can see that they all have one thing in common: the tendency to focus on yourself. Sorry about that, but it is the common denominator. If you don't buy that, just look at your list or the one on the previous page.

You're thinking about what you will say, what you will recommend, what you will ask, or what you will offer. All of this is coming from a good place. It isn't that you don't want to listen; you just want to offer a good recommendation or ask a good question or provide a good answer. The problem is that when you focus on these things it becomes difficult to listen.

A Historical Perspective

Synectics® was a pioneer in investigating the challenges associated with listening. Their focus was on creative problem solving and they became intrigued with how this impacted creative sessions. They soon realized that participants tend to think about other things, which detracted from their ability to perform at peak efficiency. Since they weren't tuned in all the time, they missed the opportunity to hear things that could trigger new ideas.

Now that wasn't all bad, since they saw the value in making what they called *connections*. Connections are simply thoughts that occur to you based on something you heard. Unfortunately, their research concluded that this could significantly impact both the quantity and quality of the ideas that were generated. So the challenge was to figure out how to do both—make connections without losing focus.

Using the work of Carl Rogers as a reference they introduced the concept of the rehearsal curve. See Figure 13.2. It may be familiar to you, since many people in academia and the training community have adopted it as a way to discuss active listening.

The folks at Synectics® realized early in the game that participants in meetings have an extraordinary ability to make these connections. These could be ideas, insights, perspectives or speculations.

Once that happened they started thinking about what they wanted to say; that is they began rehearsing their suggestion before they said it. I am sure you can relate to this. Just think of the last time you were confronted by a power figure. It's likely that you were in pure rehearsal mode as you planned

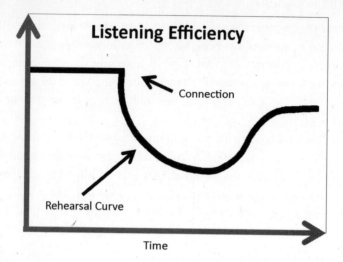

FIGURE 13.2 Listening Efficiency and the Rehearsal Effect

your defense. It's a very natural thing to do. Synectics® coined the term the *rehearsal effect* to define this.

It refers to your tendency, particularly in interactive situations, to focus on what you are thinking as opposed to listening to what others are saying. It sounds a bit harsh, but it is done with good intentions. But as you fall into this trap, you miss the opportunity to make other connections. The inevitable result is a decrease in idea generation. You can't make connections when you're rehearsing. The intent may be positive; the results are not.

In-and-Out Listening

As a result, Synectics® invented the concept of "in-and-out listening." The rationale was that every time a connection was made, the participant would drop out for a few seconds, make a note on a piece of paper, and quickly return to the meeting. Once the note was on paper, the thought was preserved and the idea was not lost. More significantly, when participants did this consistently, it resulted in their generating many additional ideas. See Figure 13.3.

When we founded Consultative Resources Corporation (CRC), we took this concept and applied it to selling situations. The dynamics are

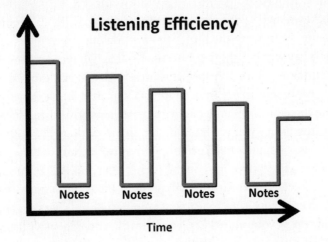

Listening Efficiency

Notes   Notes   Notes   Notes

Time

FIGURE 13.3 Listening Efficiency and "In-and-Out Listening"

exactly the same. Participants in sales calls make connections all the time. When a customer is speaking, the salespeople do precisely what is illustrated in Figure 13.2 and stop listening. They don't even know it's happening. They think about their response, whether it's an idea or a recommendation or even another question. But they are listening to themselves, not to the customer.

Now they may have stopped listening, but the customer didn't stop talking. And you know what that means—missed information and missed needs, which, of course, results in missed opportunities. It happens all the time.

Listening for Needs

The same approach that Synectics® encouraged participants to use in problem solving meetings is applicable to sales teams in customer meetings. Rather than fall into the rehearsal trap, team members are encouraged to take notes consistently.

Fred Lamparter of our team, who spent 30 years at Ogilvy & Mather likes to refer to this as *making notes* as opposed to *taking notes*. Fred is a marvelous presenter and was a pretty good stand-up comedian in his day.

Fred believes that "taking notes is what students do in the classroom as they try to capture everything the professor says. Making notes refers to writing down a few key words—those connections—that will remind you later what you were thinking. If it's on paper, it is preserved, and you can use it later as needed." That is wise advice from a former Vietnam reconnaissance pilot and worldwide director of training at a very prestigious advertising firm.

Ideally, the things you are listening for are needs. Regardless of what the customer says, if it sounds like a need, opportunity, concern, or issue, the astute team member will capture the thought. It's not a big deal. All they need to do is write down a few key words that will preserve the connection, as Fred says.

This prevents you from rehearsing your response. That's a good thing. When you review your notes later, you'll have a comprehensive list of needs. The simple act of note taking can have a major impact on the quality and the quantity of the needs you determine in your customer interactions. Again, see the similarities between problem solving and selling?

What makes all this even more important is that there is a strong tendency for most people to save the best for last. When individuals are asked open-ended questions, what they say last is usually more important to them than what they say first. This was first determined in interviewing research, but it applies to most interactive situations.

We have observed this for decades and you have probably seen this in your own experiences. If you're a bit skeptical, observe your kids when they ask for something or your colleagues when they just stop by for a minute. You'll see that what they say last is usually what is most important to them. It could be a question or suggestion or even a comment about something.

If this is true, and we believe that it is, think of how it can affect anyone in the selling role. If you drop out while the client is sharing information, and start to plan your response, the risk is that you'll never hear what might be most important. The tendency to fall into this trap probably has as significant an impact on your missing needs as anything else you do.

Speed Kills

We do not want to make light of what was an important campaign to counter drug abuse, but a participant in one of our recent sessions used the expression "speed kills" in another context. A very successful investment banker, he used the term to explain how his tendency to rush to solutions works against his success. "If we could just be more patient and let the client finish before offering our solutions, we would avoid so many pitfalls," he moaned. And he was absolutely right. Rushing to solutions and tuning out after you hear something interesting works against truly understanding the client's situation. Yes, speed kills.

Needs-Driven Ned is one of our favorite fictitious characters. We discussed him in *Selling Is a Team Sport*, and we refer to him in virtually all of our courses. He's a very likeable character, and what he does illustrates why so many professionals do not really understand their clients' needs.

Before we talk about Ned, let us share some research. Whenever we work with a new client or start a new sales training initiative, we like to send questionnaires to the participants. We have been doing this for more than 20 years.

One of the 15 to 20 questions that we ask salespeople is whether they understand all of their customers' needs. It's a very straightforward closed question. We have asked it thousands of times.

What percentage of the respondents do you think say they do? Take 10 seconds and guess.

The answer is 80 percent. That's right; four out of five sales professionals, when asked if they understand their customers' needs, say yes. That's reasonable. (Most people guess that the answer is even higher.)

We also have the opportunity speak to people on the buying side. Not as often, of course, but through surveys and focus groups we learn from the buyers also. And when we ask them what percentage of the sales professionals who call on them truly understand their needs, the answer is usually around 20 percent. That's right. Buyers tell us that only one in five truly understands their needs.

Talk about disconnects. After all these years, we still find that situation mind-boggling. We refer to this as our version of the 80/20 rule—80 percent of salespeople believe that they understand their customers' needs, but only 20 percent of those customers agree. Interesting stuff, indeed.

In a funny way both groups are correct. Salespeople do uncover many of their customers' needs. They just don't get *all* of them, for many reasons including these listening issues. Some of the responsibility falls on the customer. Often they choose not to share information, or don't tell the whole story, which is certainly their prerogative. But when they do this, they lose the right to complain if salespeople don't understand their needs.

Intuitively, we think that 80 percent is way too high; but we also think that 20 percent is probably too low. That's one of the dangers of qualitative research; you have to depend a lot on other people's perceptions. Using all this as a backdrop, let's return to our pal, Needs-Driven Ned.

Ned is an extremely bright, hardworking, conscientious guy. He's got excellent credentials and on paper he should be very successful. He prepares well, knows his products cold, and is likeable to boot. Any of us would love to have him on our team.

But he hasn't reached his potential. We had high expectations for this guy, but he just isn't cutting it. Nobody really knows why. So you, as one of our top performers, were asked to go make a joint call with him on a prospect to see if you could figure out what's wrong.

The call got off to a good start with Ned positioning the meeting in textbook fashion. He put the customer at ease, confirmed the agenda and time, and he even set the stage for questioning. You were impressed, early in the call. Then he started asking questions. They were thoughtful and provocative. They showed he knew what he was talking about. And he was sensitive in his approach.

"Well, if this guy is failing, maybe this consultative selling stuff is not all that they say it is," was what you were thinking. But then, just as you were about to write that down, it happened. A need the size of a beach ball was served up to Ned. It was obvious, it was business related, and it seemed important. And as you probably guessed, Ned jumped all over it like an old suit. He had at least three ideas to help the client address that need (see Figure 13.4).

The graphic looks a lot like the model that we introduced. Ned opened up well and positioned the meeting in textbook form. He asked questions, determined what he thought was an important need, and addressed it. His actions looked a lot like the consultative selling model.

Not really. It doesn't even come close. What Ned did is what we think most people do in selling situations. He heard the first need and attacked it. He never even heard needs number two or three or four. All he heard was the first need, which may not have even been very important to this prospect. If the tendency is to save the more important stuff for last, then Ned never even heard what really mattered to the prospective client.

The most successful salespeople and sales teams rarely fall into this abyss. They do much of what Ned did, but in direct contrast; once they hear the first need, they continue to ask additional questions and determine more needs. They stay in this mode until they learn everything they can about the client. Then and only then do they offer solutions. See Figure 13.5.

Needs Driven Ned

FIGURE 13.4 The Needs-Driven Ned Approach

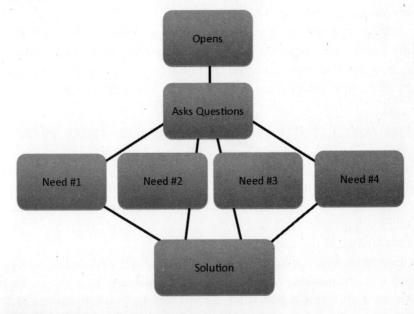

FIGURE 13.5 The Preferred Approach

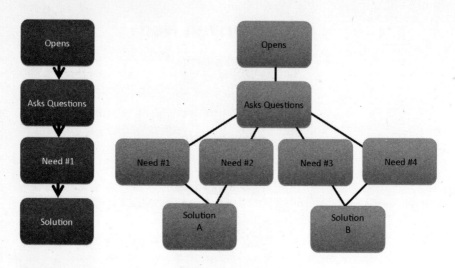

FIGURE 13.6 Comparing the Two Approaches

As a result, their solutions not only address multiple needs, but will be richer, more innovative, more client focused, and simply better than the ones Ned offered. You'll see later that most objections are unfulfilled needs. Since Ned did not uncover all the needs in his haste to provide solutions, he will invariably encounter more resistance. That's why he is not as likely to reach his potential. See Figure 13.6.

When you put the two approaches side by side as Figure 13.6 illustrates, you can see there is no comparison. Ned simply cannot compete effectively with the guy who gets all the needs. We can't encourage you strongly enough to be that guy on the right. And you can do it even better with help from your team.

Bringing It All Together: Reviewing What You Learned

Situation analysis is the most important *phase* of the selling process. Questioning is the most important *skill*. Next we'll discuss what we consider to be the most important *step* in the process. It's when you review your understanding of the client's needs.

Everything that you and your colleagues have accomplished up to this point in the relationship was done so that you could take the next step. This is when it all comes together. It's the last step in situation analysis and, as you'll see, the first step in making a fabulous presentation.

Many initial visits to clients end right here. Some organizations prohibit their people from doing any more than this on a first visit. Some even wait longer. The thinking is that you simply can't present effectively until you completely understand the client. Once you have done that, you can collaborate with your team and develop outstanding recommendations. Then and only then do you have the right to present.

Review Your Understanding of the Needs

You'll never know if you have everything right if you don't check it out. It is a very professional way to end any client meeting. If you have to present right there and then, this becomes an excellent way to segue into that phase. Just as setting the stage became a comfortable means to transition from phase one to phase two, this step serves that purpose when you transition from phase two to phase three.

As simple and straightforward as the reviewing of needs may appear, there are some guidelines that we encourage you to follow. If it is such an important step, let's be sure to apply it as best we can.

Use "I" Statements or "We" Statements

Clients love to know that you listened to what they said and understand their situation. But they don't particularly like your telling them what they need. Saying "You need this . . . " or "Here's what you said you'd like to accomplish . . . " can actually work against you.

Instead, use an "I" statement such as, "Here is my understanding of your situation," or "Thank you for all this information. I'd like to conclude by reviewing what I learned." Sometimes "we" statements are even more appropriate, particularly in team selling situations. "Here is our understanding of your objectives" sounds less threatening, doesn't it?

If you review what you heard as opposed to telling them what they said, they will probably be more receptive. And you won't get accused of trying to put words in their mouths, which is never appreciated.

Start with the Obvious

When you review needs, it is in your interest to begin with the ones that the customer came out and told you. Those are the obvious needs. You can't get into too much trouble if you simply review what they openly discussed: "It's apparent to us from our conversation that the quality requirements of the product dwarf everything else."

You have to be a bit more careful in reviewing the implied and unconscious needs. After all, they never actually said these things. You inferred them. So soften your review; and be as sensitive as you can: "You never really said this but I can't help but conclude that when you bring this to your boss you want to be confident that you are prepared to answer whatever questions she might raise."

Or, "I hope we're not reading too much into this, but since we heard you say that you never did anything like this before, we are sensitive to your need to understand precisely how it works and feel confident about its efficacy."

There's no need to go overboard and get touchy-feely. Just let them know that these are your conclusions, based on some of the things you heard. You certainly don't want to give the impression that you made these up or are manipulating them. That would destroy the credibility you worked so hard to develop.

Seek Confirmation

Finally, give the client the opportunity to correct, modify, or delete anything you said. It helps if you make that easy for them. The last thing you want to have happen is to think you understand their needs when in fact you don't. That happens too often.

Did you notice how the examples above begged for another statement at the end? Something as simple as "is that correct?" or "would you agree?" are all you need. But give them the chance to confirm what you have said.

It's a great compliment to anyone when you demonstrate that you have been listening. When you review their needs, it's possible that they may not want to correct you. They are impressed with how well you listened, so if you missed a point or two they'll let it pass. But you don't want to miss anything. The more you know, the better prepared you'll be to make a great recommendation. So give them the opportunity to clarify your understanding. They just may surprise you and offer a new need that was never discussed previously. What could be better than that?

So there it is—situation analysis. It's the heart and soul of consultative selling. Each of the four steps is important. It starts with preparing the clients for questioning. Then you ask as many questions as you can in a most professional way. As the clients respond, you listen at 112 percent to capture all their needs. And you conclude by reviewing your understanding of what you learned.

It sounds simple, doesn't it? It's not. Anyone who ever called on a customer knows that. It requires lots of work. Sales teams can play an incredible role in assuring that you are among those 20 percent who distinguish themselves and win lots more business lots more often.

The result of all this is that you'll not only impress the customer, but you'll have the ammunition required to develop terrific proposals and make outstanding presentations. That's the ultimate goal of innovative team selling.

Some Things to Consider

What

Listening is hard work. Lots of things prevent us from listening. The first step is to become aware of the issues. The next is to take concrete actions. Any individual or team member can become a better listener and therefore a better needs developer if they put in the effort.

How

At a meeting, ask each team member to look at their notes from a recent client meeting or internal discussion. Then ask them to find the needs that are buried in those notes. Some are obvious; others less so. Some are business; others are personal. But have them dissect those notes to see what new needs they can find. Share the results. Everyone will be surprised.

When

This is a fun exercise that you can do any time you are pursuing business. It is particularly useful when you are preparing for a formal presentation and want to begin by reviewing the needs.

14 The Big Day

When the alarm finally went off, Sam hoped that the team enjoyed a better night's sleep than he had. After all, today was the day they had anticipated for almost two months, and as a result he found himself staring at the ceiling in his hotel room much of the night. He never slept well in hotels, particularly on the first night, but this was worse than usual. But in spite of that restless night, he felt energized as he got ready for the big day.

From the time the initial RFP arrived, a big part of his day-to-day activities had focused on this opportunity. He knew that if they won the business, this would be the third biggest contract that his company was ever awarded. There was a lot on the line. Everybody from the CEO down knew that this was happening. He had received many encouraging e-mails from many executives over the past few days.

And today was the day when the team would finally participate in the finalist presentation. Today was when it all came to fruition.

The presentation was scheduled for 10:30 that morning. Sam's team was scheduled to present second; the first company was on at 8:30. Each had an hour and a half.

There were four finalists and he wasn't thrilled with being in the middle. "I would have loved to have been first or last, but there are things beyond your control so you play the cards you're dealt," he sighed, as he said goodbye to his wife, Jessica, before he headed out the night before.

Everyone on the team planned to arrive that night as there was no way they would let bad weather or congestion at the airport keep them from attending this huge presentation. As he got dressed Sam wondered if he should have bought a new suit for this special day. The shirt and tie were new and he felt good about how he looked. He was comfortable with his outfit, which Jessica assured him was "current." That was one of her favorite words, which he attributed to her market research background.

"You can't show up to one of these things looking like you don't belong," he mused to himself as he carefully tied his tie so the dimple was perfect. As he often did before important meetings, he gave himself an encouraging pep talk before he left the room: "You're ready, the team is prepared, we put in the time. Now let's go out there and kick some butt."

He met the team in the hotel coffee shop as planned. Everyone was there on time and after they ordered breakfast he kidded them about "what an attractive team we are." You could sense the anxiety amongst the group, but you could also see that virtually everyone demonstrated what could best be described as a quiet confidence.

And why not? They were well prepared, they had developed a great presentation, and they had rehearsed several times. They were ready. They knew that many people wanted to attend, but this was the team that was selected to represent the company. They felt privileged, even honored to be included. The team did little at breakfast other than conduct a quick review of the approach, and remind themselves about the importance of staying on point. They knew that they would defer to Sam if at any time they were not sure how to proceed.

Sam's final comment, which he said in a matter of fact way as he signed the check, was a bit surprising, but important. "I have been in many of these finalist presentations. It is possible that at some point, when we least expect it, something will happen that could derail us. It happens often. Someone might ask a question or make an unexpected remark or come on a bit strong. We can't let that undermine what we want to accomplish. You'll have to trust that I can navigate us through those choppy waters if that happens."

Everyone was encouraged by the way Sam demonstrated how he was in control of the situation. They needed that, particularly those two team members who had never done one of these before. Everyone nodded as they left and Sam could see that they were ready.

They arrived at the client's office 45 minutes before they were due to present. They passed through security in less time than they had anticipated, which was a welcomed relief, and were ushered to a small conference room where they were asked to wait. Their presentation was on a flash drive, since the client had insisted that they would provide the computer and LCD projector. Sam had extra copies of the presentation and his own computer in case anything went wrong. He also had hard copies of the slide show to distribute before they began.

While they were waiting, Harvey Buck, the sponsor who had led the RFP process, poked his head in for a minute and said "Good morning, everyone. We are right on time. Give us just a few minutes to finish debriefing the first presentation and we'll be ready for you." His tone was warm and the group felt encouraged. Before anyone could say anything, he was gone.

Ten minutes before they were scheduled to present, they were invited in to set up the conference room. A few of the client team members were huddled together outside the room where they would present, but nobody made any attempt to greet them. Sam assured his colleagues that this was fine, as the group appeared to be informally discussing the first presentation. Sam's team set up the room and to their delight, the equipment supplied by the client worked perfectly and they were ready to proceed.

The client team consisted of five people, as did Sam's. It had not been easy to decide who would participate, and the team had discussed this at length. But in the end they concluded that Manufacturing, Operations, IT, and Distribution were the functions that needed to be there to support Sales. This was based on what was included in the RFP. Sam would play the lead role but everyone would participate.

There was the typical awkward shaking of hands, exchanging of business cards, and saying hello before the meeting finally began. The clients all sat on one side of the large mahogany conference table; Sam's team had no choice but to sit opposite them. "It feels a bit like a 'Labor vs. Management' negotiation," he thought. At that very moment Harvey stood up and called the meeting to order.

Harvey was unusually gregarious and complimentary, which made several of the team members just a bit suspicious based on their previous interactions. "We are all very interested in what you have to say. As you know you are one of four finalists and we were quite impressed with your proposal. We have met with some of you before, but there are some new faces around the table, so Sam, I will ask you to introduce your team and tell us why you should be selected as our vendor."

"Showtime," said Sam to himself as he stood up to begin the presentation. As he walked to the front of the room he thought about how he could never get used to being called a vendor. "I guess I just have to demonstrate that we're better than that," he said to himself.

He was pleased that Harvey asked him to lead the introductions. Too often the client did that, which detracted from that critical moment in the meeting and prevented his team from doing it their way. It's never a great way to begin a meeting when you tell the client you'd like to do things differently than they requested. But luckily, that wasn't an issue today.

And so he began, "First of all, I would like to thank you for providing us with this opportunity and for taking the time to meet with us today. Needless to say we are very enthusiastic about the possibility of working together as you approach this exciting initiative." The vibes felt good. He continued: "As Harvey mentioned, we have met some of you before, but it's in everyone's interest to do a quick round of introductions. If each of you could please tell us who you are, what is your role in the organization, and most importantly, what you would like us to emphasize during the meeting, that will ensure that we focus on the right subjects. I'd like our team to go first, if that's okay."

Sam himself went first and modeled a short, crisp introduction. He knew that if he was brief, others would probably follow his example. His objective for the meeting, he explained, "is to demonstrate our understanding of your situation and explain how we can help you accomplish your objectives." Each of his team members reviewed their own role and explained that they were there to discuss how their function would address what was requested in the RFP.

"Just the way we rehearsed it," thought Sam. "So far, so good." Charlie went last and got a nice laugh when he said something like: "Operations always goes last; probably because that's where the buck stops. I will explain how our process works and what we will do to ensure that the performance standards you referenced are not only met, but exceeded."

Then it was the client team's turn and each person followed the approach. Some were specific; "I'd like to know how you would manage the transition if we decide to use you." Others were more vague, asking to "know how you are different," or "how you'll address the challenges outlined in the RFP." But each expressed what they wanted to get from the meeting, and that was exactly what Sam wanted. Everyone on his team took notes during the introductions and tried to memorize the names.

One challenging question was raised during intros about whether Sam's company had the resources to manage such a large project. Fortunately, the team was ready for that and had planned their response. The person who raised that issue seemed a bit antagonistic. Sam assured him that this issue would definitely be addressed during the presentation.

There were no major surprises, which was, of course, a relief for the team. When they finished, Sam graciously thanked the group. He also referenced that they knew they would have to conclude by noon and assured them that "if anyone from our team is still talking at 12 : 00 you have my permission to leave." The meeting was positioned in textbook fashion and they were off to a great start.

He then said, "Well, now it's our job to explain how we can address what each of you requested, and of course what was outlined in the RFP." He hit the button on his remote advance to activate the computer and they were off to the races. The team had put significant time into creating the slide show, and you could sense how excited they were to see how Sam led the discussion.

Before he started, he handed out what was a replication of the slide show. "We will distribute our formal proposal at the end of the meeting. The key points are covered in the slide show. This is a replication. I will encourage you not to read ahead; if you do you'll see the punch lines before we tell our story." That got little reaction from the group, but it wasn't expected.

The first slide was the cover slide. It wasn't dramatically different from most since it featured both companies' logos, the date, and a reference to the presentation. The next slide was entitled "Needs as Understood." Sam explained that, "This is our understanding of your situation based on what we have learned to date from the RFP and our subsequent discussions. We appreciate how helpful everyone has been in briefing us about the initiative. I'd like to review these and check for confirmation."

He then reviewed the list, which included 10 specific needs. There were five on each of the two slides. He discussed one at a time, and amplified each as he spoke, since they were written in headline form and needed clarification. Several times a team member would add a comment or two to enhance what he had said.

Each need was expressed as a verb and started with the word "to." Sam believed in the "five by five" approach, which suggests that a slide should include no more than five bullet points, and that each bullet point should have no more than five words. Laura Daley, author of "*Talk Your Way to the Top*" coined that expression. She is a marvelous presenter and believes that the slides should always play a secondary role. This was one of his cardinal rules that he followed whenever he developed slides. It was hard to do that when they crafted the slides that reviewed the client's needs, as they didn't want to dilute them. But the slides were crisp and they worked, even if they were longer than the team would have preferred,

Presenters need to make their slides look professional, and if you can make them different that's great, but keep them as simple as possible. And that's what Sam did. He reviewed each need and embellished them. They were short but poignant, and they were all about the client. Here are a few examples:

- To be as cost effective as possible.
- To make the transition seamless.
- To bring innovation to the process.
- To educate the impacted employees.
- To partner with a provider who is committed long term.
- To complete the transition in 60 days.

After he reviewed each need, he checked in with the client team to make sure he got the needs right. There were two that had never been stated formally, so he explained how they had concluded that these were important. He encouraged questions at the end and asked if anyone had anything to add. There were a few questions for clarification but nothing major. At this point they had used 20 of the allocated 90 minutes and were in fine shape.

Sam then gave a broad overview that described what they were recommending. He explained to the clients that he would get very specific momentarily but he wanted to keep everything in context, and he began by reviewing the big picture. He then explained how the different team members would explain in detail how these needs would be addressed in the formal recommendation.

Addressing one need at a time, Sam played the role of facilitator, almost like a master of ceremonies. He briefly reintroduced each team member before they spoke and boasted just a bit about their expertise. The four members of the team who accompanied Sam each spoke for about 10 minutes; they discussed the needs that related to their area of expertise and made significant contributions. It was clear to everyone why these people were there.

The approach was somewhat mechanical but very effective. As the team members reviewed the different needs, they explained how their recommendation addressed the objectives outlined in the RFP. They were careful to clearly explain the associated benefits.

They used a specific approach suggesting that after you reference the need, you describe your recommendation and then explain how it addresses that need. Of course you provide as much information as required, but it's no more complicated than that. The key is to demonstrate the value to the customer.

As each team member presented, they used this approach: need, recommendation, benefit, and additional information. They tried to make it conversational and engage the clients as best they could. When appropriate they lightened things up a bit. For example, when Helen talked about the transition process associated with the transformation, she listed the five worst things that could happen and what her team would do to make those things impossible. That really captured the clients' interest.

The group had been well prepped not to overload the client with too much information and to focus more on how what they presented would be of value, rather than just focusing on the products themselves. They did a good job. The rehearsals had yielded significant dividends.

As the team applied this process they encountered some tough questions and a few objections, as is always the case. Some of the questions were a bit challenging. But they managed these effectively using a specific process that they had rehearsed. The issue about their size was the big one. That could have been what Sam warned them about at breakfast. It had the potential to derail the presentation, but it didn't. They were ready for it and addressed it professionally. For the most part, their presentation proceeded extremely smoothly, and they covered almost all the points that they considered most important. Simply put, they told their story well.

Sam spoke last and reviewed the pricing and associated terms. He had to be a bit vague because this was dependent upon which option they selected. But he assured the client group that the specifics were outlined in the document that he would leave behind. When they finished and had answered all the clients' questions, they were delighted to see that they still had 20 minutes left. Again, just as they had planned. And other than that one big issue, there were no major land mines.

Now it was time for Sam to make a huge decision. The game plan suggested that if they had time at the end, they would consider going with Lesley's idea that had come up in the rehearsal session. He decided to go for it. He had thought about this a lot prior to the meeting and knew he would make the decision based on two criteria—did they have the time to do it, and did the climate in the room suggest it would be well received? He knew how risky it was, but he also knew how important it was for his team to differentiate themselves. The climate was positive, they had the time, so he pulled the trigger.

The team had decided, you may recall, that if the client discussed a problem during the meeting, they would offer to work on it right there, in real time. They would use that opportunity to demonstrate how creative they could be, and how well they worked together as a team. It was risky, but they believed that risks could lead to rewards and they were ready.

The client had raised the issue that their people would be reluctant to change. This came up during the introductions. It was mentioned again in a matter-of-fact way when Helen from IT was presenting. That's why her potential pitfalls piece was so well received. She did her best to assure the client that they would make the change process as painless and seamless as possible.

So, consistent with their plan, Sam brought this up at the end of the meeting and asked the client if it was all right to spend a few minutes addressing that issue. The client said, "Sure, it's your time," and Sam explained what they would like to do.

"We have concluded that you want to work with an organization that will not only partner with you, but will approach this initiative with creativity and innovation. Is that correct?" The clients nodded their heads like a bunch of bobblehead dolls in the back window of an old car. "So why don't we do some problem solving right now?" he asked. "We have almost 20 minutes left, and we'd like to demonstrate how we work as a team to address issues like this. And you are all welcome to participate."

Sam asked Charlie to assume the role of facilitator. They had learned during their planning meetings that he was a natural. He had facilitated many of their internal meetings and did it well. Charlie immediately stepped up and briefly explained how they would work. He asked the client a few questions about this reluctance to change, and probed further to learn why that could be an issue and what they had done previously. The group took notes, made connections, and generated about a dozen ideas, two of which came from the clients themselves. When the clients raised their hands and Charlie called them by name, they seemed quite pleased.

In the limited time available, they could not thoroughly develop any ideas, but they had a nice list and they were able to get a couple of next steps to keep them alive. They did all this in 15 minutes. The client ended with a few new ideas that they could consider using in the future, and the team had successfully demonstrated how effective a creative session could be. Needless to say, the clients were quite impressed ("blown away" was the way Sam put it afterward), and to this day he believes that this 15-minute demonstration won them the business.

It was a great way to conclude the meeting. In the few minutes that remained, the client explained how the selection process would work and when they would hear back. They still had two other companies presenting that day. Sam asked them to please call at any time if anything they had discussed required clarification.

He distributed the "pitch books"—the formal recommendation in detail that he had promised to give them earlier—and graciously thanked them for their time. Everyone shook hands and said goodbye. It was over—finally. They team kept their game faces on as they left the conference room and headed toward the elevator. But everyone knew that they had knocked it out of the park.

"Let's be cool and save the high-fives until we get back to the hotel," Sam pleaded in the elevator. "You never know who's looking out the window." He wasn't paranoid; he just wanted to be careful. Which they were, of course, but as they headed to lunch they were one very excited and satisfied group.

It's All about Differentiation

Now this is an extraordinary example. Sales teams do not demonstrate their creativity as a formalized component of a presentation. But sales teams can do marvelous things to differentiate themselves when they meet with clients.

Some put on live demonstrations to illustrate in the moment how their products perform. Others lay out different approaches based on a variety of scenarios. Still others outline potential pitfalls and explain how they would resolve them as Helen did when she spoke. Some even go so far to bring in videos highlighting their products performing brilliantly in a customer's facility.

There are companies who even bring videos quoting satisfied clients or happy end users. We know about one major financial services organization that had initiated a very successful, highly recognized advertising campaign. With that in mind, they began every presentation showing several of those ads. There are as many clever ways to enhance presentations as there are clever sales teams to develop them.

Differentiation is a critical requirement in the global commoditized world in which we live. Your clients are demanding and they insist that you bring them innovative solutions. You know that. In today's extremely competitive global marketplace, there simply is no option. The good news is that you can demonstrate your creativity in every part of the sales process.

You can do this in the way you begin your meetings; the questions you ask and how you ask them; the needs you uncover; the recommendations you make; and the answers you provide when you encounter resistance. You consistently have the opportunity to be innovative as you navigate your way through the sales process. Leveraging your resources is a marvelous way to do just that.

As you'll see in the next chapter, you can even bring your clients ideas that go beyond your products and services. Your ideas are unique and hard to replicate if you derive them yourselves based on what you learn from the client. I'll never forget an expression I learned from the late Bill Brandt, who taught at Columbia Business School: "It's not just what's in the bag; it's what's in your head."

So Sam and his team won the business. And when they heard the news they were told "it wasn't even close." They earned it. They delivered a great presentation that focused on the client. They had a great story to tell, which was the result of many hours of researching, planning, strategizing, and rehearsing. Without the time they put in early, they never could have accomplished what they did. Presentations are the final chapter of a long story. But when the up-front work is done well, great things can happen.

For most of us this is the part of the sales process we enjoy most. It's when we tell our story, and that is in many ways a microcosm of how we define ourselves. When we discuss our products and services, we are presenting what we do to earn our livelihood. That's huge. If you approach this critical moment in a customer oriented way, realize that presenting is a privilege that must be earned, and sensitively navigate your way through these meetings, you have to be successful. There is no question about that.

I was fortunate to meet Tim Seifert when he ran Sales for Prudential Annuities. You may remember that I referred to him earlier. He's the one who said, "It's not what you know; it's what you *do* with what you know." Those are wise words from an outstanding sales leader. And that expression summarizes in a few words what we just spent an entire chapter trying to explain. Those words are worth remembering.

Some Things to Consider

What

When you participate in finalist presentations, you have the opportunity to clearly differentiate yourselves in front of the client. That is because they are seeing your team in action. So many buying decisions are made primarily for personal reasons and how the client feels about the individuals involved. Do what you can to impress them . . . big time.

How

As you saw in the anecdote, the team leader plays a key role here, before, during, and after the finalist presentation. You need to be confident, in control, and as relaxed as you can. You need to let the team know that they can count on you and defer to you if necessary. Let them know you believe in them. If the team appears to work well together, enjoy each other, respect each other, and like each other, it can seriously impact the outcome. All that is up to you.

When

The next time a big opportunity presents itself to the organization, get the team involved and do what you can to transform a group of individuals into a competent, efficient team that feels good about itself and will be dedicated to the client.

15

Okay, So How Do We Do All That?

We illustrated in Chapter 14 how Sam Jamison's sales team put together an outstanding finalist presentation that won them the business. And they did that even though the odds were stacked against them. This was fictional, of course, but it is based on the kinds of things that we have observed successful sales teams do over the years. Even their demonstration was based on a real story.

The approach that you observed is applicable to any presentation, but since finalist presentations are so exciting, we used that to demonstrate the approach. What we described brings to life a specific methodology that we teach to both teams and individuals. The basic tenets have stood the test of time because they work.

The approach, which we simply refer to as the "four-box model," is used to succinctly explain what the team recommends (see Figure 15.1). It is a key component in any presentation and was conceived by Kate Reilly of CRC.

As you explore the model, we want to emphasize that it is just a model. We know that structure helps. Even in situations as complicated as creative problem solving meetings, we saw how having a road map can be very helpful. It applies here as well.

Different kinds of presentations require different approaches. But the basic components of this model, when applied appropriately, can be a valuable tool for every sales team whenever they present.

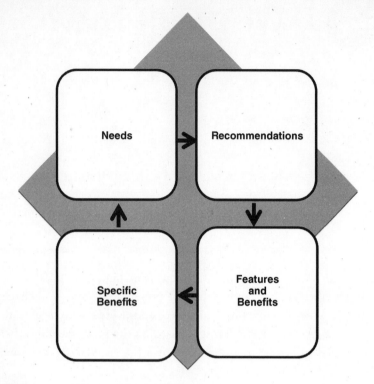

FIGURE 15.1 The Four-Box Model

The Presentation Model

The approach stipulates that all presentations, regardless of the complexity, begin by first reviewing the customers' needs. That is extremely important. Reviewing needs is the last step in situation analysis and the first in offering recommendations. That's why we call it a transition step.

If we appear somewhat dogmatic here, we'll apologize. But we'll probably never apologize for encouraging you to take this approach because we know that it works. We have heard so many buyers say they made their decision to go with a certain company based on that company's understanding of their needs. That's good enough for us and reinforces the need to begin your presentation this way.

Once the needs are reviewed and confirmed, it is time to make your recommendation. Most sales professionals offer their recommendations in terms of their *features* and *benefits*. These terms have been used to describe products and services since the 1930s. That's right, they have been around forever. But that doesn't mean they aren't relevant. They are. We tried to come up with alternative terms, but after trying for years we gave up, and were comfortable doing so. The terms work, and regardless of how sophisticated your product or service may be, they can easily be described by using those weathered but valuable terms.

Features can be defined as anything that answers the question "what"? Benefits, on the other hand, answer the question "so what"? This simple but elegant way of describing these concepts was coined by Kent Reilly of our team. A former member of our team, Hap Cooper, took the concept, amplified it, and put it in our training materials. Hap is no longer with us, but the ways we use these terms are because they work well for sales teams. If you present something and can imagine the client asking the "so what" question, you probably need to do some more work.

Features are specifications, attributes, characteristics, traits, and descriptions. They tell us what a product or service or even an idea will do and how it works. But they don't tell us anything about its value or how it may help. That's where benefits come in and that's why the "so what" question is so powerful.

Benefits explain the value of the feature. Benefits tell us why something may be in our interest. As a simple example, think about the chair you are sitting in right now. (If you're lying down or standing, pretend you are sitting.) Now take a minute and do the following exercise. Think about some of the features and benefits of your chair.

The chair may have a stiff back and soft cushion. Those are the features. It may be made of wood or stainless steel. Features again. It may even have casters or be stackable. These are all features. They come to us pretty easily. Since features are descriptions, whenever we describe something we are probably discussing its features.

But benefits aren't quite so concrete. They don't always jump out at you. If the features of your chair include that soft cushion and stiff back, the benefits could be that it will provide comfort or allow you to sit for a long period of time. When someone says a piece of furniture is comfortable, they are talking in benefit language; they are not relating features.

The fact that the chair is made of wood might add to the décor of the room; if it's made of stainless steel, it may be able to stand up to the pounding the kids will give it. Casters make it easier to move around and stackability saves space. These are all benefits. These explain why the chair may be of interest to the customer; its value; why it may help them accomplish something.

This is probably quite familiar information. But we can't discuss how to tell your story effectively without clarifying these terms. The first time any salesperson is given a briefcase and product brochure, he or she learns about the features and benefits of the product line. Rarely do organizations of any size send their salespeople into the field without providing them with the product knowledge they need to discuss their products.

This brings to our attention what is often a huge challenge for sales teams. Most subject matter experts love to discuss the features of their products and services. They want to talk about what they do; they want to explain how they work; they want to discuss the bells and whistles; and they want to demonstrate how unique or dependable or cool they are. All that's admirable. You want your resources to enthusiastically talk about their products and services as they demonstrate their expertise.

But therein lies the challenge. That same expert, who will discuss features until the cows come home, is often reluctant to discuss benefits. They aren't as comfortable when they have to explain the value or how it will help. The result is that the customer could be listening and asking him or herself the "so what" question. It happens all the time.

Let's take this one step further. Features are facts; benefits are educated guesses. Features are tangible; benefits are intangible. Features are objective; benefits are subjective. Features are concrete; benefits are amorphous. Features are easy to explain; benefits are somewhat fuzzy. See what we mean? It's just easier to talk features.

How we feel about ourselves plays a role as well. When we talk about features we sound like consultants; when we talk about benefits, we sound more like salespeople. One way to look at this is that features are about *us*; benefits are about *them*. When we discuss features we are inwardly directed; when we talk benefits we are outwardly directed.

For some members of the sales team this can be very uncomfortable. They don't want to be perceived as salespeople. We get that. But as a result they tend to talk about the features of the recommendation; not the benefits. We hear team leaders complain often about how their resources need to get past this to maximize their value.

Sales teams must understand that they will be more successful and will better demonstrate their value if they use benefit statements. They need to

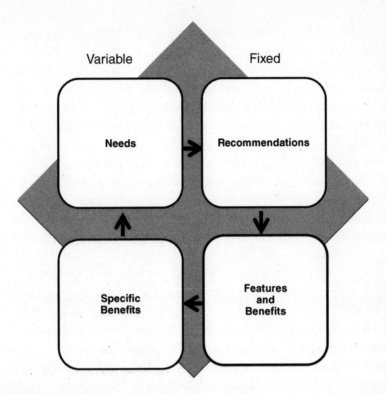

FIGURE 15.2 Variable and Fixed Components in the Four-Box Model

get past the fear of looking like Willy Loman in *Death of a Salesman*, and understand that part of their job description is to help their customers understand why they should decide to buy from this team.

Successful sales teams do exactly that. As each team member presents, they carefully explain how their part of the recommendation addresses the predetermined needs. When they do that they are using benefit language. If it's a bit uncomfortable, they'll get over it.

Now let's take all this to the next level, as shown in Figure 15.2.

What appears on the right side of the model is what we refer to as "fixed information." This information is what appears in your collateral material, brochures, spec sheets, and on your website. This data is mostly generic.

Therefore, the bottom right-hand box lists the generic features and benefits. If these were all that your clients needed to know, they would not need you. They would simply refer to the appropriate source of information and make their decision. That's one of the reasons why futurists used to predict that salespeople would dwindle over time. They were dead wrong.

Your customers do need you. They don't just make decisions based on what a product does and how that could be of value. It's much more complicated than that. They need to see the connection between what they need and what you have to offer. It's hard to conclude that from a spec sheet.

As the model suggests, the left side has the "variable components." Every client, every customer, every buyer has different needs. Sure, they may be similar at times, but they are always different. If we take the generic, fixed information on the right side of the model and use it to address the variable needs on the left side, it's like putting a round peg in a square hole. It just doesn't work.

The Specific Benefit

That is why the lower left-hand box is defined as the *specific benefit*. We define this as what your products do to address the specific needs of a specific customer. Again, clients' needs vary. Hence the specific benefits vary as well. What might be a specific benefit for one client might not apply to another. That's why we have salespeople and why salespeople need sales teams. Once you understand your customers' needs, you are much better prepared to offer recommendations in terms of their specific benefits. And specific benefits lead to closed deals.

This is yet another reason that we like to think of sales teams as needs development teams. Sales teams who work in concert to truly understand the customers' needs and then present their solutions as answers to those needs stand out. The sales teams that think in terms of specific benefits will always differentiate themselves.

Let's relate this once again to the chair you are sitting on right now. That soft cushion and stiff back may be beneficial when you are reading a book. But there are many instances where this is not a specific benefit. Think of a fast food restaurant or second grade classroom or the motor vehicle bureau. Comfortable chairs are not desirable.

Similarly, a wooden chair might not fit into an ultra modern office, just as a stainless steel chair might not work in a formal dining room. The casters aren't advisable for the deck of a boat, and the stackability factor means little to someone who doesn't plan to move the chairs from a fixed location. What is a benefit for one person may not be a benefit for another. We cannot emphasize this too strongly. It's all about the customer, right? Then we'd better be speaking to them in *specific benefit* language.

The more questions you ask, the more success you enjoy. That's because, as you ask more questions, you obtain more information, which invariably results in determining more needs. That enables you to offer more specific benefit statements. And, again, that's what eventually leads to success.

We're still not through. We're close but not quite there. You'll notice as you look at Figure 15.3 that the bulk of what your customer wants to hear falls on the left side, the variable side of the model. If you make your recommendations the same way the way you think, you would proceed in a clockwise direction. You would start by reviewing the needs, then offer your recommendation and explain the features and benefits. You would conclude with the specific benefits. Remember, your tendency is to save the best for last. That's the way most people think, so that's the way they think they should present.

But it is not the best way to present. When giving a presentation, you should explain what is important to the customer as soon as possible. This is highlighted in Figure 15.3.

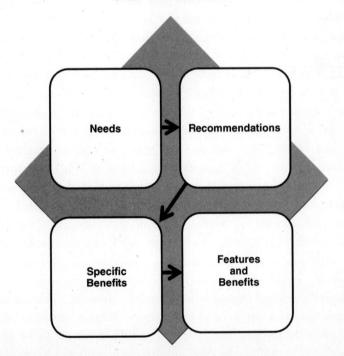

FIGURE 15.3 A Better Presentation using the Four-Box Model

If you lead up to the specific benefit with a litany of generic features and benefits, the clients may never hear what is most important to them. They could drop out before you ever get there. Attention spans are short, and if clients hear something they like, or get confused, or don't like a piece, you can lose them. And as a result, they'll never hear that specific benefit. As the model suggests, you should discuss the specific benefits first.

This is counterintuitive. It's like telling a joke and giving the punch line first. It isn't natural. But it is effective. Simply put, first you let the client know that you understand their needs and then as quickly as possible you explain how you, your team, your products, and your company can address those needs. That's the definition of a specific benefit. We discussed the "what" and "so what." Specific benefits answer the question "what's in it for me?"

This is a presentation model that sales teams can internalize and use to make great presentations. Just as Sam's team did, you should review the needs early and give an overview of what you recommend. Then have different team members explain different parts of the recommendation in terms of the specific benefits. Of course, they will discuss the generic features and benefits as necessary, but the key is for each presenter to focus on the specific benefits.

That is what each member of Sam's team did when they gave their winning presentation. They did it in a natural way, simply reviewing the relevant need and explaining how they could address that need. They were comfortable discussing specific benefits and so can you. That's what closes the loop for the customer. That's what closes deals. And that's why the futurists were wrong. We need salespeople to help their customers make that connection.

Let's relate this to a real story. What could be more fun than to highlight an example of someone buying a pre-owned car? Yep, a used car story. But it's real and will highlight many of the points we need to explore.

A former member of our team has twin daughters. When they turned 16, the parents decided they would buy the girls a used SUV. Anyone who ever had teenagers knows how scary a time it is when their kids start driving.

So the parents went to a used car lot. And sure enough, on the lot was a SUV in excellent condition that looked very much like what they wanted. An affable salesperson approached, and they explained why they were there.

Before they could say much more, the salesman ushered them over to the car they had eyed and started talking proudly about it. "This car has 415 horsepower. It has a top speed of 135 miles per hour. It can accelerate from zero to 60 in almost no time. It can. . . . " That's as far as he got. Our colleague had to get off the lot. She said she was literally sick to her stomach.

All she could visualize were her babies zooming down the highway at insanely high speeds. Needless to say, the parents did not buy that car.

Now think about how different things may have been if the salesperson had asked a few questions first. Had he known they were buying the car for teenage girls, he might have first talked about the safety features. He could have discussed the seven air bags, the antilock brakes, the steel construction, or the anti roll statistics.

Of course, he would also have to discuss how powerful the car was, but he could have done that in a more sensitive way: "Now you need to know that this is a powerful automobile, as most SUVs are. Your daughters will need to respect that, and if they are responsible this can be an asset at times like when they are getting on the highway." Again, it's all about knowing your customer. The canned pitch rarely works. This salesperson had customers who were prepared to buy and he literally scared them away.

Making Outstanding Presentations

We summarize all this in what we call the effective presentations model. Yes, another sequence. Remember, road maps help. (See Figure 15.4.)

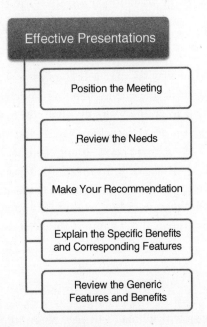

FIGURE 15.4 Effective Presentations

This sequence applies to virtually any presentation.

The four-box model gives you a way to tell your story. It is a key component of any presentation and can be most helpful in the planning process. Now we'll discuss how to bring this to life.

The model is based on the assumption that you have determined the needs of the customer prior to this presentation. We realize that sometimes you are forced to present on the first call. The model still applies. The order changes since the positioning has already happened. But everything else is the same.

Phase One: Position the Meeting

What a surprise, huh? As we've explained several times, meetings, regardless of their intent, start with positioning. It certainly applies here. As you conduct the round of introductions and learn who is there, determine how they fit in, and confirm what they want to accomplish, you create a healthy climate.

As in any meeting, you do this up front as you attempt to connect with the group. You confirm the agenda and time allocation, get the clients' names, proudly introduce your team, and set the stage for what is about to happen. In this case, that is the presentation. Then it's off to the races.

Phase Two: Review the Needs

There may be a better way to start a presentation, but we haven't quite figured that out. Assuring the clients that you understand their situation, know what they want to accomplish, and that you took the time to think through their objectives is a marvelous way to get started. It sends the message that it's all about them, as it should well be.

If you start with a "needs as understood" list or something like that, it ensures that everyone is on the same page. If it's a team presentation, encourage your colleagues to chime in every so often as you review the needs. Reviewing needs tells the clients a story about them. It has to capture their attention.

Phase Three: Offer Your Recommendation

Begin the presentation with a broad overview of the recommendation. Don't get too specific too early. Whether it's a new payroll system, a piece of manufacturing equipment, or a streamlined retirement plan, briefly explain your recommendation first. Think of this as an executive summary of what you'll present. You will get more specific as you proceed

Phase Four: Review the Specific Benefits

The clients need to know how your recommendation will add value. Whether it's the return on the investment, how it simplifies the process, or how it will motivate their people, they need to know what's in it for them. If you can relate these specific benefits to the corresponding features, that will add meat to the bones. Do this first, even though it is not natural to ensure that they hear what you have to say.

This phase presents a wonderful opportunity for the team members to demonstrate their creativity. Innovative team selling suggests that team members participate throughout the entire sales process. But in this phase they get to shine, since they can demonstrate how their expertise will help the client.

Different functions can contribute in different ways. The marketing manager can discuss trends and their potential impact on the business. The distribution head can explain their unique approach to "just-in-time inventory." The business analyst can suggest ways to improve cash flow. The technical wizard can project the next few generations of the product. Each team member can demonstrate how the whole is greater than the sum of the parts. That is yet one more advantage of sales teams.

Phase Five: Discuss the Generic Features and Benefits

You must tell the client everything they need to know, even the things they don't want to hear. (Think about the used car example.) But we suggest that you save these negative features, like cancellation fees or contract requirements or the need to shut down the plant during installation, for later in the presentation. You have to share this information, since not doing so is inappropriate, even unethical. Just save it for later.

Attention spans are short and getting shorter, so we must be sensitive to this when we present. There are cases where the customers need to know everything; there are others where they want to hear only what is important to them. The team needs to recognize which approach is proper here, and approach the presentation accordingly.

So there's your presentation model—five very specific phases. Each is critically important and each provides you with a way to distinguish your sales team. The model applies to most situations, and it provides you with a process that will help you move comfortably through your presentation, leverage your resources, and clearly tell your story.

Airtime Distribution

One thing that is important to considerer is that when you are presenting, it's your turn. You have done a marvelous job of letting the customer do most of the talking prior to presenting. But now you take center stage. This is illustrated in Figure 15.5.

The model talks about "airtime," just like on radio or TV. It demonstrates how if you give up the airtime early, you'll get it back later. We developed

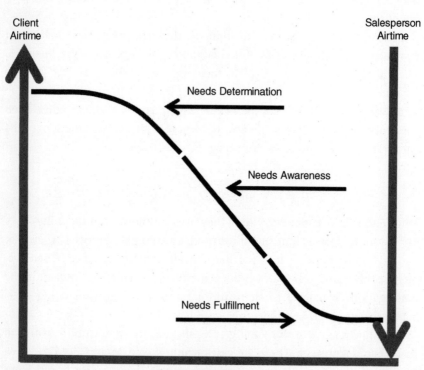

FIGURE 15.5 Airtime Distribution

this at CRC and love the way it differentiates between needs determination, needs awareness, and needs fulfillment.

When you're determining needs, the customer has the bulk of the airtime as you ask those thoughtful, provocative, open-ended questions. Needs awareness refers to when you review the customer's needs. That's more of a dialogue as you clarify the situation and make sure that everyone agrees. But when it's time to present, it's your turn and you enjoy the airtime. A wonderful way to think about presenting is to think of it as fulfilling the customer's needs. Once again, it's all about the customer and now it is time for you to do your thing.

The Unsolicited Idea

We have one last thought regarding presentations. There is something we call the *unsolicited idea*. Some of our people call it the uncompensated idea. These are ideas you offer the client strictly to enhance the relationship. They have nothing to do with your products or services. There is no revenue attached. They are simply ideas that may be of interest to the client.

You can do this as you conclude the meeting. You need to be sensitive in the way you do this. Remember, they didn't ask for the idea, so get permission first: "Betty, I have been thinking about the employee morale issue you mentioned on my last visit. If you're interested, I have an idea for you." If Betty is open to hearing your idea, go for it.

Use the same approach that we just introduced. Identify the need, confirm it, offer the idea, and give a benefit: "It sounds like the team needs to respect and appreciate one another more, is that right? I know someone who works with these kinds of groups. He'll get them out of the office on a Friday and have them do some community service work. Good stuff happens when they work together to clean up a park in a bad neighborhood, or paint an elderly couple's home. They learn that they do have more in common than they thought. It helps build relationships and often impacts morale. I'd be glad to have this guy give you a call."

Often the customer will like the idea. If not, they won't use it. But the message is clear—you care about them. That's the bottom line. Remember the David Maister line we shared earlier about customers not caring about how much you know, until they know how much you care.

We suggest that you do this as you conclude the meeting for two reasons. If you do it early and they get excited about the idea, it could derail the meeting. If they don't like it, it can put a cloud over the meeting. So save it for later.

We often tell groups we hope that when the receptionist announces that you have arrived, the customer will say something like, "I wonder what she has for me today." It's as if they expect you to bring them new and different ideas. It's simply one more way to differentiate yourselves, and that's what we have to do in this competitive environment.

And in Conclusion . . .

This chapter began by mentioning that although Sam's situation was hypothetical, it was based on real situations that we have observed. With that in mind, we'll conclude with an anecdote that involved a member of our team.

One of our people was participating in a finalist presentation by himself. We always prefer to send several people, but there was very little notice and everyone was committed, so he had to fly solo. He was scheduled to give the third of three presentations. It took place at a country club. The first team was on from 8:30 to 9:30; the second from 9:45 to 10:45; and our guy was on from 11:00 to 12:00.

When he walked into the room he encountered 16 people sitting at a "U" shaped table. They all looked a bit glassy eyed, even shell-shocked. They had just heard two consecutive one-hour presentations, and they gave the impression that they were not thrilled about having to sit through another.

What made things worse was that our representative realized that he was the only thing standing between this group and lunch, which would be followed by a round of golf. And of course the first tee was quite visible through the window adjacent to where he would speak. As he told us later, "they wanted to hear my presentation about as much as they wanted to endure a root canal."

Realizing his unfortunate predicament, he made the decision to conduct a round of introductions. That's right, even with 16 people seated around the table, he asked each person to tell him who they were, what their role was in the company, and what they wanted to get out of the meeting. Sound familiar? We do occasionally practice what we preach.

Everyone participated. It took 21 minutes, which left him less than 40 minutes to tell his story. "It was the smartest thing I ever did on a sales call," he mused later, perhaps exaggerating just a bit. "They came back to life. They had fun. There was some bantering going on. When one sales manager said he wanted to hear about how we taught listening, someone else kidded him about how much help he needed in that area. That got a big laugh. Different people wanted to hear different things, ranging from our training methodology, to how we use video, to how we reinforce the training.

When he finally presented, he did his best to address the areas of interest to the group. He made the presentation all about them. He even called a few of them by name. "I only had those 40 minutes or so," he recalled, "but it was so much better than it would have been if I had just given a one-hour presentation without hearing from them."

He won the business. He was told the vote was almost unanimous. When the job was under way several months later, the client told him that of the three finalists, he was the only one who even attempted to hear from them first. The other two just showed up and presented. They had impressive presentations prepared, and did nice jobs in explaining how they could help. But they never involved the customer. They didn't take the time to position the meeting. They made no attempt to connect with the group. As a result they lost. This happens all the time.

Presentations. Pitches. Showtime. Telling our story. Call this part of the process whatever you like. It may be the part of the process you like best, but it is complicated and requires lots of thought and preparation. But when it works and proceeds as you had planned, it's one of the best experiences you enjoy in business. Nothing compares with winning the business, which, of course, is the objective behind every presentation.

Some Things to Consider

What

The Presentation Model we introduced—what we call the "four-box model"—applies to any sales presentation. Whether it's a simple recommendation in the course of a discussion, or a formal presentation, the approach applies. That's because it is all about the client as it explains how your products, services, and ideas address their needs.

How

When you and/or your team are planning for a presentation, take out a piece of paper and draw a line down the middle both vertically and horizontally, so you have four boxes. This resembles the model we introduced. Start with the top left-hand box and capture the needs. Next, determine what you will present and put that in the top right-hand box. Under that, in the bottom right-hand box, list the relevant features and benefits. And finally, in the remaining box in the lower left, list the specific benefits.

Remember that what is on the right side is fixed information about us, and what is on the left side is variable information about them. Start your presentation by reviewing the needs; explain what you will recommend, and be sure to put most of your energy into discussing those specific benefits. That is what matters most to the client and that is the key to a successful presentation.

When

Any time you present anything, this model is useful to help you plan the process. Remember, specific benefits explain how your recommendation addresses the client's needs. That's the key point you need to make.

16 What Do You Mean You Don't Like It?

No matter how great your presentation may be, you will encounter resistance. Even if every member of your team performs brilliantly, and everything goes perfectly according to plan, your clients will object. It's a fact of life. We hear many salespeople complain that "it's human nature" to push back. Even if someone is convinced that they want to buy, they will resist at some level.

When most people hear new ideas or have to deal with the possibility of change, they resist. That's the way it is. For many reasons, when it's time to make decisions, the tendency is to focus on the negative. And as a result, people object. Yes, it's human nature.

If you don't agree, take a look at what you are wearing at this very minute. We would bet that if it's an article of clothing, a piece of jewelry, or even your pajamas, you resisted buying it initially. Either the price was too high or the color wasn't right or it didn't fit the way you liked. But you did buy it. After going through some deliberation process, you did that. And you're probably glad you did.

That's the way it works. Most people tend to look for the flaws when they make decisions. They do it with the things they buy just as with everything else. It is how their minds work. If you're still skeptical, think back to the last time you asked someone to do something differently, whether it was a colleague, a friend, a significant other, or a kid. Chances are they pushed back. I doubt we're telling you something you don't know. One more time, it's human nature.

When people are in the buying mode, this tendency to resist increases as the ticket price gets higher. You're less likely to resist as quickly when buying a toaster as when it's a computer. We hear often how people start second-guessing their big purchases before they get to their car in the parking lot.

That's why the advertising folks tell you that you are more likely to read the ad for the car the day *after* you purchase it than the day before. You're looking for confirmation. You are uncomfortable. So reading the ad, which tells you how wonderful the car is, can be very comforting.

You buy things yourself, of course, so much of this is familiar. You have experienced these feelings. The realtors call it *buyer's remorse*. The advertising folks call it *cognitive dissonance*. It speaks to the fact that when buyers make major decisions, they find themselves in a state of disequilibrium. Part of them is confirming that they made a good decision; the other is questioning what they just did. It can be quite disconcerting.

As a result, people in the buying mode will object even if they are inclined to buy. They know they'll react later, so they object now. Use your own experience to test this theory. How do you feel after making a big purchase? A bit uncomfortable, perhaps? Most people do. Your customers are no different, and this is something that every member of every sales team must remember.

That is why it is so important to be more visible the day after the customer buys than the day before. Remember Ted Levitt of Harvard and our comment about how the real selling starts after you win the business. Many sales managers will tell you that anyone can get the first order; it's the ones who get the second, third, and fourth that deserve your attention.

So let's accept that objections are raised regardless of the situation. The challenge is how sales professionals react when they encounter them. Ideally, they will take all this into consideration and work with their client to resolve the differences. Sadly, that's often not what happens. Instead, most people find themselves acting somewhat reptilian. That primitive part of the brain kicks in, and they behave in a self protective way. The result is that they become defensive, or aggressive, or passive. They react the way any species might when they encounter danger: they either fight, take flight, or freeze. It is basic psychology.

None of these behaviors work when you try to resolve conflict. Think about it. Who wants to work with someone who goes on the attack, or someone who overreacts, or someone who simply gives up?

Okay, maybe you don't behave that way. Good for you. But do any of the following reactions seem familiar when you or your colleagues encounter resistance?

"No, no, no, you don't understand. . . . "
"I'm sorry; I wasn't clear. I'll try again. . . . "
"Can't you see how this will help?"
"I was only responding to what you asked for."
"You'll be missing a big opportunity. . . . "
"You're right. It's not what you really need."

Sure, these examples are exaggerated. But you have probably heard salespeople react precisely this way when they encounter resistance. You may have reacted this way as well. After all the effort you put in to get to this point in the process, if your ideas are rejected, you react. Sometimes you might overreact. This is understandable, even forgivable, but it rarely turns things around.

The good news is that sales professionals and their team members can learn to behave differently when this occurs. If they use their problem solving skills, they can work with their clients to resolve whatever issues arise. Sales teams can work in concert when they encounter these uncomfortable situations if they know what to do and are comfortable with each other.

Ask yourself how you hope you react when you encounter resistance, regardless of the situation. Take a few minutes and invent your own objection resolution process. Come on. It's one of our last exercises.

When you thought about your own behavior when you encounter resistance, there's a good chance you realized that you, like most people, can become a bit defensive or aggressive. The inclination is there; you can't control it. You've got a couple of million years of DNA working against you. But there are many things you can do to manage your behavior. That's part of the learning process.

Process awareness can help. So can applying some kind of framework. That's why we asked you to think about this. Our approach appears in Figure 16.1. Chances are that it is quite similar to what you came up with on your own. Check it out.

You'll see very quickly that it encompasses many of the skills introduced earlier. Like any model, it is meant to assist you or guide you, not to direct you. Every step is important, but not every one is used every time.

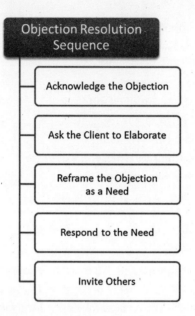

FIGURE 16.1 The Objection Resolution Sequence

Acknowledge the Objection

Any time a client objects or asks an intimidating question or comes on aggressively, it will calm things down immediately if you acknowledge what they say. Acknowledging is a life skill and applies to so many of your daily activities, whether you are interacting with your loved ones, your colleagues, or your clients. Acknowledging sets the tone for what will eventually happen, regardless of the situation.

Acknowledging is different from agreeing and should not be interpreted as acquiescing. Don't confuse it with patronizing. Acknowledging is simply letting the other person know that you have heard them, that they have the right to object, and that you are available to work with them. It's a wonderful way to demonstrate both empathy and willingness to problem solve. It prevents you from becoming aggressive or defensive.

So when the client says "your price is too high," the acknowledgment could be, "I know you are under pressure to reduce costs." If a client says they are happy with their current supplier, the acknowledgment might sound like "I appreciate loyalty as much as anyone." If they complain about the time required, you could acknowledge by saying, "I know you want to get this done as quickly as possible."

You'll figure out the words. The key is to let the other person know that you heard them, want to work with them, and have no desire to argue. It can be quite disarming, and it sets the stage for everything that is about to happen.

Elaboration

We have explored the importance of questioning at length throughout the book. Questions can also help resolve objections. Asking the client to elaborate on their objections is the most important step in resolving them. You'll never get below the surface, and truly understand the essence of an objection, if you don't allow your customer to elaborate. And it is an excellent time to leverage your resources.

Questioning can be like a double-edged sword. As important as it is, it carries a lot of baggage. Most people are suspicious of questions. So as important as it is to encourage the client to speak out when they object, you have to be cautious in the way you go about it. You have to be straightforward, direct, and honest. You don't want to be perceived as being manipulative or conniving. This is a tense moment, and you must be extremely sensitive.

You and your colleagues can follow certain guidelines when you ask your customers to elaborate. Keep your questions open ended. Don't come across as judgmental. Avoid asking questions that are really ideas. For example, a question like, "Do you think we can meet the person who didn't like the proposal?" is really an idea, not a question.

Try to make your questions "contentless," which means they should not be guesses about the buyer's concern. Often people ask questions like "is it our size?" or "are you worried about the quality?" or even "was it because of that unfortunate article?" These kinds of questions can bring up issues that the customer never considered. They do nothing to enhance the process.

Another trap to avoid is the multiple-choice question. Leading the witness doesn't work in the courtroom, and offering possible responses detracts from interviews. When people give two or three possible answers to a question before getting the response, they not only detract from the process, but also can insult the person being asked the question.

We have all seen a sport reporter ask a football coach questions like "why he changed quarterbacks?" or a soccer coach "why did you change goaltenders?" If that were all they asked, these would be terrific open-ended questions. But too often, they just can't stop there. They immediately follow it with the possible answers: "Was it to send a message to the team, or to change the approach, or to surprise the opponent's defense?" When they do this, they might show how much they know, but it detracts from the quality of the answers, as the person being interviewed doesn't have to think much about what was asked.

It is important for you to see how asking these multiple-choice questions can prevent you from getting the answer you really want. Too many believe that they can get a client to open up by offering several options as to why they are pushing back. But the results are usually the opposite.

Think about the salesperson who encounters resistance when he asks a question like "is it our higher price, the disappointing service, or my style that is creating this reluctance?" Of course we are exaggerating here, but the message is clear. There is no need to complicate this step in the process.

So keep those questions open-ended, direct, contentless, straightforward, nonmanipulative, and please, please avoid those multiple-choice questions. What you want to do is acquire information, not play games. The intent is to encourage the customer to open up and speak freely about their concerns. That's what will get you to the core of the objection. As with most interactive skills, simplicity helps.

Can you be more specific?
Would you please elaborate on that?
I'm not sure what you mean regarding. . . .
Could you say more about that?
Can I ask why?

You'll figure out the questions that work best for you. And if you can't, your team members will. When you experience any kind of pushback, your colleagues can help, both in the preparation by anticipating possible objections, and contributing when they are present at the meeting.

Envision a customer objecting to a recommendation during a client visit. The individual who was on the receiving end of the objection would be the one to acknowledge what the customer said. But then team members could step in and ask the necessary questions.

They need to be sensitive when they do this, since you don't want everybody firing questions at the customer like in some kind of stress interview. But often when someone is blindsided, they can have difficulty coming up with the questions they would like to ask. That's when team members can help. Knowing that your colleagues "have your back" is very comforting, particularly when resistance occurs.

Since elaboration is such a key step, we'd like to dig a bit deeper. David Michelson of our team came up with an interesting concept years ago. He is an outstanding facilitator as well as an extraordinary instructional designer. He's also a heck of a songwriter. One day he showed up and introduced us to "double-clicking." Let me explain.

If you hear a key word in the customer's complaint, double-click on it as you might when doing some research online. For example, if a client says something like "this is inconsistent with our strategy," you might ask, "in what way is it inconsistent?" You chose to double-click on "inconsistent." You could have double-clicked on "strategy" and asked, "what components of the strategy haven't we addressed with our recommendation?" Both would get you more information.

The rationale is that you take a key word that the customer used and ask them to expand on their concern. Even when things get somewhat testy this can help, as you are using their words, not yours. If a client says something challenging like "this is ridiculous" it would be very easy for anyone to get defensive. But after acknowledging it, if you ask why they think it's ridiculous, it can calm things down and begin the process of getting to the core of the issue.

Envision three of you on a sales call having just recommended something. The client seems annoyed and says something like "you guys really missed the boat on this one." The presenter would acknowledge it with something like "that's disappointing to hear, as we thought we were on target." Then a team member can step in and ask a specific question like "it would be very helpful to understand why you think we missed the boat," or if they didn't want to double-click, they might say, "could you say more about why you feel that way?" When team members step in, it immediately takes the pressure off the person getting bombarded and starts the customer talking. That's precisely what you want to happen.

Finally, be sure you know when to stop. As important as the elaboration step is, you need to know when enough is enough. We suggest that it's better to ask two or three questions too few than one too many. Be careful not to cross the line, as this is an uncomfortable moment in the sales process. By all means, ask the questions you need to ask; just know when to stop.

One way to look at this is to think of an algebraic equation. (Sorry about bringing up bad memories for some of you.)

If *n* represents the number of questions that annoy the customer, how many questions do you ask?

Think about this for 30 seconds.

Our answer is $n - 1$. It's our silly way of letting sales teams know that as important as it is to ask questions when you encounter resistance, don't wear out your welcome. Let the customer know that you appreciate their help, let them know why you need the information, and make this process as comfortable as possible. But at the same time do whatever you can to make this an open and honest discussion, not an interrogation.

Reframing

Once you have acknowledged the objection and think you understand it, it's time to address it, right? Not exactly. There is one additional step to take prior to offering your response—*reframing*.

Most objection resolution processes encourage the sales professional to restate the objection before responding. You probably had something like this in the model you developed earlier. If you do this you will be different from most of the people out there. But you can go beyond this. That's where reframing comes in.

Reframing, as we define it in objection resolution situations, is *transforming the objection to a need*. Put another way, it allows you to think of objections as unfulfilled needs. That's an important assumption. Objections are needs that have not been satisfied. By reframing objections, you transform them into needs. It is easier to address a need than to challenge an objection. So if you do this you increase the likelihood of obtaining buy-in.

One concern about simply restating objections is that in some cases it can actually work against you. When you restate an objection, and use the client's words, it almost validates what they said. For example, if a client says "your price is too high" and your response is "so you think our price is too high," they hear their negative words come out of your mouth. It adds credence to their concern. It can even sound silly. You can do better.

Again, we make the assumption that objections are really unfulfilled needs. When you transform objections into needs, it makes them more resolvable. You need to get that elaboration first, of course, but if someone complains that your price was too high, the reframe might focus on their need to know what they are getting for the additional cost. Perhaps it's their need to see the value in what you offer. It could even be their need to see why paying you more is a good business decision. But each of these examples highlights the need that has yet to be addressed.

Reframing builds on what we learned from successful problem solvers. Recall how we introduced the concept of *invitational language* when we discussed idea development. We compared someone expressing a concern like "it will take too long," with how another might say "how can we get it done in less time?" or "how do we get the time line extended?" The great problem solvers look at ways to get things done as opposed to focusing on why they can't. You can apply this thinking to objection resolution through reframing.

Reframing provides sales teams with another way to contribute to client interactions. Once again, they can do this before and during sales calls. When we talked about getting our acts together, we mentioned that part of the planning process includes anticipating objections.

When sales teams anticipate what objections might occur during a sales call, they can give serious thought to how to acknowledge them, how to seek elaboration, and yes, how to reframe them. This doesn't mean they script their responses, but it does mean they work together to ensure that they are prepared to respond if necessary.

We'd be disingenuous if we said that reframing is easy to do. It's not. But like anything else, it is something everyone can learn to do. Sales teams who are comfortable with reframing can perform admirably when they encounter resistance.

When we discussed listening, we explained that one of the most significant barriers to listening is our tendency to think ahead; to rehearse our response. We warned about the danger of doing that and discussed the need to fight this tendency, even though it may be coming from a good place. Remember our pal, Needs-Driven Ned? He was the guy who heard the first need the customer expressed and jumped all over it before he understood their entire situation. As a result, he never reached his potential.

After saying all that, we will now contradict those words a bit. We're not being hypocritical. It is beneficial to do some rehearsing at this moment in the process. To drop out and take advantage of your ability to think faster than the client can talk is perfectly appropriate. After all, you worked hard to determine the client's needs and you made a solid recommendation. Yet now you are encountering resistance. If you do some rehearsing, we can live with that.

You constantly find yourselves thinking about how you'll address an objection while the customer is answering your questions. It is difficult not to do this. But you can go even further. From the minute the customer starts answering your questions and elaborates on the concern, see if you can determine what the *need* is that you haven't satisfied.

Everyone on the team can contribute if they challenge themselves to find the need that is buried in the objection. If you can figure that out, most of your work is done. Because once you understand the need, your ability to comfortably reframe is assured.

When it's time to reframe, you can use the same approach that was introduced when we explained how to review the customer's needs:

Use an "I" statement.
Express the objection as a need.
Seek confirmation.

This looks familiar, doesn't it? When you reframe, and review your understanding of the objection in needs language, you are doing precisely what you did when you concluded situation analysis. You are reviewing in your words your perception of what the customer has expressed.

That's why the "I" statement is so important, even more so than during the needs review. When you reframe an objection, you are changing the tone, even the scope of what was said. So it's important to express what you heard, which is somewhat different from what the client said. The customer said the price was too high and you say something about justifying the cost. The words are different. That's why the "I" statement is necessary.

When you reframe objections, be sure to express what you say in needs language. Use verbs, think in terms of what they hope to accomplish, and focus on the client. And since you have changed the scope, be very careful to seek their confirmation:

"So if I understand you correctly, you need to _____, is that correct?"

There are dozens of ways to reframe objections. What appears above is one simple example. But as you can see, the example includes an "I" statement, the objection is expressed as a need, and there is an attempt to receive confirmation. Those are the three key steps in reframing.

If someone was unhappy with your performance in the past, the need could be "to feel confident that what happened in the past won't happen in the future." If they are content with their current provider, the need could be "to see why it's in their interest to consider a second source." Or if they complain about how difficult it will be to change systems, the need might be "to feel comfortable that the transition will be seamless."

It is easier to address needs than to challenge objections. If you and your team can successfully reframe objections, you will dramatically increase the likelihood of resolving them. And you'll differentiate yourself every time you try.

One final thought. There will be times when your reframe is not quite on target. That's fine. If you didn't get it completely right, simply ask what you missed. Then try again. Eventually you'll get there. And the client will appreciate your efforts.

Address the Need

Once the objection has been reframed and confirmed by the customer, it's time to address it. Ironically, this is the least challenging part of the resolving objections process. That's because you know the answers. The challenge is to favorably predispose your customer to accept your answer. You can accomplish that by applying the first three steps. And once you get there, it's simply a matter of giving your best answer.

These answers are always situational. It's up to you to determine what they are. What we can do is list some of the options available. But the answers are up to you and your team:

- Talk about your team.
- Sell the company.
- Review the benefits.
- Modify your original recommendation.
- Discuss parallel situations.
- Offer referrals or testimonials.
- Suggest an idea.
- Ask the customer for their thoughts.
- Call a time out.

The list goes on and on. There are as many ways to address objections as there are clever sales teams. If you believe in what you are selling, and have put together a solid recommendation, once you reframe the objection successfully, you'll have the answer.

Team members can be very helpful here. When objections come up, the individual who was confronted will usually acknowledge it. Different members of the team can help get the customer talking and assist in the reframing. They can also help with the answer. If they plan this beforehand they can operate like a well-tuned machine.

That's exactly what happened with Sam's team. Consistent with the warning he gave them at breakfast, an unexpected objection came up. It happened when Jerry from Manufacturing was discussing the quality standards that they had established. Just as he started to explain their "zero defects" process, one of the customers said, "Well, that's all well and good, but we are genuinely concerned about your capacity and your ability to deliver, particularly in crunch time."

The room got very quiet. But the team was well prepared and Jerry immediately acknowledged what was said: "That's a fair question. Our ability to deliver the goods is critical." And then he immediately asked a question: Can you tell us why you are so concerned? The customer talked about how their current provider had twice as much capacity as their company did. Sam then jumped in and asked a question about the antici-pated volume during crunch time. Jerry asked another question about lead time, and even Charlie from Operations joined in with a question about the desired turnaround time. The customers responded openly and honestly.

Sam realized they had enough information and came through big time with a poignant reframe. He had told the group at breakfast that they could count on him if something like this happened and he delivered: "I want to be sure that we understand your concern. It appears to me that you need to feel confident that if we are fortunate to work with you that we will be able to meet your delivery requirements, particularly during crunch time. Your current provider is larger than us and they had problems in the past and you need to know we can deliver. Is that correct"?

It was absolutely correct. When the customer confirmed what he said, Sam deferred to Jerry and Charlie, who gave great answers. They were ready. They had prepared. They had data to back up what they said, with projections, inventory configurations, and even contingency plans. They had the answers. Because they took those first few steps, they clearly confirmed what the real issues were and converted them into needs. That allowed them to offer a strong response. They nailed it and the customers were extremely impressed.

Invite Others

There is a final step in the issue resolution process. It's called *inviting others*.

Every time you resolve an objection, we encourage you to find out if there are others. We don't do this to open up what some people call "Pandora's

Box." We do this for two reasons. You need to ensure that there aren't other issues that require your attention. If there are, you will eventually hear them; so you might as well get them on the table now when you and your colleagues are there to address these issues.

The other reason is that inviting others sets the stage for closing. If the customer doesn't have a reason not to buy, then you can assume they are ready to buy, and when appropriate you can ask for the business right there and then. It doesn't necessarily happen after formal presentations, but it can happen on more typical customer visits.

It's Really Problem Solving

When we discussed problem solving we introduced the four levels of idea response. We repeat the graphic we introduced at that time; see Figure 16.2.

You'll recall that the model explains how we can respond differently to ideas we don't like. What the objection resolution process we introduced attempts to do is "walk the client up the staircase" (see Figure 16.3).

As you can see, when you acknowledge what a client says and ask them to elaborate, you get them from level one to level two. Reframing will help you walk them to level three. And if your answer is accepted, and they see value in your recommendation, you have elevated them to level four. The objection resolution process helps you prevent the customer from missing a great opportunity—the opportunity to work with you and your team.

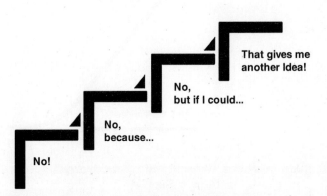

FIGURE 16.2 The Four Levels of Idea Response

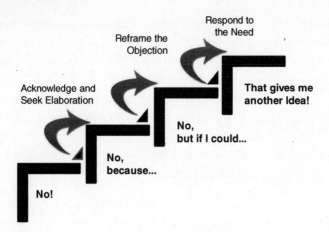

FIGURE 16.3 Walking the Client Up the Staircase

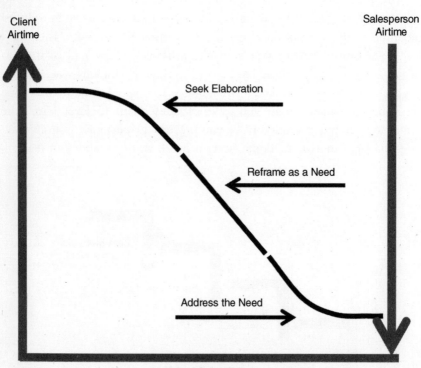

FIGURE 16.4 Airtime Distribution in Objection Resolution

Airtime Distribution—Again

We previously discussed how giving up airtime early results in your getting it back with dividends later. We introduced a chart that discussed needs determination, needs awareness, and needs fulfillment.

The exact same model applies to objection resolution; see Figure 16.4.

Just as in needs determination, if you let the client enjoy the majority of the airtime early as they elaborate, and share the airtime as you reframe their concern, you'll have your turn when it's time to respond. As you look at this graphic, it may occur to you that in many ways objection resolution is a microcosm of the entire consultative selling approach.

Sales Teams Rule

Sales teams can do many great things. They can connect with their counterparts early in the relationship. They can transform themselves into needs development teams and play a major role in analyzing their customers' situations. They can play a major role in giving outstanding presentations. And as you just saw, they can elevate the process of managing resistance and resolving objections.

As we move toward competing this journey, it is important to understand that there is no part of the process that cannot be enhanced if you leverage your resources effectively before, during, and after meeting with your customers and prospects. It is a big mistake not to do this all the time.

Some Things to Consider

What

Remember that the most professional salespeople can turn into pit bulls when they encounter resistance. As good as they are, when clients push back the tendency is to get aggressive or defensive. Sometimes salespeople even just give up. None of these work. But applying the objection resolution process can help dramatically.

How

A great exercise for any sales team is to take some time and anticipate the client's objections. They begin by writing up the potential objection in the client's words. Then together they can discuss ways to apply each step in the model. They can look at different ways to acknowledge what the client might say. They can explore how to ask appropriate questions so the client will elaborate. And together they can draft ways—several if possible—to reframe the objections. Then as a team they can use their creativity to develop ways to successfully address these objections. It is a good use of time for any sales team when they plan their calls.

When

Do this before any client meeting that you anticipate encountering resistance and for major presentations in particular. Start doing this on Monday.

17 Bringing Home the Bacon

You just read an entire chapter dedicated to explaining how to resolve objections. We explained how clients object even if they are inclined to buy. We reviewed how most salespeople react when they encounter resistance. And we introduced a process to use any time you are in these challenging situations. We even demonstrated how Sam and his team resolved a difficult objection during their finalist presentation. We hope it all made sense.

But we'd be kidding you if we didn't admit that this is a difficult thing to do. Even the most seasoned sales professionals will admit quite readily that this is the most challenging part of the sales process. When sales professionals and sales teams fail, it is often because they were not able to resolve the issues that they encountered. That's what kept them from winning the business.

Resolving issues is directly connected to every phase of the sales process. This phase does not stand alone. That is why objections can occur any time. If you encounter objections it could be because you did not do the necessary planning. It may be the result of not connecting with the customers or conducting effective meetings. Most often it's because you did not totally understand the customer's needs. Remember, most objections are unfulfilled needs. And of course, if your presentation is off base, the customer has no choice but to object. So even though we made the point that clients object even when they are inclined to buy, the objection itself is often the result of how the team fell short and did not meet the client's expectations.

One way to think about closing the sale is to realize that from the time you finish making your recommendation and ask the customer for feedback, you are in the closing process. That's right; it begins earlier than you think. Everyone makes such a big deal out of the closing process. We get that. There are dozens of names and titles for different closing techniques, most of which are nonsense. You may recall the expression "ABC" from the play, *Glengarry Glen Ross*: "Always be closing." That is not exactly what we would call a customer-focused expression. If all you think about is closing, it's all about you. Bad form.

So as we begin to look at the closing process, whether we call it *gaining commitment*, or *seeking closure*, or simply *closing the deal*, we must realize that this phase is inextricably connected to resolving objections. We know that at some point you have to ask for the business and close, but at the same time it is critically important for any sales team to realize that closing is the result of everything that has happened previously. That's why hearing salespeople discuss this ABC nonsense is so maddening.

We know that any team that wants to can learn how to apply this process when they encounter resistance. Acknowledging, seeking elaboration, and reframing are all very learnable skills. If sales teams practice the skills, plan and rehearse before they make major presentations, and anticipate the objections that they might encounter, they can effectively apply this process. But in many ways it's counterintuitive.

Remember, the tendency is to fight or take flight or freeze. It is a lot easier said than done. It is usually dependent on how disciplined you are when you find yourselves in this kind of situation. That's right, it's really dependent on your ability to be disciplined as much as anything else.

One situation that demonstrates this is the story of a sales call that my former business partner and I made. We had won a major piece of business after a grueling RFP process. It was an exciting opportunity and we were thrilled to have been selected. You have all been there. You get the call, spread the word, and everybody is thrilled. High-fives, fist pumps, even an occasional whoop or two are heard all over the place. Those are the best days in the career of any salesperson or sales team. This book began by talking about how that happened to Sam Jamison and his team.

My partner and I were still enjoying the afterglow a week later when we received another phone call from the same person who had originally relayed the good news. He was the director of management development, and we'll refer to him as Marvin for reasons of confidentiality. He had coordinated the

RFP process from start to finish. We had connected well with him from the beginning, and when he awarded us the business you could tell that he was genuinely pleased.

This call was less upbeat. You could tell from the sound of his voice that he was a bit troubled. He informed us that yes, we had been selected to do the job, but that the SVP of Sales and Marketing wanted to meet us prior to signing the contract. "It's a chemistry test," he said. When asked to elaborate, Marvin explained, "He just wants to meet you and make sure the chemistry feels right. After all, it's his sales force and he wants to be comfortable with the people who are providing the training."

Well, that seemed perfectly reasonable. He certainly had the right to do that. We wished he had done it sooner and been involved in the decision, but that wasn't the way it happened. It meant another trip for us, and it meant that the deal wasn't really completed, but we realized we had no choice, and we made the trek to their facility on the day they requested. We were confident that we would pass his test.

When we arrived and greeted Marvin, we could see that he was a bit tense. He was pleasant as always, and very engaged as we talked about the project and the action plan that we submitted two days after getting his call. He let us know he was impressed with how quickly we put that comprehensive document together, and told us again how pleased he was that we were selected. He told us he hoped we could leave with a signed contract, which had been sent to the SVP. We were glad to hear that, but there was this unsettling chill in the air.

What made matters worse was that the SVP was late. Five minutes became 10 and then 15. That's never a good sign. Finally he walked in. You could see immediately that this was going to be a serious discussion, as he wasn't friendly, and he made no effort to apologize for his tardiness. He did not have anything that resembled a contract. The vibes did not feel good. My partner and I looked at each other and without saying a word; we both knew things were heading south.

Marvin was a pro and he did what he could to get things moving in a positive direction. He introduced us and explained why we were selected. He talked about what he thought were our points of difference. He even went so far as to share the results of the vote, which leaned heavily in our direction. He then asked us to explain how we planned to approach the project. We were well prepared to do that and for the first time felt a bit less nervous about what was happening.

We began by asking the SVP if there was anything of particular interest to him and he said, "not really; why don't you just do what Marvin asked." That was fine, even if a bit cold. He wanted to hear from us and that was his prerogative.

I began to explain our game plan and review the document we had submitted after wining the business. But shortly after I began, the SVP interrupted me and said in a rather harsh tone, "I'm sure you guys are great and it's obvious that you impressed the committee, but after reviewing your proposal I have decided not to move forward with your company. I regret that you put in all this time and effort to get to this point, but I really don't want to move in this direction."

Yikes! Talk about a letdown. We had worked so hard to win the business, got the good news, celebrated the victory, developed an action plan, and allocated resources. We had probably already spent some of the money. And now this power figure appears from nowhere and fires us before we even began. It seemed surrealistic. How could this be happening? In all the years we had been in business we never encountered anything quite like this. To win a job and then have the rug pulled out from under you before you start, with no notice and no reason, was mind-boggling.

We both looked at Marvin, who was surprisingly calm. We guessed he had some inkling that this was happening prior to this meeting. When he heard the remarks, he turned to the SVP and asked, "Can you tell us why? This is clearly not what we expected to hear." I was quite impressed with his courage as he confronted the senior manager in front of us. It was obvious that he had encountered difficulty with this guy before.

Many people in his position would have just accepted the decision and ended the meeting. Good for Marvin.

The SVP responded immediately: "I just don't believe in this videotape nonsense. It's a lousy way to train sales professionals and I don't want to subject my people to this." That was also something we did not expect to hear. In planning for the meeting, we had thought long and hard about the chemistry issue and anticipated as best we could what might come up. This never occurred to us. We use video as a training vehicle in virtually all of our programs. Giving participants the opportunity to practice the skills they learn in role-play simulations is one of the highlights of our courses. This was one of the points of difference that won us the job, and the committee was very enthusiastic about this approach.

As soon as I heard him complain about the video, I responded. He had hit a hot button and I was ready to jump on it. I tried to be cool, but that wasn't going to happen. I looked him right in the eye and said something like "I'm surprised to hear you say that. We have been using video as a training vehicle for 20 years and what we have learned is that . . . ." That's as far as I got. My partner interrupted me. He literally grabbed my arm and said, "Excuse me, Eric." I could see he was quite serious, as the blood had virtually stopped circulating in my arm. "Of course" was all I could say, and I deferred to him.

Now it was my partner's turn to address the client, but he took a much smarter approach. Rather than get defensive and go on the attack as I had, he responded by saying "We want you to be comfortable with the training methodology. Can you tell us what the problem is with videotape?" As soon as he said that, my cheeks got very hot. I realized that I had just contradicted everything we teach about conflict resolution. Rather than acknowledge the objection and ask the client to elaborate, I immediately jumped in with my pitch. Not very impressive.

My partner did exactly what I should have done. I felt like a jerk, but was glad he had bailed me out. As the SVP started talking, we realized that he didn't have a clue as to what we had outlined in the proposal. He had concluded we were going to bring in tapes of actors and actresses making perfect sales calls and use them to demonstrate to the group what the process looks like. "Our people will watch the tapes, which will probably be unrealistic, and conclude that they could never replicate what they were watching. It will demotivate them, it will give them the impression that this is what we want them to do, and it works against what we are trying to accomplish. I simply can't buy into this approach."

We listened carefully as he expressed his dissatisfaction with what he thought was our approach. Now it was time to reframe. I sat there quietly feeling quite sheepish and watched my partner come through big time. "I have to apologize," he said. "We obviously were not clear in our proposal. You are under the impression that we plan to show your people how to apply the skills we'll introduce with demonstration tapes. And if I heard you correctly, you want them to realize that there is no one right way to sell. Each individual has his or her own unique approach, and you need the training to reinforce that, not dilute it. Do I have it right?"

The SVP could only say one word: "Exactly." My partner continued, "We would never do that in our courses, even when asked, for the same reasons you just gave us. What we plan to do is put your people on video practicing the skills. The intent is for them to test the efficacy and applicability of the concepts that we introduce. We want them to see how each person has their own style and how each will use the concepts differently. Philosophically we agree with you 100 percent."

I just sat there saying nothing. What could I possibly contribute? There was nothing to add.

"You mean you use video for *practice*, not *demonstrations*," he sighed, appearing a bit embarrassed. "Exactly," said my partner, hoping he was not deliberately repeating what the SVP said earlier. He continued, "We are as opposed to using orchestrated sales tapes to teach these concepts as you. It's just not a good way to teach adults."

Well, to make a long story short, we officially closed the deal that day. The SVP accepted our approach and was surprisingly gracious in welcoming us to the team. Within three days we received a signed contract.

I'll skip the details about what the ride home was like. It wasn't very pleasant, as you can imagine. Of course, we were pleased with the fact that we had turned things around. My partner felt good about how he took over and literally saved the day. And I was gratified that he stepped in and bailed me out of the hole I was about to dig for myself.

But needless to say, he was quite animated in expressing what a pathetic job I had done in reacting to the SVP's objection. I mean the guy had barely raised the video issue, and I started addressing it without having a clue as to what the real concern was. Remember what we said earlier about how "speed kills." This was an example where it almost killed a big opportunity for our company.

As I look back at that day I still shudder. All the skills that we teach and try to practice went down the tube in a New York minute. The process sensitivity we preach about was nowhere to be seen. The objection resolution process that is so powerful might as well not have existed. I heard an objection, I had the answer, and I jumped all over it like a cheap suit. If my partner hadn't been there, we would probably have blown the deal.

Now why do we take the time to tell you this story, particularly now as we wind down our exploration of innovative team selling? It certainly isn't because I want you to know that I had a bad day. All of us have had many of those, and I don't want to lose credibility, especially now. There are some important messages that we can take from my experience.

First of all, don't expect too much of yourself when you first try to use these skills. Though many are what David Hauer calls "applied common sense," in the heat of battle they can to be hard to use. Everything introduced here is applicable to your world, and with practice this body of knowledge can become a collection of valuable tools that you can use every day. Just don't try to do too much too soon.

Second, never lose sight of the power of your resources and how you can almost always count on them to bail you out. Teams outperform individuals. Even if it's just you and a colleague, look to that person for help. Feel confident that he or she has your back. Take advantage of the gift of resources. Don't be afraid to ask for help; it's a sign of strength, not weakness. When I was about to screw up big time my partner stepped in. As embarrassed as I was, it was gratifying to know that he was there. Team members need to always be on the alert and available to help when needed.

Remember that much of what we introduced are *disciplines*. Sure, we introduced skills and techniques and approaches, but so much of this is about being disciplined in your approach, even when you are looking for innovation. We can give you sequences and models and even sample quotations, but when you are applying these concepts it's all about being disciplined. Whether you are planning, conducting meetings, or interacting with customers, discipline consistently impacts your outcome. Had I demonstrated a bit of that, my partner would never have needed to rescue me.

Finally, we want you to see how from the minute you conclude a presentation and ask the customer for feedback, you are in the closing process. Closing begins when the customer objects. That may appear counterintuitive when you look at the sequence. It suggests that you resolve the issues and then close. Agreed. But the closing process begins when you encounter resistance. After all, if you successfully resolve the issues, you should be able to close.

You'll recall that the fifth step in the objection resolution model suggests that you invite other objections. We referenced that in the last chapter and explained that we don't do this to open the floodgates. We do this for a very specific reason: to close the deal. Inviting other objections results in one of two things—either the customer still has concerns or they don't. If they do, you'll attempt to resolve them. If they don't, it's time to ask for the business.

The Assumptive Close

Kate Reilly of CRC coined the term *the assumptive close*. It has a nice ring to it, doesn't it? The thinking is that if a customer cannot give you a reason not to buy, then they are ready to buy. If that's the case, you can comfortably ask for the business. The assumption is that they are ready to commit and take the next step. We know all the expressions out there badmouthing assumptions. In this case, assumptions work.

Every time you resolve an objection, ask the client if they have others. If they do, you need to hear them while you are there. If they don't have any, it provides you with a very comfortable way to ask for the business.

There are some guidelines to consider. One is that we encourage you to use neutral language, such as:

Is there anything else we need to discuss?
Do you have any additional questions?
Anything else on your mind?
Is there anything I did not answer to your satisfaction?

Notice how we don't use words like "objections" or "concerns" or "worries." If you ask a customer if they have any other concerns, you may give the impression that you know something they don't, and that does very little to move you to closure. So you simply provide the client with the opportunity to raise other issues. If they do, repeat the process. Go right back to step one, acknowledge what they say and start again. But if they don't have any additional concerns, its time to ask for the business.

You: Is there anything else we need to discuss?
Client: No, it seems like you've answered my questions.
You: So what we have recommended meets your criteria?
Client: Yes, it looks good.
You: That's great. Then I guess we can begin to formalize the agreement.

It may not go quite that smoothly, but you get the gist. You simply ask if there are other objections, using neutral language. If the answer is no, you ask for the business and hopefully close the deal. If they aren't ready to commit, then you ask why and go back into objection resolution mode. It's no more complicated than that.

The ultimate objective in any selling situation is to close the sale. Asking for the business in a less aggressive way is a terrific way to do that. Most of us don't like to ask for the business. There is a ton of data to support this. But it's part of our job description; we have to do it. The assumptive close makes it less frightening.

If you are looking for tricky ways to close the sale you won't find them here. The "Ben Franklin" close, the "Puppy Dog" close, the "Either/Or" close, the "Pro/Con" close, and the "What If" close are among the scores of approaches that have found a place in the sales world. These just aren't commensurate with the relationship-oriented approach introduced here.

If you follow these principles, there is no reason to coerce customers into doing something they may not want to do. It's not necessary. Show them the value that you, your colleagues, your recommendations, and your company bring to the table, address their concerns, and close the deal. QED.

Big "C" and little "c"

Kent Reilly, a highly respected and acclaimed trainer and facilitator, has been part of our team since the beginning. That's almost 30 years. His company, Kidder Reilly, has done some outstanding work in training salespeople and their managers. He is the first person I ever heard use the terms big and little "c."

Big "C" refers to when we close the sale. That doesn't happen too often during formal presentations, as clients need to get together and discuss the different providers and decide which to select. Usually you hear the news afterwards. But in the course of everyday relationships you'll often have the opportunity to close in real time in the customer's office. When you do, it's important to express your appreciation, and clarify the next steps using the approach that appears below.

Little "c" is a bit different. The only time you fail in sales is when you don't get a next step. The key is to make your next steps specific and clear. There isn't a whole lot of value in being fuzzy. Make sure you know who is responsible for what. And put some target dates on all your deliverables. Some people call this the interim close. It says that you're not there yet but have made progress towards eventually gaining commitment.

Enter the Four W's

We strongly advocate that groups end their meetings with very specific action plans. Whether it's a creative session, a strategy development meeting, a weekly staff meeting, or a sales call, we encourage teams to develop next steps with associated accountabilities. When they don't, the likelihood of their implementing their solutions simply isn't high.

The "Four W's" ensure that each next step clearly states *what* needs to be done, *who* is responsible, *when* they will complete the task, and *who* is available to help. In internal meetings the facilitator or team leader assigns the next steps and those responsible commit to follow through.

It's a little trickier in sales calls. Again the facilitator, usually the sale professional, makes it happen. Ending a sales call without next steps simply isn't acceptable. Even if they are nebulous, they are critically important. If a prospective customer tells you that the project won't happen for six months, you may think you don't have to get any next steps now. You should rethink that.

If nothing is expected to happen for six months, agree to check in three months from now and to stay in touch consistently. You could offer to review the status in a letter within a week and to keep the customer advised regarding developments at your end. Out of sight is out of mind as the old cliché goes; don't let that happen to you.

Sometimes you'll end with a commitment to move forward. That's great. Other times you'll conclude with an action plan that keeps the momentum going. The reality is that you'll do better if you end with that action plan. You may not get the commitment today, but this is a step in that direction.

Closing. Bringing home the bacon. Delivering the goods. Winning the business. Whatever term you use, that's what the sales team wants to eventually accomplish. It doesn't have to be manipulative. It doesn't require complicated approaches. Closing is an extension of the objection resolution process. If you apply that, resolve one issue at a time, and eventually ask for the business, you'll close more deals than you ever imagined. And you'll do it in a way that feels good for everyone involved.

Some Things to Consider

What

The ultimate objective of any sales team is to close the sale. There have been dozens—perhaps scores—of different closing approaches described over the years. But when push comes to shove, we believe in one simple approach—ask for the business. If you follow the tenets of consultative selling this is a very natural step in the process. It is nothing more than a continuation of the resolving objections process.

How

As we explained, whenever you successfully resolve an objection, it is important to invite others. If the client has other objections, you need to hear them. If you don't hear them now, you will hear them later. If when you do this the client raises another objection, repeat the process. But if they don't give you a reason not to buy, assume they are ready to buy and ask for the business. It's that straightforward.

When

ABC—"Always be closing" may have worked in the *Glengarry Glen Ross* world, but it does not work in yours. Closing prematurely sends a poor message to the client. Close when it is appropriate. Never forget that it is the last step in the process, and is only appropriate when all the objections are resolved.

18

One Last Time: It's All About Differentiation

We conclude our story where we began—talking about the power of sales teams. We have spoken at length about how teams typically do better than individuals. We explained how, when sales teams leverage their resources, they outperform the competition. Teams have an extraordinary ability to thoroughly understand each of their customers' needs. They can use what they learn to craft exciting and innovative solutions. As a result they can clearly distinguish themselves. If one company is pursuing an opportunity using a collection of individuals, and another is using a well organized sales team, it won't be much of a contest. The team should win almost every time.

As we wind down, let's review some of the ways that teams can differentiate themselves. The following dozen thoughts summarize much of what was discussed throughout this book. Even more significant, you will notice how these activities enable sales teams to play a major role in pursuing and winning new business opportunities.

Everyone knows that competition gets tougher every day. The global marketplace in which we find ourselves has made conducting our business more difficult than we ever imagined. Technology moves at such a rapid pace that today's solutions are almost obsolete overnight. But as daunting as all this is, we can never forget that the single biggest differentiator that any company has is its people. That is an asset that only your company has. You and your colleagues are what make your organization unique. Nobody can replicate that. The key is to leverage those resources and stay ahead of your competition.

So let's look at some of the things we introduced and see if these concepts give you ways and means to demonstrate just how different you can be.

Differentiating the Sales Team

Conducting Productive Internal Meetings

A key variable in the formula for any sales team's success is their ability to work together productively. Most of this happens in their day-to-day meetings, whether it's two people or the entire team. Meetings can be very frustrating, and people complain often about how the time they spend in meetings is wasted. If teams gain an understanding of meeting dynamics and follow certain guidelines, they can get so much more out of the time they spend together. It can be as simple as starting and ending on time, or as complicated as drawing out reluctant participants. Teams can learn how to make their meetings work.

Sales teams need to understand basic guidelines. They must approach meetings with reasonable objectives. They can use a specific process such as the interactive meeting model. They need to create a healthy climate by treating others with respect. They should involve everyone and encourage participation. And they have to conclude their meetings with action plans and assign next steps.

Conducting successful meetings results from taking many small steps. Often things that seem insignificant can in the long run have major implications. Rejecting someone's idea in one meeting could result in that person not participating in a future meeting. Sales teams need to understand that every action they take in a meeting can have a reaction down the road. They must be sensitive to how their behavior impacts others. If they are aware of principles like these, their meetings will be more effective, they will do great work and the results will speak for themselves.

The Art of Facilitation

Keep in mind the difference between content and process. *Content*, you will recall, focuses on the "what." In internal situations this refers to the agenda, the objectives, the issues, and the conclusions. In external situations, it includes things like the questions you ask, the recommendations you make, and the answers you give when customers object. Most individuals do very well with content.

Process is the reason that groups don't reach their potential. This happens both internally and externally. Process is the "how." Process refers to things like how you listen, how you ask questions, how you offer ideas, and how you manage conflict. It includes subtle concepts like how comfortable people feel, how ideas are treated, and how safe it is to take risks. When groups don't reach their potential, process issues are usually the cause.

That's why it helps to appoint a facilitator in every meeting. In internal meetings you can divide those tasks among the participants. In external meetings it's the responsibility of the sales professional or whoever manages the relationship. The facilitator is the person who clarifies the agenda and time frame and creates a healthy climate. The facilitator does what is required to involve everyone and distribute the available time. The facilitator protects ideas and acts as a catalyst in internal meetings, and he or she leads the issue resolution process in external meetings.

The facilitator acts like a traffic cop or a quarterback, and their primary responsibility is to manage the flow of the meeting and ensure that the objectives are accomplished. Regardless of the situation, the presence of a facilitator results in more productive outcomes.

Enhancing Creative Sessions

You don't always need to think creatively. Nor does every action you take require innovation. George Prince believed that it's all about good thinking and that sometimes good thinking is routine and other times it's creative. Both are necessary; the situation determines when to use which kind of thinking.

When it is time to get creative, there are many things you can do to enhance the approach. Paying attention to process is critical, and having a facilitator will always help. Establishing an environment in which people are free to speculate and take risks is imperative. Suspending evaluation plays a major role, since people are more willing to offer creative ideas if they don't have to worry about defending them.

When individuals go beyond just offering ideas they'll have more raw material to use in attacking the task at hand. Ideas are always welcomed, of course, but they can go further. Beginning ideas, idea fragments, absurd ideas, silly ideas, directional ideas, and even illegal, immoral, and unethical ideas are encouraged early in any problem-solving situation. When a group gets stuck, using idea generation techniques like thinking in terms of metaphors, analogies, and absurdity can be energizing. Ideas are only ideas, and the ideation process needs to be freewheeling, fun, and risk free. There is always time to evaluate later. First you need to develop exciting, rich, raw material.

When it's time to evaluate, select the ideas that intrigue you the most. Treat them with tender loving care. Identify the value first and then work together to resolve the concerns. Be diligent and tenacious. Give that new and different idea every chance to become a solution. The most exciting solutions are often a fourth or fifth cousin of the original idea. When groups use approaches like these to transform ideas into solutions, the results can be new, different, and yes, quite creative.

Making the Planning Process Work

Remember that article that Kate Reilly and I wrote about planning sales calls. She wrote the great opening line, "Mention the word planning and sales-people start to yawn." After all, planning is not high on any sales professional's list of favorite activities. The same applies to sales teams. Managers often complain that the teams just don't put in enough planning time before they visit the client.

That's a big a mistake. Sales calls are analogous to performances. No actor would go on stage without rehearsing. No singer would prepare for a concert without getting comfortable with the band. No politician would consider debating without doing the necessary prep work. And no athlete would prepare for a game without putting in the required practice time. The same applies to sales teams. It seems ludicrous for any team to approach an important meeting without devoting time to preparing. But it happens much too often.

That's why we introduced the "reporter's approach to planning." If a team asks themselves the "who, what, where, when, why, and how" before every client meeting, they'll be much better prepared. If they review the history and ask those questions, everyone will be on the same page. If they do some rehearsing they'll be in a much better position to make it a great show. Rehearsing may not be cool but it is critically important. And planning may not be fun, but teams that carefully plan before their customer meetings stand out every time.

Leveraging Your Resources

Simply put, leveraging resources is what team selling is all about. The best sales teams are the ones who know how to tap into the expertise of the organization.

Whether you are a 10-person family business or a Fortune 25 company, you have tons of talent available to utilize. The challenge is to do it.

Sales teams can be either temporary or permanent. Some groups work together all the time in managing client relationships; others are assigned to work together for a specific opportunity. The fictitious example we used in the book was about a temporary team. They were assembled for this one particular initiative. Since it was a significant RFP opportunity, a senior person from each function was actively involved. This is common in many organizations.

When determining your resources, look at what the customer wants to accomplish and then put together the best team possible. Even permanent teams can reach out for additional resources. Do whatever you can to make sure that the expertise you need is available when you need it. Usually the people you ask will respond. If potential resources aren't willing to help and you need their contributions, you may have to remind them about what is at stake and what's best for the company. They are part of something bigger than themselves, and that is what should drive their decision. If all else fails, go over their heads. It may not be wise politically, but sometimes the ends do justify the means.

Cross-functional teams work best. Get as many different functions involved as possible. Heterogeneous teams tend to develop more innovative solutions than homogenous teams. Tap into that experience and remember that naiveté can be a marvelous source of expertise. If you identify great thinkers in your organization who know little about the task at hand, invite them to your creative sessions, since they often provide valuable new and different perspectives. The single most powerful asset any organization has is its people. Your people are what makes you unique. Leveraging them will only make you more successful.

Connecting with Clients

Empathy is the key to establishing relationships. Every survey we have ever seen talks about how critical this behavior is in developing meaningful relationships. The ability to see things from the customer's perspective, to relate to their issues, to try to understand how they feel, is paramount. It is not just the sales professional's responsibility; it's every team member's responsibility.

Connecting can happen before, during, and after sales calls. Different team members need to relate to their counterparts. They need to figure out how to connect. Everyone has to listen at 112 percent in order to hear both what the customers say and what they don't say. They have to demonstrate their understanding, and be sensitive to the customer's concerns, worries and even fears. As complicated as the sales process may appear at times, people still buy from people they like, people they enjoy, people they trust, and yes, people who truly understand them.

Adding Value

We introduced the value pyramid when we first discussed the sales process. There are different levels of relationships that salespeople and sales teams develop with their clients. The levels range from simply implementing what the client requests at one extreme, to becoming strategic advisors at the other. Most sales professionals have relationships at all four levels; the objective is to get to higher levels.

Sales teams can add significant value to the customer in many ways. It's not just their ability to discuss how their products can help address the customer's needs, although that is important. Bringing in the experts always helps them do better at telling their story. But it goes beyond that.

Resources can offer perspectives, insights, and ideas that the customer might never know about if not for them. They have unique forms of expertise, and each has his or her own experiences to draw from when speaking with customers. They can offer specific examples, share war stories, and identify parallel situations. All this adds significant value.

We hear stories about how a customer's production manager will call a technical resource from the supplier on their own without involving the salesperson. Sometimes a customer's marketing manager will give the supplier's market research director a call. Even the portfolio manager from a hedge fund will call the investment bank's analyst to get some relevant information about a particular industry.

It can become the norm for the customer's key players to be so comfortable with their counterparts that they'll call for help when needed. There have to be ground rules established, of course, but when those kinds of relationships exist, and the credibility and trust levels of the counterparts are solid, the value sales teams can add is almost incalculable. This results in deep, secure, and long-term relationships.

Understanding the Power of Positioning

When we first mentioned positioning we admitted that it was a funny word. But it is significant whenever you find ourselves in interactive situations. It is a powerful concept, and managing it is the responsibility of the person who called the meeting. When meetings are not positioned properly they will not accomplish their objectives. Or put less kindly, when people don't bother to do this, they set themselves up to fail.

The irony is that this is not a hard thing to do. Positioning is nothing more than explaining what the meeting is all about and getting everyone involved. Most professionals know what needs to be done, whether it's an internal or external meeting. The problem is that too often they just don't take the time to do it. Whether they forget or they are in a rush or they just don't know any better, it doesn't happen. And even when people attempt to do this, most don't do it nearly as well as they could.

Positioning addresses concepts like creating a healthy climate to ensure that everyone is comfortable and knowing who the participants are. Positioning includes things like clarifying the agenda and ensuring that you know what everyone hopes to accomplish. Positioning ensures that you determine how much time is available so you can be respectful of others' time constraints. It even allows you to brag a little about your colleagues when you introduce them, or at least explain what they bring to the meeting.

And positioning allows you to set the stage for what will happen in the meeting. If it's internal, it could be as simple as getting status reports from the participants. In external meetings, it could be preparing a customer for questioning or teeing up a formal presentation. Managing expectations is so important. We have all been on sales calls, whether we are selling or buying, when we didn't have a clue as to why we were there. Effective positioning precludes this from happening and gives you yet another way to differentiate yourselves.

Understanding the Client

When you think about sales teams as *needs development teams*, you aren't just being clever. It's a very different way to think about the role of sales teams. Most organizations think that the primary role of the sales teams is to work together to develop outstanding solutions for their customers. This is admirable and it is certainly a big piece of what they are tasked to do. But it's only part of the picture. If you don't use sales teams to help you understand precisely what the customer wants to accomplish, then you are underutilizing them and they'll never reach their full potential.

The sales team members' job descriptions should include something about determining needs. Different team members, because of their backgrounds, experience, and expertise, will hear the same thing and reach different conclusions. Though everyone might agree on the obvious needs, when it comes to the implied or unconscious needs, each team member will have different perspectives. In some cases the differences will be significant. Since situation analysis is the most important part of the sales process, you had best get your entire sales team involved in understanding the clients' needs.

This doesn't apply only to what they hear. Questioning may be the most important skill of all. Sales team members can help tremendously by asking questions that the sale professional didn't know enough to ask or wasn't comfortable asking. They are better prepared to react to the answers. Just their presence often leads to more thorough needs assessments. Every colleague can become a terrific contributor to the needs determination process because of their knowledge and expertise.

These resources can help before, during, and after the sales call. Whether they are reviewing correspondence, studying an RFP, listening in on a conference call, or participating in a sales call, they can help determine the needs of that customer. When teams get together to debrief what they heard, and share perspectives as they plan for presentations, each member of the team needs to contribute and express their understanding of the customer's needs.

Making Fabulous Presentations

This will get the least attention here because we devoted two full chapters to it already. Presentations in general, and finalist presentations in particular, may be your most exciting moments. It's analogous to opening night on Broadway. It's like the playoffs. Some might even compare it to the Olympics or the World Cup. The comparisons can go on and on. When its time to present, all the work, all the meetings, all the research, and all the effort come to fruition. It's finally time to tell your story.

It will be a much better story if you use your resources. Plan carefully for the presentation. Rehearse. Do some tweaking when necessary. Come up with a new idea or two if appropriate. Make sure everyone knows what is expected of them, and what they can expect from each other. Be sure to have contingency plans ready if necessary. And when the bell rings, go out and knock their socks off. Everything you do is to get to this place; you might as well do a brilliant job.

Dealing with Resistance

Resolving objections is the most challenging part of the selling process. Most professionals don't respond as well as they'd like when they encounter resistance. The tendency to become aggressive or defensive or passive doesn't help.

The process that was introduced was in many ways familiar. The way acknowledging was suggested, or the concept of reframing might have been new, but you understand how to resolve differences. You need to get the other guy talking, demonstrate that you understand the issue, and give it your best answer. If you can reframe the objection as a need, it increases the likelihood of success. It's a viable process. You know that.

But what a luxury it is to have colleagues there to assist you when you find yourself under the gun. Knowing that someone else can help draw the client out or reframe the objection is very comforting. If they can help you with a great response, so much the better. If resources step in when you get blindsided, you'll be very grateful. Anticipating objections beforehand, and determining who will do what, helps tremendously. If ever there is a time you'll appreciate your resources it's when the client objects. When you work together, objection resolution can become a beautiful thing.

Following Through Professionally

Finally, sales teams need to realize that the real selling starts after they win the business. Anyone can get the first order; we put our money on the guy who gets the second, third, and fourth.

I remember a sales manager who preached, "Everyone follows up; the best of the best follow through." I didn't really know what he meant the first time I heard that, but it became clearer as time passed. Of course we do what we said we would do. That's the *follow-up*. It's the things we do that go beyond that, the *follow through*, that really differentiate you.

It's the action plan that arrived before anyone asked for it. It's the article you sent that the recipient did not expect. It's the visit you made just to check in, or the phone call you made to alert them about industry issues that they needed to understand. It's the idea you gave them that had nothing in it for you, but something of interest for them. And it's that meeting you conducted, which focused strictly on their situation with virtually no reference to what you could do for them.

Every team member can help when it comes to following through. They can stay in touch with their counterparts. They can help expedite the next steps. They can consistently ask themselves what they can do to help the customer. When ideas occur to them, they can channel them through the team leader or discuss them with the assigned "champions."

We like to say that it's all about the customer. That's easy to say. The words have become a very common phrase. They can appear shallow, even insincere, if you don't back them up. By following through consistently, you demonstrate that this isn't just another catchy phrase, but that you have their best interests in mind. And following through provides you with yet another way to differentiate yourself and your team.

Some Parting Thoughts

As we conclude our time together, let us say we hope that you will consider using many of these concepts. Don't try to do everything at once and don't try to do too much too soon. Much of this was familiar to you, and some was new. You'll decide what to use and when.

Sam Jamison and his team gave us a way to demonstrate how these concepts come together. Of course, his story was fictitious. But every reference to Sam was based on our own experiences and those that we observed or learned about from others. For Sam's team to win that business, which at first glance was out of their league, they had to use every one of the 12 principles described earlier. And more.

So can you. There is no reason why sales teams cannot accomplish miracles. They can develop relationships that seemed unlikely. They can learn things about their clients that seemed unattainable. They can develop solutions that they thought were unimaginable. They can put together presentations that looked implausible. They can overcome challenges that seemed insurmountable. And they can win business that appeared impossible. They really can.

You can do this as well. Just leverage your resources. They are there; tap into their expertise. Look at *Innovative Team Selling* not just as the name of a book or a clever term. It can become a collection of operating principles within your organization. It can enable you to accomplish great things. It can help your colleagues grow to new heights and derive tremendous satisfaction from their accomplishments.

David Richter is an extremely perceptive underground philosopher and a long-time friend. He said, "The first thing you have to do to make your dreams come true is to get out of bed." It is one of my favorite quotes ever.

You can't accomplish anything without getting started. No matter how long the road may be, it all begins with that first step. On that note we conclude our story, with the hope that you'll take that first step and begin the process of making innovative team selling a way of life for you, your colleagues, and your customers. The investment required will yield significant returns. Enjoy the journey.

About the Author

Eric Baron, founder of The Baron Group, has more than 35 years of experience in sales, sales management, and sales training. Educated as a chemical engineer, Eric began his career at Union Carbide Corporation where he held positions in sales, sales management, marketing and sales training. He left Carbide to join the prestigious consulting firm Synectics Inc.®, where he researched and taught creative problem solving and innovation. It was at Synectics that he became fascinated with the connections and similarities between problem solving and selling, which led him to form in 1981 what is now The Baron Group.

Eric is an internationally known public speaker and his firm provides sales and sales management training programs for numerous companies around the world including UBS, Ogilvy & Mather, Prudential, JPMorgan Chase, Kraft, BNP Paribus, New York Life, Onyx, and BNY Mellon. He is an adjunct professor at Columbia Business School, where he teaches his popular course, Entrepreneurial Selling Skills, to second-year MBAs. He was awarded the Dean's Teaching Excellence Award in 2010.

Innovative Team Selling is his third book; *Selling Is a Team Sport* was published in 2000, and *Selling* in 2009. He has also published many chapters and articles throughout his career. He has been active in the March of Dimes for more than 30 years and served as chairman of the Fairfield County Board for four years. He is an avid runner, softball player, and fly fisherman. His hobbies include woodworking, gardening, and studying presidential politics.

He lives in Weston, Connecticut, with Lois, his wife of more than 40 years. He has two grown children, Andrea and Deborah, and four grandchildren, Logan, Sage, Jonah, and Tess.

About The Baron Group

The Baron Group (TBG) is a research-based consulting firm that devotes most of its time and energy to providing training programs for its clients in sales and sales management skills, techniques, and approaches.

Their curriculum includes a variety of selling skills programs, including *Consultative Selling, Team Selling, Negotiation Skills, Prospecting, Effective Finalist Presentations,* and *Relationship Management.* Sales management programs include *Coaching for Improved Sales Performance, Sales Management 101, Sales Action Planning,* and *Conducting Effective Sales Meetings.*

Eric Baron and his team speak regularly at national sales meetings, trade association events, recognition programs, and industry conferences. Their offerings are customized for the specific event, as are all of their training programs.

TBG programs are highly participative, interactive, and skill-based. Skill sets fall into five categories: interpersonal, communications, presentation, problem solving, and facilitation. Videotaped simulations and role plays are included in virtually every program to provide participants the opportunity to test the efficacy of the concepts they learn while increasing their self-awareness and confidence.

The Baron Group has had the opportunity to work with the world's most prestigious companies including American Express, AT&T, Citigroup, Pepsi, Hewlett-Packard, Pfizer, Research International, JPMorgan, Prudential, PricewaterhouseCoopers, Ogilvy & Mather, Bristol Meyers Squibb, UBS, Chiron, Publicis, Morgan Stanley, and Merrill Lynch.

Acknowledgments

I t all begins with Lois, my wife of more than 40 years. I know that most acknowledgments usually save the comments for their loved ones for the end. I get that. But there's no way I can thank anyone before I express my appreciation and love for my best friend. Lois thinks of everyone else before herself, almost to a fault. She can be tough as nails when necessary, but is nurturing, loving, and encouraging every single day. Since she is a writer herself, her editing is always appreciated, and her suggestions and perspectives have been helpful and valuable throughout this process.

My grown children and their children are gifts that I cherish. I don't quote Paul Anka very often, and most of you don't have a clue as to who this singer from the 50s and 60s is. He sang a relatively unknown song about being the father of girls. The line I remember most goes something like " . . . as the father of boys, you worry; as the father of girls you pray." My prayers were certainly answered. Andrea Cooper and Deborah Rubin have grown up to be extra-ordinary adults, and their husbands, Jon and Howie, are outstanding young men. All are making meaningful contributions to the world and I am so proud of them. And of course my precious grandchildren, Logan, Sage, Jonah, and Tess, have taught me to experience feelings that I never imagined.

Dan Ambrosio, formerly with John Wiley & Sons, called me one day, after having done some research about my work, and asked if I would be interested in writing another book. Within 60 days we had a deal, and four months later I submitted the manuscript. One of the few regrets I had during this project was Dan's decision to move on, and therefore he could not finish the project with me. I wish him only good things and thank him for his support. The Wiley team understands the value of teamwork, and I am grateful for the advice, counsel, and contributions from Shannon Vargo, Linda Indig, and Tiffany Colon. They have been there for me throughout this initiative, and their perspectives and support are very much appreciated. Thanks to you all.

As I did in my first book, I refer to Synectics,® Inc., now Synecticworld, throughout *Innovative Team Selling*. That is because so much of what I do, and so much of who I am, results from what I learned at Synectics.® The late George Prince was my mentor and friend, and his wisdom and insights literally changed my life. Rick Harriman, who built the organization into a serious global entity, has been a dear friend for over 35 years, and more than anyone I know, opened doors that led to what I have been able to accomplish.

There are members of our team that do so much day in and day out to make The Baron Group successful. But Doris Anderson and Francine Mendence are the two people who literally keep the place humming and cover for me every single day. Barbara Vahsen is our stabilizing influence and we all benefit from her perspectives and insights. And when I was focused on the book and was a bit preoccupied, our Director of Sales, Troy Fowler, was always there ready to step in and do what was needed.

You'll see me refer to many members of our team throughout this story, since each has made significant contributions to who we are, what we offer, and how we do it. Ralph Bellrose, Greg Conderacci, Laura Daley, Fred Lamparter, David Michelson, Reggie Pearse, Kent Reilly, and Jim Schwarz are among the many people who help make The Baron Group the client focused company we try to be.

It's risky business to mention clients when you thank those who helped because you can't avoid leaving people out inadvertently who deserve mention. But it's worth the risk, as I couldn't ignore people, past and present, who have contributed to our success. I am so grateful to Paul Beideman, Tamasine Bogle, Steve Bohnenkamp, Barbara Brooks, Fernando Costa, Eric Dale, John Gibbons, Steve Harty, Kathryn Hounsell, Matt Kissner, Linda Knox, Mark Lipson, Sylvia Mahlebjian, Jeff Neubert. Janice O'Neill, Darcy Pierson, Scott Posner, John Prael, Jodi Rabinowitz, Virun Rampersad, Dave Renke, Paul Ruane, Steve Samuels, Damien Sauter, Glenn Starkman, Jeffrey Stiefler, Chuck Sulerzyski, Kip Testwuide, Ed Valencia, Steve Vickers, Bill Voelkel, Geoff von Kuhn, John Ward, and Zac Zeitlin.

Of course, I will forever be grateful to my parents. My father, Sydney S. Baron, imbedded in me an awareness of the importance of hard work and personal sacrifice. My loving mother, Sylvia Baron, was the perfect role model, particularly in teaching me the importance of showing other people the respect they deserve. And finally, my late sister-in-law, Sandi Rotkoff, to whom this book is dedicated, taught me an incredibly important life lesson—"assume that people are trying to do the best that they can." That is great advice for everyone.

I thank all of you, and the many people I have not mentioned, for your support, your perspectives, and your friendship. Nobody does this kind of thing alone, and you are living proof that groups outperform individuals.

Index